Book of Sun and Moon
(I Ching)

日月經

Traditional Perspectives on Divination and Calculation
for the *Book of Changes* (Volume II)

Translation and Commentaries
by Stuart Alve Olson

Valley Spirit Arts
Phoenix, Arizona

Copyright © 2014 by Stuart Alve Olson.

All rights reserved. No part of this publication may be reproduced or used in any form or by any means, electronic or mechanical, including photocopying, recording, or by any information storage and retrieval system, without prior written permission from Stuart Alve Olson and Valley Spirit Arts LLC.

ISBN-13: 978-1-5032-9129-4
ISBN-10: 1-5032-9129-4

Valley Spirit Arts
Phoenix, Arizona
www.valleyspiritarts.com
contact@valleyspiritarts.com

Book design, charts, and graphics by Patrick Gross.

Fu Xi (circa 2852 BCE) is one the Four Great Sages of the *Book of Sun and Moon*. He is credited with creating the Eight Trigrams and assigning correlations to them.

Preface

This volume contains the translation of the original *Book of Sun and Moon* (易經, *Yi Jing*). Each of the Sixty-Four Hexagrams includes the following sections, which provide insights into both the divination and calculation methods for interpreting any given hexagram and how it may pertain to a particular question or situation in a person's life:

1. *The Prediction* by King Wen and *The Lines* by Duke of Zhou (with commentaries).
2. Alternate English Translations of the Hexagram (see list of books below).
3. *The Great Symbolism* by Confucius.
4. Sexagenary Placement:
   - Heavenly Stem
   - Earthly Branch
   - Chinese Animal Astrological Year
5. Trigram Correlations for the Upper and Lower Trigrams.
6. Associated Developed Hexagrams *(The Seen* and *The Unseen* Triangulated Hexagrams):
   - Before Heaven Hexagram
   - Contrasted Image Hexagram
   - Eight Gates Hexagram
   - After Heaven Hexagram
   - Sun, Moon, or Eclipse Hexagram
   - Ruling Line Hexagram
   - Inner Hexagram

Together, these sections provide a wide spectrum of information to help one better interpret a hexagram casting. No matter the question put to the *Book of Sun and Moon*, it is either asking for a divination about some future event (such as should I get married?) or trying to see when to do something by calculating the date and location. So, depending on whether a question is based on divination or calculation, the information given with each hexagram should be examined accordingly. See *Book of Sun and Moon*, volume I, for more information on each section, as well as how to use the *Book of Sun and Moon* by casting and calculating a hexagram.

Alternate English Translations of the Hexagram
Alternate translations for the hexagrams are listed from eleven popular and available works. Together, these books show the varying interpretations of the Chinese characters

used for each of the individual Sixty-Four Hexagrams. Nothing is incorrect about these translations. They just offer differences in opinion. Although numerous other works can be examined, the following translations represent some of the best works on the subject of the *Book of Sun and Moon*. Note that the original translation work of James Legge, *Book of Changes* (Clarendon Press, 1899), is not listed below. The reason for this omission is that Legge did not include translations of the names of the hexagrams in that work, rather he simply presented the romanizations of the Chinese characters. However, in 1964 an edition using James Legge's translation was edited and published by Ch'u Chai and Winberg Chai. To date, this work is still one of the best *Book of Sun and Moon* translations existing, and it includes all *Ten Wings*. The reason for the excellence in Legge's translation work was a result of his highly learned Confucian handlers, both in China and Scotland. Hence, the Ch'u Chai and Winberg Chai translations of the hexagrams represent Legge's translation work.

[B]   *I Ching: The Book of Change* by John Blofeld (Dutton/Plume, 1968).

[C]   *The Taoist I Ching.* Translated by Thomas Cleary (Shambala Publications, Inc., 1986).

[CC] *The I Ching Book of Changes.* Translated by James Legge, edited with an introduction and study guide by Ch'u Chai with Winberg Chai (Bantam Books, 1986).

[CS] *The Astrology of I Ching.* Translated from the 'Ho Map Lo Map Rational Number' Manuscript by W. K. Chu. Edited, and commentaries added, by W. A. Sherrill (Penguin Books, 1993).

[H]   *The Complete I Ching* by Taoist Master Alfred Huang (Inner Traditions International, 1998).

[K]   *I Ching: The Classic Chinese Oracle of Change.* Translated by Stephen Karcher (Vega, 2002).

[L]   *I Ching Coin Prediction: How to Consult the I Ching to Predict Your Future* by Da Liu (Harper & Row Publishers, 1975).

[N]   *I Ching: The Book of Changes and the Unchanging Truth,* Revised Edition by Hua-Ching Ni (SevenStar Communications Group, Inc., 1983).

[RS] *The Original I Ching Oracle* by Rudolf Ritsema and Shantena Augusto Sabbadini (Watkins Publishing, 2005).

[S]   *The Text of Yi King: (and Its Appendixes) Chinese Original With English Translation* by Z. D. Sung (The China Modern Education Company, 1935).

[WB] *The I Ching, or, Book of Changes* (Bollingen Series XIX) by Richard Wilhelm and Cary F. Baynes (Princeton University Press; 3rd edition, 1967).

Contents

Upper Book (Images 1 thru 30)

1. Creativity of Heaven (乾, Qian) 2
2. Receptivity of Earth (坤, Kun) 6
3. Beginning Difficulties (屯, Chun) 10
4. Untaught Youth (蒙, Meng) 14
5. Hesitation (需, Xu) 18
6. Contending (訟, Song) 22
7. The Army (師, Shi) 26
8. Union (比, Bi) 30
9. Small Accumulation (小畜, Xiao Chu) 34
10. Treading (履, Lu) 38
11. Peacefulness (泰, Tai) 42
12. Adversity (否, Pi) 46
13. People United (同人, Tong Ren) 50
14. Great Possession (大有, Da You) 54
15. Modesty (謙, Qian) 58
16. Joyful Ease (豫, Yu) 62
17. Following (隨, Sui) 66
18. Inner Destruction (蠱, Gu) 70
19. Approaching (臨, Lin) 74
20. Contemplation (觀, Guan) 78
21. Mastication (噬嗑, Shi He) 82
22. Adornment (賁, Bi) 86
23. Removing (剝, Bo) 90
24. Returning (復, Fu) 94
25. Innocence (无忘, Wu Wang) 98
26. Great Accumulation (大畜, Da Chu) 102
27. Nourishment (頤, Yi) 106
28. Great Passing (大過, Da Guo) 110
29. The Abyss (坎, Kan) 114
30. Distant Brightness (離, Li) 118

Lower Book (Images 31 thru 64)

31. Attraction (咸, Xian) 124
32. Constancy (恒, Heng) 128
33. Retreating (遯, Dun) 132
34. Great Strength (大壯, Da Zhuang) 136
35. Advancement (晉, Jin) 140
36. Diminishing Light (明夷, Ming Yi) 144
37. The Family (家人, Jia Ren) 148
38. Opposition (睽, Kui) 152
39. Difficult Obstruction (蹇, Jian) 156
40. Liberation (解, Jie) 160
41. Sacrifice (損, Sun) 164
42. Increase (益, Yi) 168
43. Decision (夬, Guai) 172
44. Pairing (姤, Gou) 176
45. Collecting (萃, Cui) 180
46. Ascending (升, Sheng) 184
47. Oppression (困, Kun) 188
48. The Well (井, Jing) 192
49. Revolution (革, Ge) 196
50. The Cauldron (鼎, Ding) 200
51. Arousing Movement (震, Zhen) 204
52. Determined Stillness (艮, Gen) 208
53. Gradual Movement (漸, Jian) 212
54. Marriageable Maiden (歸妹, Gui Mei) 216
55. Prosperity (豐, Feng) 220
56. The Wanderer (旅, Lu) 224
57. Submission (巽, Xun) 228
58. Joyousness (兌, Dui) 232
59. Dispersion (渙, Huan) 236
60. Regulating (節, Jie) 240
61. Inner Truth (中孚, Zhong Fu) 244
62. Small Passing (小過, Xiao Guo) 248
63. After Completion (既濟, Ji Ji) 252
64. Before Completion (未濟, Wei Ji) 256

Book of Sun and Moon

Upper Book

上 經
Shang Jing

[Images #1 thru #30]

Qian 乾 — *Creativity of Heaven* — 1

Qian (Heaven) above
乾上
Qian Shang
Qian (Heaven) below
乾下
Qian Xia

Image of the Male Dragon-Horse   Sun/Yang Image

The Prediction (象, Tuan)

Creativity of Heaven:
Great, persevering,
advantageous, and correct.

乾.元亨利貞.

This hexagram predicts using boldness and strength to achieve success. Heaven is naturally strong and auspicious, and it represents creativity. Heaven reveals the activities of the Hun Spirits[1] and spiritual development. The Dragon seeks to fly into the Heavens and achieve clarity. This hexagram is auspicious for predicting the future and acquiring good fortune.

The Lines (爻, Yao)

First Nine (初九, Chu Jiu)
Hidden dragon is without use.

潛龍無用.

A dragon is lurking about, looking for the right opportunity to show its abilities. No opportunity has risen, so the skills of the dragon remain hidden. Be patient as the time is not yet right for accomplishing things.

Second Nine (九二, Jiu Er)
Dragon seen in the fields.
It is beneficial to see an elder.

見龍在田.利見大人.

When you see a dragon, consult the master to find out what should be done.

---

[1] *Hun* (魂, Heavenly Spirit) are the three immortal spirits that influence a person's spiritual nature.

Third Nine (九三, Jiu San)
A superior person is actively innovative and creative until the end of the day. In the evening, appears respectful. Discipline. Without fault.

君子終日乾乾.
夕惕若. 厲. 无咎.

A dragon is diligent all day long, but dares not relax in the evening from fear of danger. The dragon's fear is useless because there is no pending injury or harm. Being disciplined and respectful is without mistake. Be creative and cautious.

Fourth Nine (九四, Jiu Si)
Perhaps leaping into an abyss. Without fault.

或躍在淵. 无咎.

A dragon has no fear when leaping in and out of deep water. There is no mistake being made when doing so.

Fifth Nine (九五, Jiu Wu)
Dragon flying in the Heavens. It is beneficial to see an elder.

飛龍在天. 利見大人.

A dragon can fly up into the vast sky. When it reaches the Heavens, this is the moment the master appears, and when the master appears everyone will follow him.

Topmost Nine (上九, Shang Jiu)
An arrogant dragon has regret.

亢龍有悔.

The high-flying and willful dragon is filled with regret because of heated conflict with other dragons. Arrogance always leads to remorse and a downfall.

Usefulness of All Nines (用九, Yong Jiu)
A multitude of dragons are seen without heads. Auspicious.

見羣龍无首. 吉.

None of these dragons considers itself the master, and so they are called the "sovereign dragons." The dragons are seen without heads because they are flying into the Heavens and only their tails can be seen. This signals a very auspicious time.

Alternate English Translations for the Hexagram of Qian, 乾

Firmness Symbolizes Heaven [S]
The Creative Principle [B]
The Creative [L] [WB]
Initiating [H]
Force/Dragon [K]

Heaven [C]
Creative (Innovatory) Action [CS]
Positiveness—The Creative [N]
Energy [RS]
The Symbol of Firmness [CC]

The Great Symbolism (大象, Da Xiang) says,

Heaven's movement is strong.   天 行 健. 君 子
Superior persons, according with this,   以 自 彊 不 息.
strengthen themselves unceasingly.

Trigram Correlations

Upper Gua (Heaven)

Qian 乾   **Represents:** Heaven, Sky, Male, Father, Emperor
Actions: Creative Principle, Persisting, Forceful
Influences: Blessings, Good Fortune, Strength, Spiritual Power
Shape: Circle   **Color:** White
Body: Head   **Season:** Summer (Summer Solstice)
Moon Phase: Full Moon
Animals: Earthly Horse, Celestial Red Phoenix
Directions: South (BH), Northwest (AH)
Nine Palaces Numbers: Fu Xi: 2
   Yu the Great: Ho River Map, 9—Lo River Script, 6
Internal Alchemy: Clarity, Illumination
   Qi Center: Ni Wan (Mud Pellet)
   Qi Meridian: Du Mai (Control Vessel)

#1 Creativity of Heaven (Qian)

Lower Gua (Heaven)

☰ **Qian** 乾

Represents: Heaven, Sky, Male, Father, Emperor
Actions: Creative Principle, Persisting, Forceful
Influences: Blessings, Good Fortune, Strength, Spiritual Power
Shape: Circle **Color:** White
Body: Head **Season:** Summer (Summer Solstice)
Moon Phase: Full Moon
Animals: Earthly Horse, Celestial Red Phoenix
Directions: South (BH), Northwest (AH)
Nine Palaces Numbers: Fu Xi: 2
   Yu the Great: Ho River Map, 9—Lo River Script, 6
Internal Alchemy: Clarity, Illumination
   Qi Center: Ni Wan (Mud Pellet)
   Qi Meridian: Du Mai (Control Vessel)

Associated Developed Hexagrams of Qian

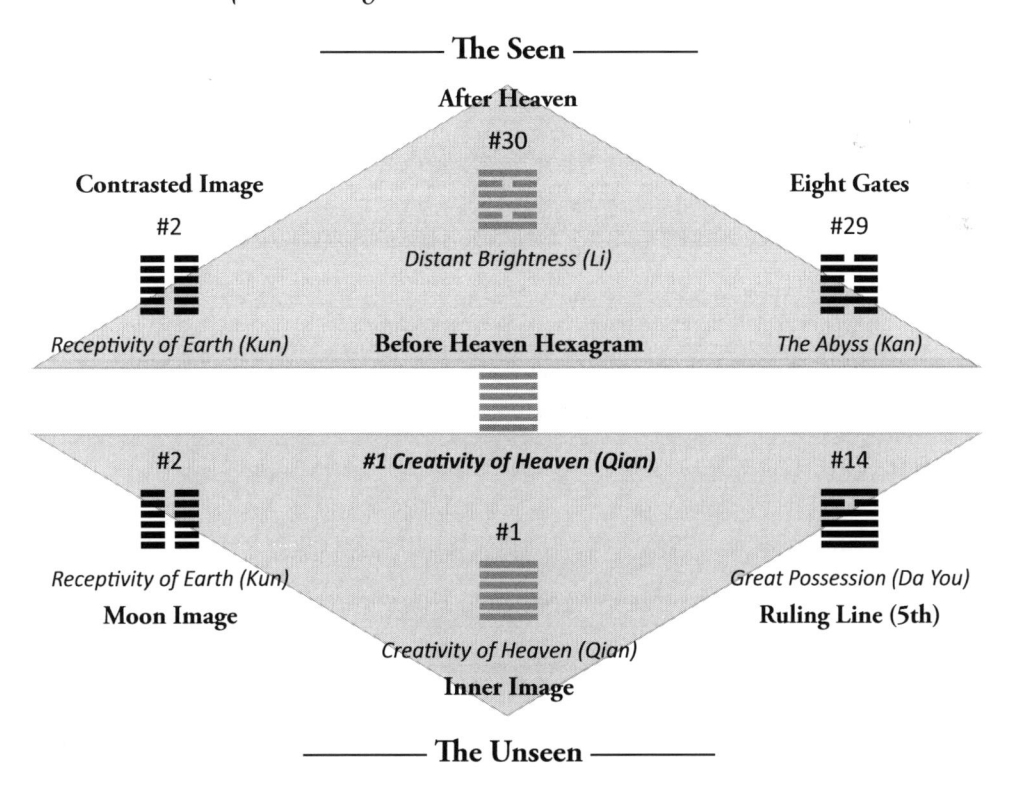

——— **The Seen** ———

After Heaven
#30
Distant Brightness (Li)

Contrasted Image
#2
Receptivity of Earth (Kun)

Eight Gates
#29
The Abyss (Kan)

Before Heaven Hexagram
#1 Creativity of Heaven (Qian)
#1
Creativity of Heaven (Qian)
Inner Image

#2
Receptivity of Earth (Kun)
Moon Image

#14
Great Possession (Da You)
Ruling Line (5th)

——— **The Unseen** ———

Kun 坤

Receptivity of Earth 2

Kun (Earth) above
坤 上
Kun Shang
Kun (Earth) below
坤 下
Kun Xia

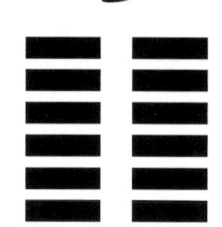

Image of the Female Dragon-Horse

Moon/Yin Image

The Prediction (象, Tuan)

Receptivity of Earth:
Great and persevering. Advantage in the correctness of a mare. The superior person has somewhere to go. At first going astray, but later finds the master. Advantage in obtaining friends in the Southwest. Friends will be lost in the Northeast. Quiet resoluteness is auspicious.

坤.元亨.利牝馬之貞.
君子有攸往.先迷後得主.
利西南得朋.東北喪朋.
安貞吉.

This image shows being resolute in action, but also to be cautious in those actions. Things are smooth at the beginning, but there is a foreboding, so it is better to ride a mare. Earth reveals the activities of the Po Spirits [2] and spiritual intuition. The horse seeks to roam the Earth and achieve tranquility. A person traveling on horseback, even if getting lost will in the end find the way. Traveling will help locate treasures in the Southwest, but treasures in the Northeast will be missed. Tranquility is auspicious because the mind can then correctly predict the future.

The Lines (爻, Yao)

First Six (初 六, Chu Liu)
Treading upon hoarfrost, solid ice is close.   履霜堅冰之.

When feeling frost under one's feet, freezing days are approaching. This is a time for waiting until the ice becomes solid enough to cross.

---

[2] *Po* (魄, Earthly Spirits) are the Seven Earthly Spirits that influence a person's more carnal or emotional activities.

Second Six (六 二, Liu Er)
The straight and square are great.   直方大. 不習无不利.
With no repeated actions
everything is beneficial.

Galloping into the open fields and finding yourself in unfamiliar territory brings no misfortune. Nature guides itself and so should a person.

Third Six (六 三, Liu San)
Restrained excellence through being resolute.   含章可貞. 或從.
Complying with the king's affairs is without   王事无成有終.
success in the end.

Virtuous people can be employed as fortunetellers or people can follow their master. Even if they achieve no great accomplishments they still have a good end. The wise person will gladly leave the ambition for fame to others.

Fourth Six (六 四, Liu Si)
A tied-up sack.   括囊. 无咎无譽.
Without fault and without praise.

Those who seek restraint by tying themselves into a sack too tightly experience neither trouble nor do they receive credit for their deeds. Just hold back whether in quiet solitude or in upheaval.

Fifth Six (六 五, Liu Wu)
The lower garment is yellow.   黃裳. 元吉.
Great auspiciousness.

Wearing a yellow robe brings good fortune, for it is the color of being neutral and so is a constant reminder to be moderate in your affairs. Wisdom reveals itself through discretion.

Topmost Six (上 六, Shang Liu)
Fighting dragons in the wild.   龍戰于野. 其血玄黃.
Their blood is black and yellow.

The excited dragons are fighting in Heaven and on Earth. From the deep blue sky down to the yellow Earth their blood is spilling. Be well aware of your position to avoid conflict.

The Usefulness of all Sixes (用九, **Yong Liu**)
Perpetual resoluteness is beneficial. 利永貞.

This is a very suitable time to make long-term plans and predictions because all six mares are in attendance.

Alternate English Translations for the Hexagram of Kun, 坤

Submission Symbolizes Earth [S]
The Passive Principle [B]
The Receptive [L] [WB]
Responding [H]
Field [K]

Earth [C]
Receptiveness (Responsiveness) [CS]
Receptiveness [N]
Space [RS]
The Symbol of Submission [CC]

The Great Symbolism (大象, Da Xiang) says,

The root-condition of the Earth is Kun. 地勢坤.君子以.
The superior person, according with this, 厚德載物.
supports all things through generosity
and virtue.

Trigram Correlations

Upper Gua (Earth)

☷ **Kun** 坤   **Represents:** Earth, Soil, Fields, Female, Mother, Empress
Actions: Receptive, Expanding, Yielding
Influences: Relationships, Love, Submission
Shape: Square   **Color:** Yellow
Body: Stomach   **Season:** Winter (Winter Solstice)
Moon Phase: New Moon
Animals: Earthly Ox, Celestial Black Tortoise
Directions: North (BH), Southwest (AH)
Nine Palaces Numbers: Fu Xi: **10**
     Yu the Great: Ho River Map, **1**—Lo River Script, **2**
Internal Alchemy: Tranquility, Void
     Qi Center: Hui Yin (Returning Yin)
     Qi Meridian: Ren Mai (Function Vessel)

Lower Gua (Earth)

▬▬ ▬▬ **Kun** 坤

Represents: Earth, Soil, Fields, Female, Mother, Empress
Actions: Receptive, Expanding, Yielding
Influences: Relationships, Love, Submission
Shape: Square   **Color:** Yellow
Body: Stomach   **Season:** Winter (Winter Solstice)
Moon Phase: New Moon
Animals: Earthly Ox, Celestial Black Tortoise
Directions: North (BH), Southwest (AH)
Nine Palaces Numbers: Fu Xi: **10**
  Yu the Great: Ho River Map, **1**—Lo River Script, **2**
Internal Alchemy: Tranquility, Void
  Qi Center: Hui Yin (Returning Yin)
  Qi Meridian: Ren Mai (Function Vessel)

Associated Developed Hexagrams of Kun

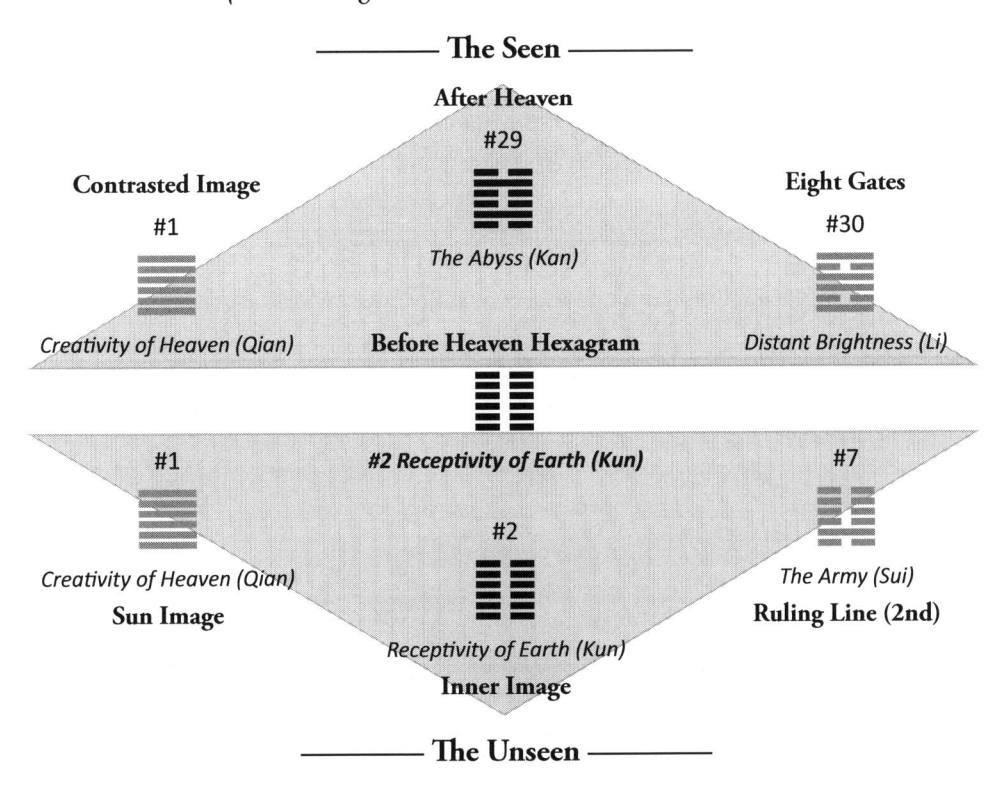

The Seen

After Heaven
#29
The Abyss (Kan)

Contrasted Image
#1
Creativity of Heaven (Qian)

Eight Gates
#30
Distant Brightness (Li)

Before Heaven Hexagram
#2 Receptivity of Earth (Kun)

#1
Creativity of Heaven (Qian)
Sun Image

#2
Receptivity of Earth (Kun)
Inner Image

#7
The Army (Sui)
Ruling Line (2nd)

The Unseen

Chun

屯

Beginning Difficulties

3

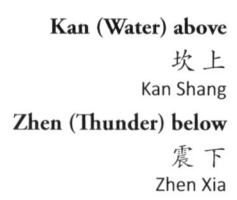

Kan (Water) above
坎 上
Kan Shang
Zhen (Thunder) below
震 下
Zhen Xia

Sun/Yang Image

The Prediction (象, Tuan)

Beginning Difficulties:
Great, persevering, advantageous, and correct. No use in having somewhere to go. Advantage in establishing the feudal princes.

屯. 元 亨 利 貞.
勿 用 有 攸 往.
利 建 侯.

To make friends is beneficial as they will come to your aid later. Not going anywhere brings ease and prosperity. It is a good time to plan for the future. No actions should be taken at this time, rather one should stay and serve the master so to bring order from the confusion.

The Lines (爻, Yao)

First Nine (初 九, Chu Jiu)
Hesitation. Advantage in remaining resolute. Advantage in establishing the feudal princes.

磐 桓. 利 居 貞. 利 建 侯.

When in doubt, it's better to remain quiet than to take action. Good time for planning and to attend to the needs of the master. This is a good time to procure helpers so to persevere through all the obstacles.

Second Six (六 二, Liu Er)
Hard and difficult to proceed.
Leaving by riding a horse. A robber wants to take a second wife. The daughter is correct, but no son. After ten years she bears children.

屯 如 邅 如. 乘 馬 班 如.
匪 寇 婚 媾. 女 子 貞 不 字.
十 年 乃 字.

Riders on horses are galloping towards you. First you question who they are. Then you see they are not robbers, but have come with the purpose of seeking a concubine. The daughter is proper, but unable to become pregnant. After ten years she will bear children. Be cautious and prepare for a long period of patient waiting.

Third Six (六 三, Liu San)
Tracking deer without a forester. Getting lost in the midst of the forest. The superior person is ingenious and not likely to go home. To move on brings regret.

卽鹿无虞.惟入于林中.
君子幾不如舍.往吝.

Chasing a deer too deep into the forest will bring misfortune. Give up the chase; otherwise, one will get lost and encounter trouble. Look carefully at the signs (the tracks of the deer) and restrain from movement at this time.

Fourth Six (六 四, Liu Si)
Leaving by riding a horse. Seeking to take a wife. To move on is auspicious. Everything is beneficial.

乘馬班如.求婚媾.
往吉.无不利.

Going to ask for a lady's hand in marriage on horseback is auspicious. Overcoming your pride attracts those who will come to your aid.

Fifth Nine (九 五, Jiu Wu)
Beginning Difficulties in dispensing riches. Moderate resoluteness is auspicious. Extreme resoluteness brings misfortune.

屯其膏.小貞吉.
大貞凶.

Store up food and money. Saving small amounts brings good fortune; hoarding is unfortunate. A gentle push is far more productive than a forceful one.

Topmost Six (上 六, Shang Liu)
Leaving by riding a horse.
Bloody streams of tears flow.

乘馬班如.泣血漣如.

Ride slowly as the tears from sobbing blind one's way. Do not persist in such conditions.

Alternate English Translations for the Hexagram of Chun, 屯

The Symbol of Bursting [CC] [S]
Difficulty [B] [C]
Difficulty at the Beginning [WB]
Beginning [H]
Sprouting [K]

Difficulty in Infancy [CS]
To Be Stationed—To Assemble [N]
Sprouting [RS]
Difficulty in the Beginning [L]

The Great Symbolism (大象, Da Xiang) says,

Clouds and Thunder. This is Chun.
The superior person, according with this,
sorts the silk threads into a fabric.

雲雷.屯.君子以經綸.

Sexagenary Placement

Heavenly Stem: Ji 己 (6th Stem, Yin)—**Earth** (土, Tu)
Earthly Branch: Si 巳 (6th Branch, Yin)—**Snake** (蛇, She)
Represents the *Year of the Earth Snake* (6th Year of the Sixty-Year Cycle)
Years: 1869 – 1929 – 1989 – 2049

Trigram Correlations

Upper Gua (Water)

Kan 坎   **Represents:** Water, Moon, Springs/Streams, Middle Son
              Actions: Peril, Danger, and Difficulty.
              Influences: Abysmal Life Path and Vocation
              Shape: Wave   **Color:** Black
              Body: Ears   **Season:** Autumn (Autumn Equinox)
              Moon Phase: First Quarter
              Animals: Earthly Pig, Celestial White Tiger
              Directions: West (BH), North (AH)
              Nine Palaces Numbers: Fu Xi: 4
                    Yu the Great: Ho River Map, 7—Lo River Script, **1**
              Internal Alchemy: Essence, Jing, Lead
                    Qi Center: Shuang Guan (Double Pass)
                    Qi Meridian: Chong Mai (Penetrating Vessel)

#3 Beginning Difficulties (Chun)

Lower Gua (Thunder)

Zhen 震　**Represents:** Thunder, Earthquake, Eldest Son
Actions: Arousing, Shaking, Initiating
Influences: Foundations, Past Actions, Excitement.
Shape: Vertical Column　　**Color:** Green
Body: Feet and legs　　**Season:** Beginning Winter
Moon Phase: Waning Crescent
Animals: Earthly Dragons, Celestial Dragon-Horse
Directions: Northeast (BH), East (AH)
Nine Palaces Numbers: Fu Xi: **3**
　Yu the Great: Ho River Map, **8**—Lo River Script, **3**
Internal Alchemy: Mind-Intention
　Qi Center: Dan Tian (Elixir Field)
　Qi Meridian: Yin Qiao Mai (Yin Heel Vessel)

Associated Developed Hexagrams of Chun

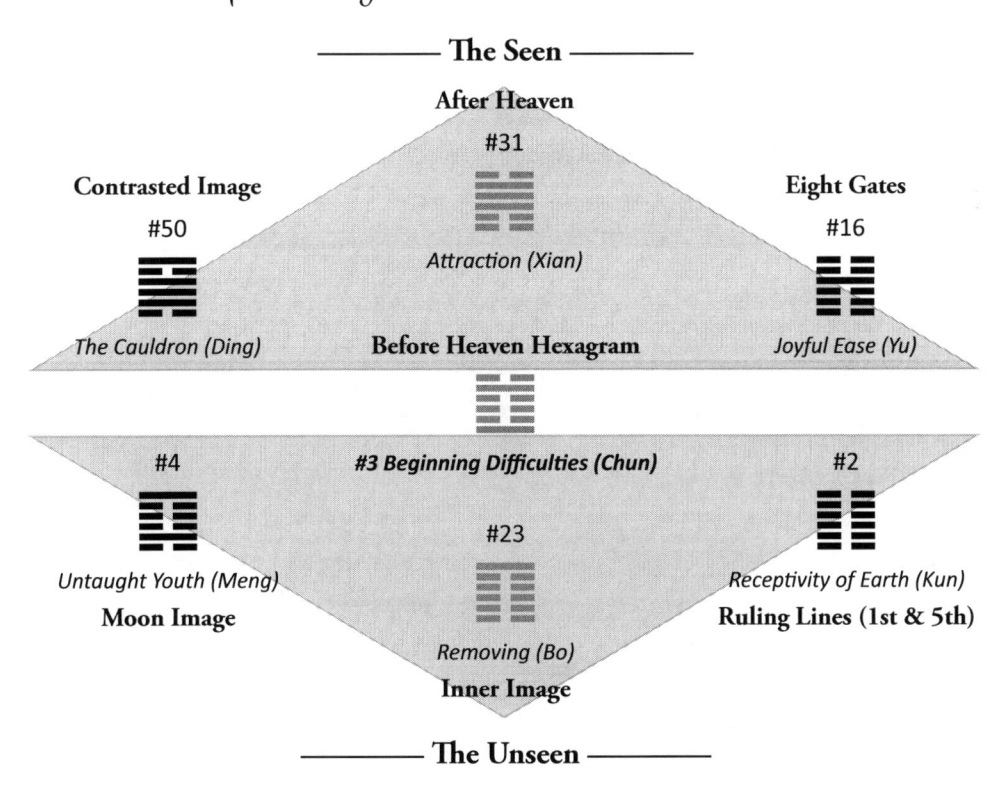

────── **The Seen** ──────

After Heaven
#31
Attraction (Xian)

Contrasted Image
#50
The Cauldron (Ding)

Eight Gates
#16
Joyful Ease (Yu)

Before Heaven Hexagram

#3 Beginning Difficulties (Chun)

#4
Untaught Youth (Meng)
Moon Image

#23
Removing (Bo)
Inner Image

#2
Receptivity of Earth (Kun)
Ruling Lines (1st & 5th)

────── **The Unseen** ──────

Meng
蒙

Untaught Youth

4

Gen (Mountain) above
艮 上
Gen Shang
Kan (Water) below
坎 下
Kan Xia

Moon/Yin Image

The Prediction (彖, Tuan)

Untaught Youth:
Perseverance. I do not seek the Untaught Youth. The Untaught Youth seeks me. First instructing divination by stalks. But a second or third time it is annoying. I do not instruct the annoying. Advantage in being resolute.

蒙．亨．匪我求童蒙．
童蒙求我．初筮告．
再三瀆．
瀆則不告．
利貞．

Adhere to acceptable conventions, but do not accept what is wrong with a fool, for this is folly in itself. Strengthening what is right in the fool is a worthy spiritual undertaking. Dispelling ignorance can bring harmony and success. However, do not ask to foretell an ignorant person's future. Wait for one to come to you. The first divination is auspicious, but when a person comes back and asks a second or third time, it shows he or she is not sincere and the answers will not be correct. This person is only looking for the answer he or she wants.

The Lines (爻, Yao)

First Six (初 六, Chu Liu)
Instruct the Untaught Youth.
Beneficial to apply punishments.
Useful to remove the fetters and manacles.
Moving forward brings regret.

發蒙．利用刑人．
用說桎梏．
以往吝．

Show the convicted person to warn the ignorant. This can prevent them from having their own hands and feet fettered. Even so, their past transgressions will not be without misfortune. There is vast difference between showing discipline and acting as a tyrant.

Second Nine (九二, Jiu Er)
Guide the Untaught Youth.   包蒙. 吉. 納婦吉. 子克家.
Auspicious. To receive a wife is auspicious.
The son is capable in family affairs.

It is auspicious to conceal the son's shortcomings at this time so he can take a bride. The son must provide for the family. Teaching tolerance is the most expedient means for teaching him responsibility.

Third Six (六三, Liu San)
No use in acquiring a wife.   勿用取女. 見金夫.
Seeing a man of gold,   不有躬. 无攸利.
there is loss of one's own self.
Nowhere is beneficial.

Do not marry the girl as she has no regard for people of influence and knowledge when she meets with them. This will cause you misfortune. It is best to use your own standards and rules to measure yourself.

Fourth Six (六四, Liu Si)
Restraining the Untaught Youth. Regret.   困蒙. 吝.

Trying to restrain the ignorant only invites more trouble. Persisting in ignorance will only result in humiliation and remorse.

Fifth Six (六五, Liu Wu)
The Untaught Youth is pure. Auspicious.   童蒙. 吉.

It is auspicious that the child is naive and innocent.

Topmost Nine (上九, Shang Jiu)
Striking the Untaught Youth. No benefit   擊蒙. 不利為寇. 利禦寇.
in doing harm. It is beneficial to resist harm.

Making mistakes when punishing the ignorant turns them into rebels. If punished correctly, they will become agents who oppose rebels. Never punish the ignorant with anger, rather show understanding and teach positive, productive discipline.

Alternate English Translations for the Hexagram of Meng, 蒙

The Symbol of Covering [S]
Immaturity, Uncultivated Growth [B]
Youthful Folly [WB]
Childhood [H]
Darkness [C]
The Symbol of Obscurity [CC]

Immaturity [CS]
The Undeveloped One [N]
Enveloping [RS]
Youth [L]
Enveloping Ignorance [K]

The Great Symbolism (大象, Da Xiang) says,

From beneath a Mountain, a Spring issues forth. This is Meng. Superior persons, according with this, are resolute about their actions and in nourishing virtue.

山下出泉. 蒙.
君子以果行育德.

Sexagenary Placement

Heavenly Stem: Ji 己 (6th Stem, Yin)—**Earth** (土, Tu)
Earthly Branch: Mao 卯 (4th Branch, Yin)—**Rabbit** (兔, Tu)
Represents the *Year of the Earth Rabbit* (16th Year of the Sixty-Year Cycle)
Years: 1879 – 1939 – 1999 – 2059

Trigram Correlations

Upper Gua (Mountain)

Gen 艮
- **Represents:** Mountain, Towers, Youngest Son
- **Actions:** Stillness, Binding, Stopping
- **Influences:** Knowledge, Wisdom, Skill, Determination
- **Shape:** Vertical Column   **Color:** Blue
- **Body:** Hands and arms   **Season:** Beginning Autumn
- **Moon Phase:** Waxing Crescent
- **Animals:** Earthly Dog, Celestial Vermilion Snake
- **Directions:** Northwest (BH), Northeast (AH)
- **Nine Palaces Numbers:** Fu Xi: 7
  Yu the Great: Ho River Map, **6**— Lo River Script, **8**
- **Internal Alchemy:** Hun (Heavenly) Spirit

Qi Center: Jing Men (Essence Gate)

Qi Meridian: Yang Qiao Mai (Yang Heel Vessel)

Lower Gua (Water)

☵ Kan 坎

Represents: Water, Moon, Springs/Streams, Middle Son

Actions: Peril, Danger, and Difficulty.

Influences: Abysmal Life Path and Vocation

Shape: Wave   **Color:** Black

Body: Ears   **Season:** Autumn (Autumn Equinox)

Moon Phase: First Quarter

Animals: Earthly Pig, Celestial White Tiger

Directions: West (BH), North (AH)

Nine Palaces Numbers: Fu Xi: 4

Yu the Great: Ho River Map, 7—Lo River Script, 1

Internal Alchemy: Essence, Jing, Lead

Qi Center: Shuang Guan (Double Pass)

Qi Meridian: Chong Mai (Penetrating Vessel)

Associated Developed Hexagrams of Meng

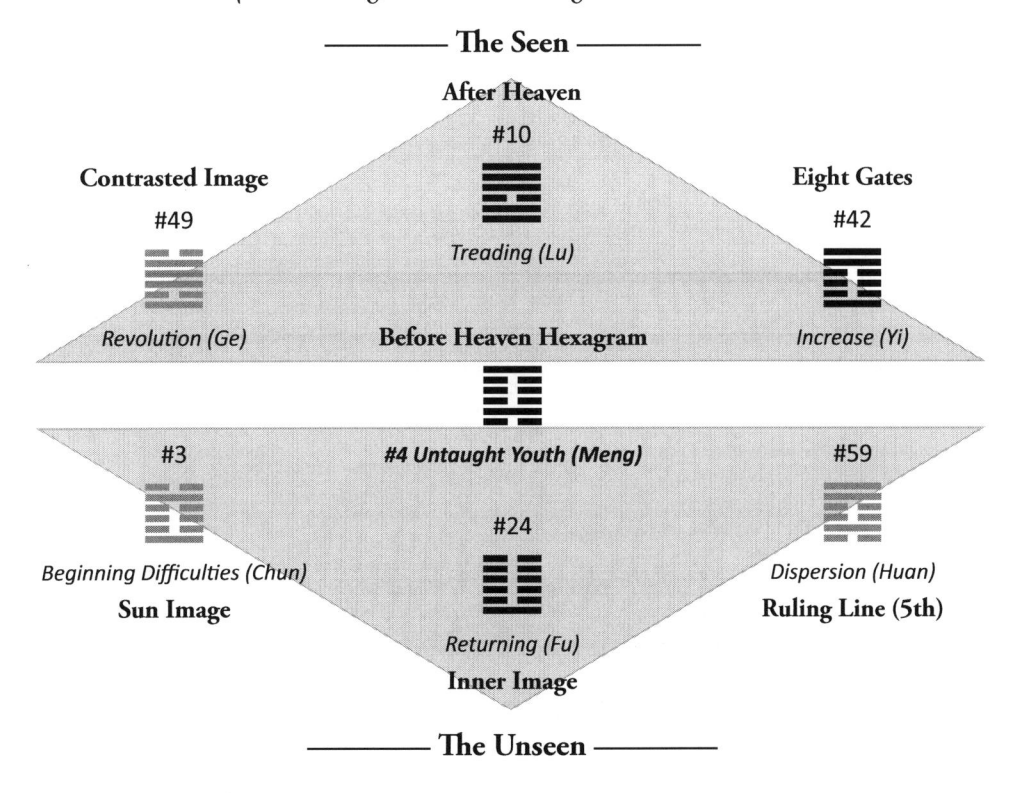

——— **The Seen** ———

After Heaven

#10

Treading (Lu)

Contrasted Image   **Eight Gates**
#49   #42

Revolution (Ge)   *Increase (Yi)*

Before Heaven Hexagram

#3   **#4 Untaught Youth (Meng)**   #59

Beginning Difficulties (Chun)   *Dispersion (Huan)*

Sun Image   **Ruling Line (5th)**

#24

Returning (Fu)

Inner Image

——— **The Unseen** ———

Xu

Hesitation

5

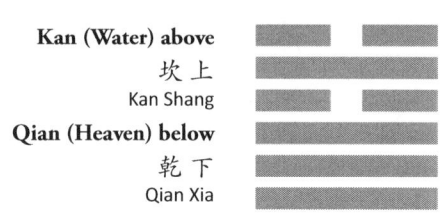

需

Kan (Water) above
坎上
Kan Shang
Qian (Heaven) below
乾下
Qian Xia

Sun/Yang Image

The Prediction (象, Tuan)

Hesitation:
There is sincerity, brightness, perseverance, correctness, and auspiciousness.
Advantage in fording the great stream.

需. 有孚光亨貞吉.
利涉大川.

This hexagram shows that boldness incites opposition. Wait in patience and contemplation. Something will appear showing greatness and harmony. Planning is auspicious at this time. It will reveal a way to cross the river.

The Lines (爻, Yao)

First Nine (初 九, Chu Jiu)
Hesitation on distant borders.
There is advantage in being constant.
Without fault.

需 于 郊. 利用恆. 无咎.

Waiting on the edge of things, adopt a strategy for defending the outside of the city and see what changes occur. Just observe and remain still. This is beneficial.

Second Nine (九 二, Jiu Er)
Hesitation in the sand.
Having few words. The end is auspicious.

需 于 沙. 小有言. 終 吉.

Lay in ambush in the sand fields at the bank of the river and keep silent. Stay calm even though things are uncertain. This is auspicious.

#5 Hesitation (Xu)

Third Nine (九 三, Jiu San)
Hesitation in the mud.
Brings about the arrival of injury.

需 于 泥. 致 寇 至.

Do not stay in a damp and muddy place. Bandits will arrive. Use extra caution as this situation is very unfavorable.

Fourth Six (六 四, Liu Si)
Hesitation in blood.
Get out of the cave.

需 于 血. 出 自 穴.

Fight the enemy head-on. This is the time to order the troops to come out of the trenches and surprise the enemy with a sudden attack. This situation shows great danger, so use caution when taking action.

Fifth Nine (九 五, Jiu Wu)
Hesitation with food and wine.
This is correct and auspicious.

需 于 酒 食. 貞 吉.

Providing the soldiers with wine and food brings an auspicious future. There is a lull in the situation so it is auspicious to nourish the body and spirit.

Topmost Six (上 六, Shang Liu)
Enter the cave. Without any urging
three uninvited guests are arriving. Treat
them with respect. The end is auspicious.

入 于 穴. 有 不 速 之 客 三 人 來.
敬 之. 終 吉.

Moving back into your camp, three strangers are inside the cave. Be careful with them and things will be beneficial. Blinded at first by despair, it's hard to see friends who can come to your aid.

Alternate English Translations for the Hexagram of Xu, 需

The Symbol of Waiting [CC] [S]
Waiting [C] [CS]
Calculated Inaction [B]
Waiting (Nourishment) [L] [WB]

Needing [H]
Waiting—Stagnation—Hesitation [N]
Attending [K] [RS]

The Great Symbolism (大象, Da Xiang) says,

Clouds ascending into the Heavens [sky]. 雲上於天.需.
This is Xu. The superior person, 君子以飲食宴樂.
according with this, eats and drinks
joyfully at the feast.

Sexagenary Placement

Heavenly Stem: Ding 丁 (4th Stem, Yin)—**Fire** (火, Huo)
Earthly Branch: Wei 未 (8th Branch, Yin)—**Goat** (羊, Yang)
Represents the *Year of the Fire Goat* (44th Year of the Sixty-Year Cycle)
Years: 1847 – 1907 – 1967 – 2027

Trigram Correlations

Upper Gua (Water)

Kan 坎 **Represents:** Water, Moon, Springs/Streams, Middle Son
Actions: Peril, Danger, and Difficulty.
Influences: Abysmal Life Path and Vocation
Shape: Wave **Color:** Black
Body: Ears **Season:** Autumn (Autumn Equinox)
Moon Phase: First Quarter
Animals: Earthly Pig, Celestial White Tiger
Directions: West (BH), North (AH)
Nine Palaces Numbers: Fu Xi: 4
  Yu the Great: Ho River Map, 7—Lo River Script, 1
Internal Alchemy: Essence, Jing, Lead
  Qi Center: Shuang Guan (Double Pass)
  Qi Meridian: Chong Mai (Penetrating Vessel)

Lower Gua (Heaven)

Qian 乾   **Represents:** Heaven, Sky, Male, Father, Emperor
Actions: Creative Principle, Persisting, Forceful
Influences: Blessings, Good Fortune, Strength, Spiritual Power
Shape: Circle   **Color:** White
Body: Head   **Season:** Summer (Summer Solstice)
Moon Phase: Full Moon
Animals: Earthly Horse, Celestial Red Phoenix
Directions: South (BH), Northwest (AH)
Nine Palaces Numbers: Fu Xi: **2**
  Yu the Great: Ho River Map, **9**—Lo River Script, **6**
Internal Alchemy: Clarity, Illumination
  Qi Center: Ni Wan (Mud Pellet)
  Qi Meridian: Du Mai (Control Vessel)

Associated Developed Hexagrams of Xu

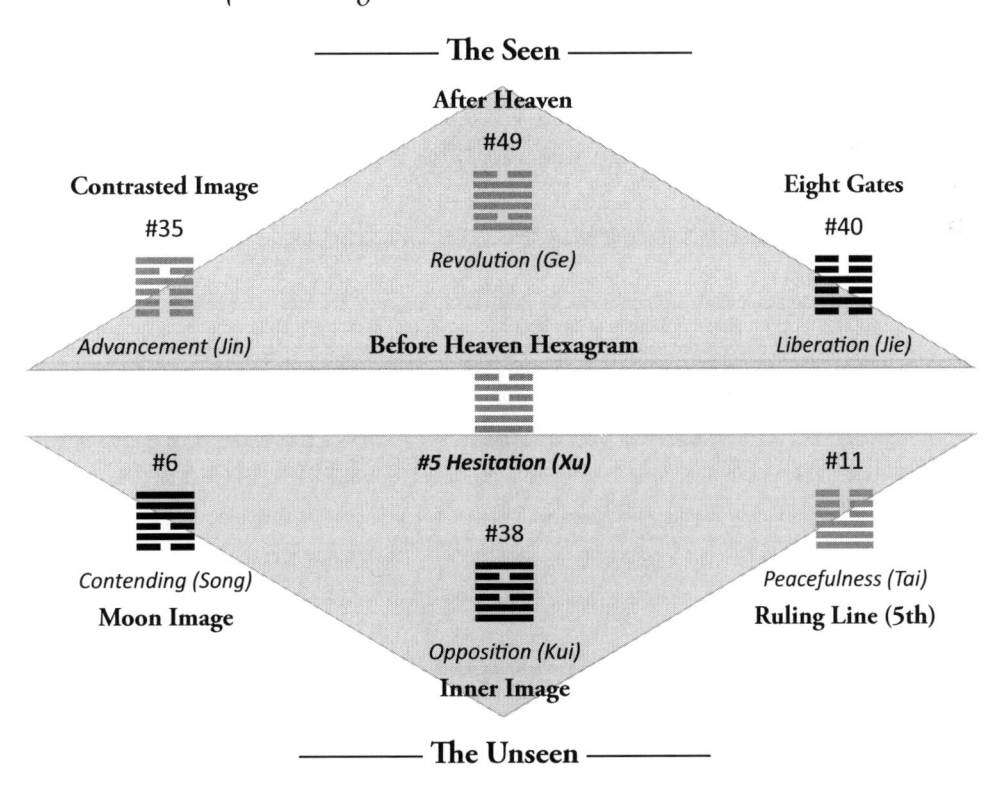

—— **The Seen** ——

After Heaven
#49
Revolution (Ge)

Contrasted Image
#35
Advancement (Jin)

Eight Gates
#40
Liberation (Jie)

Before Heaven Hexagram
#5 Hesitation (Xu)

#6
Contending (Song)
Moon Image

#38
Opposition (Kui)
Inner Image

#11
Peacefulness (Tai)
Ruling Line (5th)

—— **The Unseen** ——

Song

訟

Contending

6

Qian (Heaven) above
乾上
Qian Shang
Kan (Water) below
坎下
Kan Xia

Moon/Yin Image

The Prediction (象, Tuan)

Contending:
Having sincerity and obstruction.
Auspicious to cherish the middle.
In the end, misfortune.
Advantage in seeing the elder.
No advantage in fording the great stream.

訟.有孚窒.惕中吉.終凶.
利見大人.不利涉大川.

Avoid making rash decisions as there is a latent conflict. Be hesitant about contending. Involve yourself in proper litigation. Even though an award is received there is still a feeling of loss and regret. The middle of the situation is good, but the end is bad. It is good to go see people of power and influence, but do not attempt to overcome big obstacles.

The Lines (爻, Yao)

First Six (初 六, Chu Liu)
Not perpetuating one's affairs.
Having few words. In the end, auspicious.

不永所事.小有言.終吉.

Don't complain and argue about a litigation, and cease even talking about it. Best to just drop the whole matter. In the end there will be a good result.

Second Nine (九 二, Jiu Er)
Incapable of Contending.
Retiring and taking sanctuary.
There are only three hundred families
in the city. There is no injury.

不克訟.歸而逋.
其邑人三百戶.无眚.

After failing to win a litigation, tell all the villagers (all those involved—the three hundred families) they should retreat and escape to find sanctuary. Disaster can then be avoided.

Third Six (六 三, Liu San)
Repay kindness to the aged. This is correct. 食舊德.貞.厲終吉.
Harshness, but the end is auspicious. 或從王事.无成.
Perhaps attending to the affairs of the king.
Without success.

Sit at your leisure and enjoy the benefits of your accumulated past merits and virtue. Danger was predicted, but the situation turned out auspicious. The strength of your character brings a good result for others. Attend to and follow the master, but you will not achieve any great successes.

Fourth Nine (九 四, Jiu Si)
Incapable of Contending. 不克訟.復即命.渝安貞.吉.
Return to accord with [one's] **destiny.**
To change and rest is correct. Auspicious.

After failing to win the litigation, re-examine yourself, the present situation, and change your strategy. Reject the easy path and stay in harmony with your destiny. Be still and quiet, use your intuition, and you will obtain an auspicious future.

Fifth Nine (九 五, Jiu Wu)
Contending. Great auspiciousness. 訟.元吉.

From the beginning, involvement in the litigation has been auspicious. Seeking advice from a wise person will settle any contention.

Topmost Nine (上 九, Shang Jiu)
Perchance a leather belt is granted. 或錫之鞶帶.終朝三褫之.
By the end of the morning it is stripped
away three times.

It is likely a belt (showing status and promotion) will be presented three times within one day, but it will be taken away three times in one day as well. Winning the litigation quickly results in attracting more conflict.

Alternate English Translations for the Hexagram of Song, 訟

Symbol of Contention [S]   *Contending (Litigation)* [N]
Conflict [B] [CS] [L] [WB]   *Arguing* [K] [RS]
Contention [C] [H]   *The Symbol of Contention* [CC]

The Great Symbolism (大象, Da Xiang) says,

Heaven and Water moving apart from one another. This is Song. The superior person, according with this, considers the beginning before acting on affairs.

天與水違行. 訟.
君子以作事謀始.

☰ Sexagenary Placement

Heavenly Stem: Gui 癸 (10th Stem, Yin)—**Water** (水, Shui)
Earthly Branch: Chou 丑 (2nd Branch, Yin)—**Ox** (牛, Niu)
Represents the *Year of the Water Ox* (50th Year of the Sixty-Year Cycle)
Years: 1853 – 1913 – 1973 – 2033

Trigram Correlations

Upper Gua (Heaven)

☰ **Qian** 乾
- **Represents:** Heaven, Sky, Male, Father, Emperor
- **Actions:** Creative Principle, Persisting, Forceful
- **Influences:** Blessings, Good Fortune, Strength, Spiritual Power
- **Shape:** Circle **Color:** White
- **Body:** Head **Season:** Summer (Summer Solstice)
- **Moon Phase:** Full Moon
- **Animals:** Earthly Horse, Celestial Red Phoenix
- **Directions:** South (BH), Northwest (AH)
- **Nine Palaces Numbers:** Fu Xi: **2**
  - Yu the Great: Ho River Map, **9**—Lo River Script, **6**
- **Internal Alchemy:** Clarity, Illumination
  - Qi Center: Ni Wan (Mud Pellet)
  - Qi Meridian: Du Mai (Control Vessel)

#6 Contending (Song)

Lower Gua (Water)

☵ **Kan** 坎

Represents: Water, Moon, Springs/Streams, Middle Son
Actions: Peril, Danger, and Difficulty.
Influences: Abysmal Life Path and Vocation
Shape: Wave   **Color:** Black
Body: Ears   **Season:** Autumn (Autumn Equinox)
Moon Phase: First Quarter
Animals: Earthly Pig, Celestial White Tiger
Directions: West (BH), North (AH)
Nine Palaces Numbers: Fu Xi: 4
    Yu the Great: Ho River Map, 7—Lo River Script, 1
Internal Alchemy: Essence, Jing, Lead
    Qi Center: Shuang Guan (Double Pass)
    Qi Meridian: Chong Mai (Penetrating Vessel)

Associated Developed Hexagrams of Song

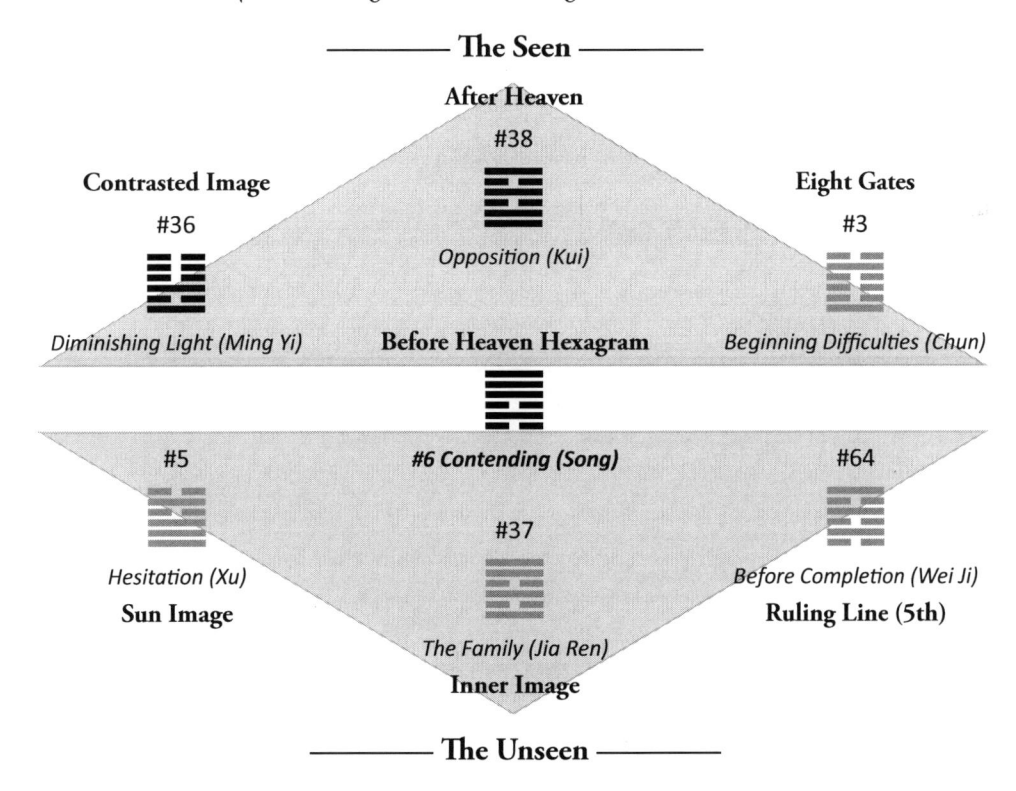

——— **The Seen** ———

After Heaven
#38
Opposition (Kui)

Contrasted Image
#36
Diminishing Light (Ming Yi)

Eight Gates
#3
Beginning Difficulties (Chun)

Before Heaven Hexagram

#6 Contending (Song)

#5
Hesitation (Xu)
Sun Image

#37
The Family (Jia Ren)
Inner Image

#64
Before Completion (Wei Ji)
Ruling Line (5th)

——— **The Unseen** ———

25

Shi 師

The Army 7

Kun (Earth) above
坤上
Kun Shang
Kan (Water) below
坎下
Kan Xia

Sun/Yang Image

The Prediction (象, Tuan)

The Army:
Resoluteness. An elderly leader of the people is auspicious. Without fault.

師. 貞. 丈人吉. 无咎.

This image shows the advantage of having an open mind. Divine to choose an elder commander of the troops and the future will be bright and without catastrophe. The path you've chosen is correct and your actions show discipline. There is no reproach and good fortune results.

The Lines (爻, Yao)

First Six (初 六, Chu Liu)
According to the law, The Army goes forth. It is not right. Misfortune.

師出以律. 否藏. 凶.

Set the troops to marching discipline and maintain a well-planned strategy before moving forth. If the soldiers have no discipline, a violent and vicious end will result.

Second Nine (九 二, Jiu Er)
Dwelling in the midst of The Army. Auspicious. Without fault. Thrice the king conveys his decrees.

在師中. 吉. 无咎. 王三錫命.

To be the commander is auspicious and there will be no disasters. The emperor bestows commendations often. Remain centered and you can share your good fortune with others.

#7 The Army (Shi)

Third Six (六 三, Liu San)
Perchance corpses are within
The Army carriages. Misfortune.

師或輿尸.凶.

Military carriages carrying corpses signals misfortune. Rely on the strength of your own self, as this will bring benefit to your cause and to others.

Fourth Six (六 四, Liu Si)
The Army needs aid at camp.
Without fault.

師左次.无咎.

If the troops are stationed on the left and the commander on the right, there will be no harm. Leave no detail unresolved, then there can be a good end.

Fifth Six (六 五, Liu Wu)
Having captured the field. Advantageous
to pronounce it. Without fault.
The eldest son commands The Army.
The youngest son tends the corpse carriages.
Even though correct, misfortune.

田有禽.利執言.无咎.
長子帥師.弟子輿尸.
貞凶.

Catching animals in the field to feed the troops will not bring misfortune. If the commander sends his eldest son to lead the troops and his youngest son to collect corpses, this will bring misfortune, even though it is correct. Better to cease further action or even go into retreat, otherwise defeat will ensue

Topmost Six (上 六, Shang Liu)
The great prince issues his decrees.
Establishes states and vests the worthy
with high official rank. Inferior people
need not be employed.

大君有命.開國承家.
小人勿用.

The prince confers nobility, wealth, and lands to the commander and his family, but the commander must not put on airs. There must be a sharing of the victory with others.

27

Alternate English Translations for the Hexagram of Shi, 師

The Symbol of Multitude and of Army [S]
The Army [B] [C] [L] [WB]
Multitude [H]
Legions/Leading [K]

Military Expedition (The Army) [CS]
Military Leadership [N]
The Legions [RS]
The Symbol of Multitudes [CC]

The Great Symbolism (大象, Da Xiang) says,

There is Water within the Earth. This is Shi.
The superior person, according with this,
forgives people and nourishes the multitudes.

地中有水. 師.
君子以容民畜衆.

Sexagenary Placement

Heavenly Stem: Yi 乙 (2nd Stem, Yin)—**Wood** (木, Mu)
Earthly Branch: Si 巳 (6th Branch, Yin)—**Snake** (蛇, She)
Represents the *Year of the Wood Snake* (42nd Year of the Sixty-Year Cycle)
Years: 1845 – 1905 – 1965 – 2025

Trigram Correlations

Upper Gua (Earth)

Kun 坤
Represents: Earth, Soil, Fields, Female, Mother, Empress
Actions: Receptive, Expanding, Yielding
Influences: Relationships, Love, Submission
Shape: Square   **Color:** Yellow
Body: Stomach   **Season:** Winter (Winter Solstice)
Moon Phase: New Moon
Animals: Earthly Ox, Celestial Black Tortoise
Directions: North (BH), Southwest (AH)
Nine Palaces Numbers: Fu Xi: **10**
    Yu the Great: Ho River Map, **1**—Lo River Script, **2**
Internal Alchemy: Tranquility, Void
    Qi Center: Hui Yin (Returning Yin)
    Qi Meridian: Ren Mai (Function Vessel)

Lower Gua (Water)

Kan 坎 **Represents:** Water, Moon, Springs/Streams, Middle Son
Actions: Peril, Danger, and Difficulty.
Influences: Abysmal Life Path and Vocation
Shape: Wave **Color:** Black
Body: Ears **Season:** Autumn (Autumn Equinox)
Moon Phase: First Quarter
Animals: Earthly Pig, Celestial White Tiger
Directions: West (BH), North (AH)
Nine Palaces Numbers: Fu Xi: 4
   Yu the Great: Ho River Map, 7—Lo River Script, 1
Internal Alchemy: Essence, Jing, Lead
   Qi Center: Shuang Guan (Double Pass)
   Qi Meridian: Chong Mai (Penetrating Vessel)

Associated Developed Hexagrams of Shi

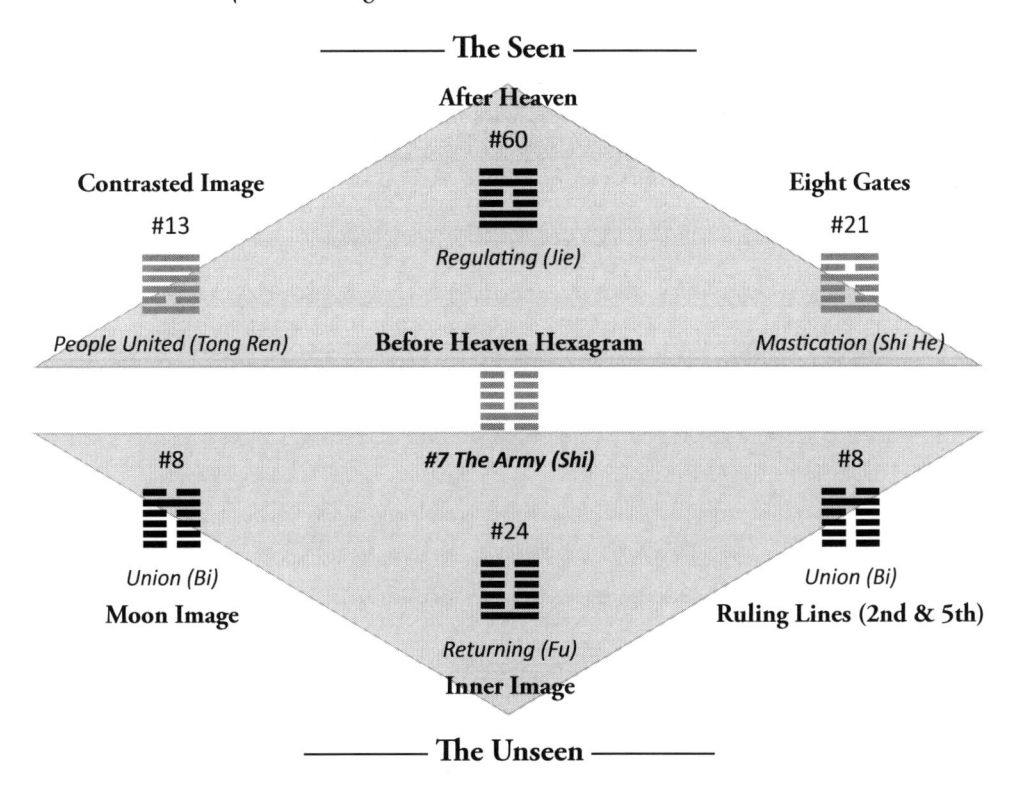

——— **The Seen** ———

After Heaven
#60
Regulating (Jie)

Contrasted Image
#13
People United (Tong Ren)

Eight Gates
#21
Mastication (Shi He)

Before Heaven Hexagram

#7 The Army (Shi)

#8
Union (Bi)
Moon Image

#24
Returning (Fu)
Inner Image

#8
Union (Bi)
Ruling Lines (2nd & 5th)

——— **The Unseen** ———

Bi

比

Union

8

Kan (Water) above
坎 上
Kan Shang
Kun (Earth) below
坤 下
Kun Xia

Moon/Yin Image

The Prediction (彖, Tuan)

***Union*:**
Auspicious. The principles of divining
by stalks are great and perpetually correct.
Without fault. Those without peace will
come. Those who come too late
suffer misfortune.

比.吉.原筮元永貞.无咎.
不寧方來.後夫凶.

Scheming and using unworthy intentions will bring misfortune. Union is auspicious if the leader is strong and creates unity. Consult the stalks again to make two separate plans, one long-term and one short-term, then disasters can be avoided. Someone who has angered you is coming to attack. Trouble will come if your actions are too slow, so be prepared to give as much as you take.

The Lines (爻, Yao)

First Six (初 六, Chu Liu)
Union having sincerity. Without fault.
Sincerity has filled the earthenware.
In the end, others arrive. Auspicious.

有孚比之.无咎.
有孚盈缶.
終來有他.吉.

Be kind to prisoners of war. Provide them with wine and food. From this, misfortune can be turned into good fortune. Even if the unexpected happens it will be auspicious. Nothing unites people better than the expression of unity.

Second Six (六 二, Liu Er)
Union within one's own self.
Correct and auspicious.

比之自內.貞吉.

Internal harmony and uniting the self and spirit is auspicious. The unity of internal matters will attract successes of external matters.

Third Six (六 三, Liu San)
Union with the wrong people.   比之匪人.

You have not chosen your friends well. Only form unions with those of your position and interests.

Fourth Six (六 四, Liu Si)
Union from without. Correct and auspicious.   外比之. 貞吉.

Choosing friends from outside your circle is auspicious. Find a master, but always remember who you are.

Fifth Nine (九 五, Jiu Wu)
Illustrious Union. The king uses   顯比. 王用三驅失前禽.
but three sides. Allowing the animals   邑人不誡. 吉.
in front to escape. The people of the city
need no warning. Auspicious.

Everyone is in harmony and on good terms if there is no coercing and all are allowed to exist by their own free will. When hunting with the king, it is honorable to leave one area open for animals to escape. Even though some game is lost, the citizens will not worry about their ruler's character. All is auspicious.

Topmost Six (上 六, Shang Liu)
Union without anyone at the head of it.   比之无首. 凶.
Misfortune.

The people are in harmony, but they are without a leader. If there is no leader, there can be no unity. The prospects foretell of misfortune.

Alternate English Translations for the Hexagram of Bi, 比

The Symbol of Subaltern Assistance [S]   *Union* [H] [L]
Holding Together (Union) [WB]   *Uniting* [CS]
Unity, Coordination [B]   *Fellowship* [N]
Accord [C]   *Grouping* [K] [RS]
The Symbol of Collaboration [CC]

The Great Symbolism (大象, Da Xiang) says,

The Earth and above it there is Water. This is Bi. The ancient kings, according with this, established all the states and cultivated good relations with the princes.

地上有水. 比.
先王建萬國親諸侯.

Sexagenary Placement

Heavenly Stem: Ding 丁 (4th Stem, Yin)—**Fire** (火, Huo)
Earthly Branch: Mao 卯 (4th Branch, Yin)—**Rabbit** (兔, Tu)
Represents the *Year of the Fire Rabbit* (4th Year of the Sixty-Year Cycle)
Years: 1867 – 1927 – 1987 – 2047

Trigram Correlations

Upper Gua (Water)

Kan 坎   **Represents:** Water, Moon, Springs/Streams, Middle Son
Actions: Peril, Danger, and Difficulty.
Influences: Abysmal Life Path and Vocation
Shape: Wave   **Color:** Black
Body: Ears   **Season:** Autumn (Autumn Equinox)
Moon Phase: First Quarter
Animals: Earthly Pig, Celestial White Tiger
Directions: West (BH), North (AH)
Nine Palaces Numbers: Fu Xi: 4
    Yu the Great: Ho River Map, 7—Lo River Script, **1**
Internal Alchemy: Essence, Jing, Lead
    Qi Center: Shuang Guan (Double Pass)
    Qi Meridian: Chong Mai (Penetrating Vessel)

#8 Union (Bi)

Lower Gua (Earth)

⚏ **Kun** 坤   **Represents:** Earth, Soil, Fields, Female, Mother, Empress
Actions: Receptive, Expanding, Yielding
Influences: Relationships, Love, Submission
Shape: Square   **Color:** Yellow
Body: Stomach   **Season:** Winter (Winter Solstice)
Moon Phase: New Moon
Animals: Earthly Ox, Celestial Black Tortoise
Directions: North (BH), Southwest (AH)
Nine Palaces Numbers: Fu Xi: **10**
  Yu the Great: Ho River Map, **1**—Lo River Script, **2**
Internal Alchemy: Tranquility, Void
  Qi Center: Hui Yin (Returning Yin)
  Qi Meridian: Ren Mai (Function Vessel)

Associated Developed Hexagrams of Bi

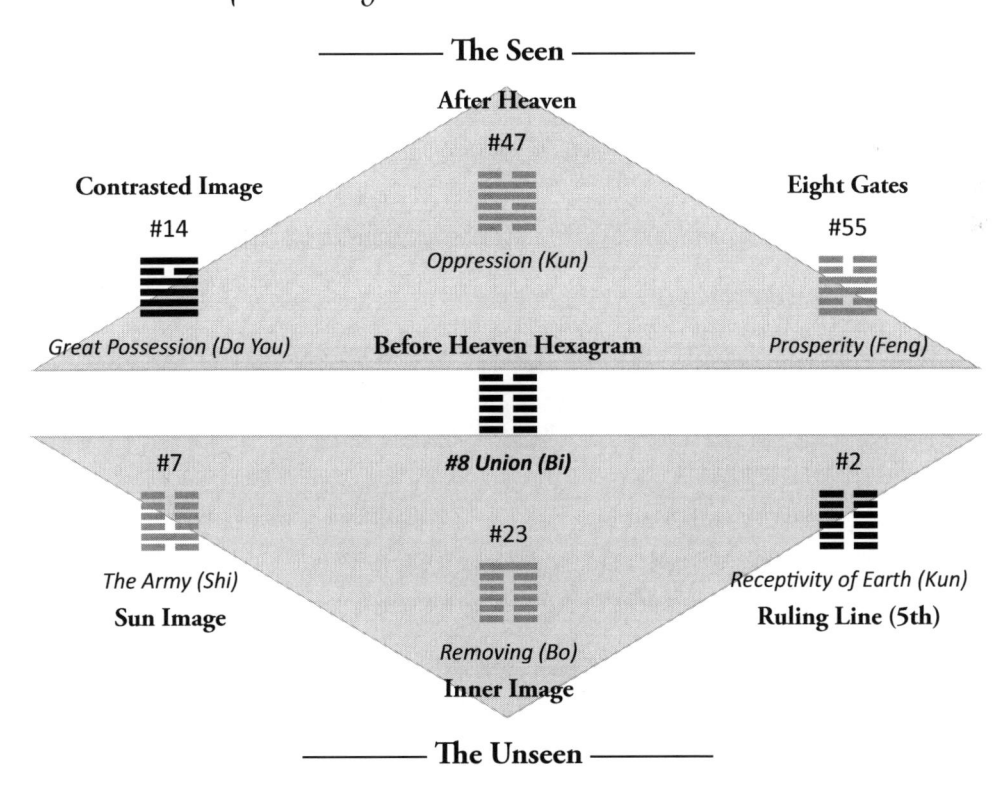

——— **The Seen** ———

After Heaven
#47

Contrasted Image   **Eight Gates**
#14   #55

Oppression (Kun)

Great Possession (Da You)   **Before Heaven Hexagram**   Prosperity (Feng)

#7   **#8 Union (Bi)**   #2

#23

The Army (Shi)   Receptivity of Earth (Kun)
Sun Image   **Ruling Line (5th)**

Removing (Bo)
Inner Image

——— **The Unseen** ———

Xiao Chu *Small Accumulation* 9

Xun (Wind) above
巽上
Xun Shang
Qian (Heaven) below
乾下
Qian Xia

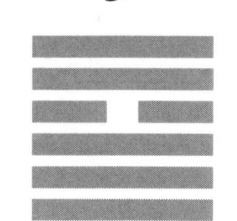

Sun/Yang Image

The Prediction (彖, Tuan)

Small Accumulation:
Perseverance. There are dense clouds, but no rain from my western borders.

小畜.亨.密雲不雨.自我西郊.

Knowing your limitations can eliminate great troubles. Having little accumulation of things will bring ease to your life. Do not make major decisions or changes, use the power of yielding and find success in victories. Rain-bearing clouds coming in from the western outlining areas shows that progress is coming.

The Lines (爻, Yao)

First Nine (初 九, Chu Jiu)
Returning to the Way [Dao].
Of what fault is this? Auspicious.

復自道.何其咎.吉.

A person looks unhappy returning on the same road, but doing so is auspicious. If adhering to the actions of small advances and small retreats there will be no remorse.

Second Nine (九 二, Jiu Er)
Drawn into returning. Auspicious.

牽復.吉.

It is auspicious to be led back by the master, who will show you how to retreat constructively.

Third Nine (九 三, Jiu San)
The spokes come out of the carriage wheels.
Man and wife roll their eyes.

輿說輻.夫妻反目.

The wheels have fallen off the carriage. The husband and wife fall out of the carriage and are dismayed. This is a situation of disorder, but all can be repaired.

Fourth Six (六 四, Liu Si)
Possessing sincerity. Blood vanishes and fear goes. This is without fault.

有孚.血去惕出.无咎.

Enemies in war have been captured, so both the need for worry and vigilance are gone. Everything is free of trouble now. Be confident that the truth will in the end prevail.

Fifth Nine (九 五, Jiu Wu)
Possessed with sincerity and drawn to others. Wealth comes through neighbors.

有孚攣如.富以其鄰.

Some enemies are captured and act as servants, and some go to serve your neighbors. In devotion lies loyalty, and in trust there is sincerity.

Topmost Nine (上 九, Shang Jiu)
The rain has ended and there is rest. Full of virtue, the wife is correct to have fear. The moon is nearly full. The wise person conquers misfortune.

既雨既處.尚德載.婦貞厲.
月幾望.君子征凶.

It had rained for a long time, but now it has stopped. Do not just presume this means everything will be successful, as much work lies ahead. Yet, you can now transport goods by cart. A woman forebodes a coming danger, so there is misfortune for a husband to set out on travels or expeditions when the moon is full.

Alternate English Translations for the Hexagram of Xiao Chu, 小畜

The Symbol of Small Restraint [S]
The Taming Power of the Small [WB]
The Lesser Nourisher [B]
Nurturance by the Small [C]
Little Accumulation [H]
The Symbol of Taming Force [CC]

Small Power [CS]
Small Accumulation [N]
The Small Accumulating [RS]
Taming the Small Powers [L]
Small Accumulating and Nurturing [K]

The Great Symbolism (大象, Da Xiang) says,

The Wind moving above Heaven. This is Xiao Chu. The superior person, according with this, admires those who conceal their virtue.	風行天上. 小畜. 君子以懿文德.

Sexagenary Placement

Heavenly Stem: Wu 戊 (5th Stem, Yang)—**Earth** (土, Tu)
Earthly Branch: Shen 申 (9th Branch, Yang)—**Monkey** (猴, Hou)
Represents the *Year of the Earth Monkey* (45th Year of the Sixty-Year Cycle)
Years: 1848 – 1908 – 1968 – 2028

Trigram Correlations

Upper Gua (Wind)

Xun 巽
- **Represents:** Wind, Wood, Eldest Daughter
- **Actions:** Gentleness, Grounding, Penetrating, Spreading
- **Influences:** Prosperity, Abundance, Wealth
- **Shape:** Rectangle   **Color:** Purple
- **Body:** Waist and hips   **Season:** Beginning Summer
- **Moon Phase:** Waxing Gibbous
- **Animals:** Earthly Fowl, Celestial Golden Rooster
- **Directions:** Southwest (BH), Southeast (AH)
- **Nine Palaces Numbers:** Fu Xi: **9**
  - Yu the Great: Ho River Map, **2**—Lo River Script, **4**
- **Internal Alchemy:** Breath and Mobilizing Qi
  - Qi Center: Yu Zhen (Jade Pillow)
  - Qi Meridian: Yin Wei Mai (Yin Preserving Vessel)

#9 Small Accumulation (Xiao Chu)

Lower Gua (Heaven)

Qian 乾   **Represents:** Heaven, Sky, Male, Father, Emperor
Actions: Creative Principle, Persisting, Forceful
Influences: Blessings, Good Fortune, Strength, Spiritual Power
Shape: Circle   **Color:** White
Body: Head   **Season:** Summer (Summer Solstice)
Moon Phase: Full Moon
Animals: Earthly Horse, Celestial Red Phoenix
Directions: South (BH), Northwest (AH)
Nine Palaces Numbers: Fu Xi: 2
  Yu the Great: Ho River Map, 9—Lo River Script, 6
Internal Alchemy: Clarity, Illumination
  Qi Center: Ni Wan (Mud Pellet)
  Qi Meridian: Du Mai (Control Vessel)

Associated Developed Hexagrams of Xiao Chu

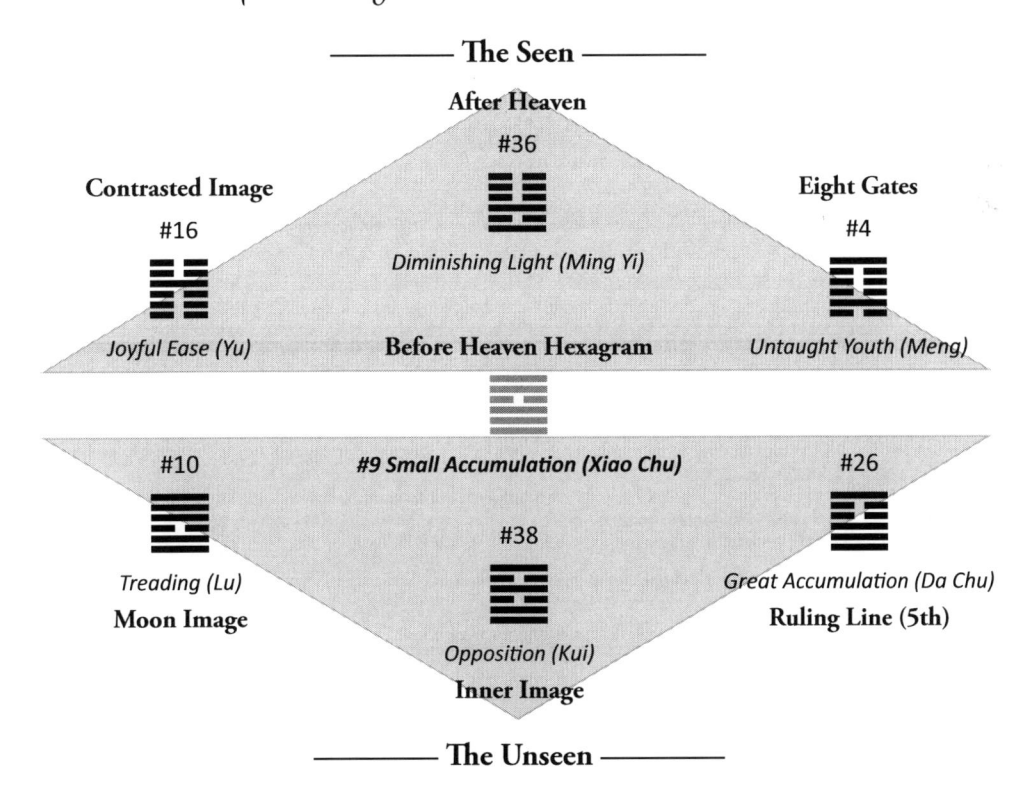

— **The Seen** —

After Heaven
#36
Diminishing Light (Ming Yi)

Contrasted Image
#16
Joyful Ease (Yu)

Eight Gates
#4
Untaught Youth (Meng)

Before Heaven Hexagram

#9 Small Accumulation (Xiao Chu)

#10
Treading (Lu)
Moon Image

#38
Opposition (Kui)
Inner Image

#26
Great Accumulation (Da Chu)
Ruling Line (5th)

— **The Unseen** —

Lu

履

Treading

10

Qian (Heaven) above
乾上
Qian Shang
Dui (Valley) below
兑下
Dui Xia

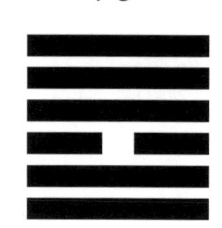

Moon/Yin Image

The Prediction (彖, Tuan)

Treading:
Treading on a tiger's tail, but does not bite the man. Perseverance.

履. 履虎尾. 不咥人. 亨.

This image shows the need for a person to be useful, industrious, and tactful. You have stepped on the tail of a tiger and did not get bitten or killed. This is very fortunate. Keep relationships cheerful and without any contention so the stronger person can only act by yielding to the weaker person.

The Lines (爻, Yao)

First Nine (初 九, Chu Jiu)
Treading towards simplicity.
Without fault.

素履往. 无咎.

Do as you wish, your future is secure. But act through the truth and seek to simplify things.

Second Nine (九 二, Jiu Er)
Treading the level and peaceful Way [Dao].
If the recluse is firm, auspicious.

履道但但. 幽人贞吉.

You are walking along a smooth and level road. Even a recluse feels that his prospects are auspicious when he doesn't seek things nor wants things from others.

Third Six (六三, Liu San)

The one-eyed person is able to see. The lame person is capable of Treading. Treading on the tiger's tail. If the person is bitten, there will be misfortune. Brave people act on the part of the great prince.

眇能視. 跛能履. 履虎尾.
咥人凶. 武人為于大君.

Even though the eyes are weakened, one can still see. Even though the foot is injured, one can still walk. Stepping on a tiger's tail will surely mean being bitten and attacked. This is unfortunate. The brave person does what the ruler should have done, staying within one's limitations.

Fourth Nine (九四, Jiu Si)

Treading on the tiger's tail. This causes many complaints, but in the end it is auspicious.

履虎尾. 愬愬終吉.

First there is fright and then accusations of blame, but proceed in caution as though holding the breath. The end result will bring fortune.

Fifth Nine (九五, Jiu Wu)

Resolute Treading. Correct to be fearful.

夬履. 貞厲.

Determined to go on the journey, but soon you sense danger. Be resolute in your actions as this will overcome the danger.

Topmost Nine (上九, Shang Jiu)

Watchful Treading while examining the good omens. Return is great and auspicious.

視履考祥. 其旋元吉.

Contemplate and observe the roads you have walked. All has been done correctly but it is only auspicious to return to where you had started from.

Alternate English Translations for the Hexagram of Lu, 履

The Symbol of Stepping Carefully [S]
Treading (Conduct) [B] [CS] [WB]
Treading [C] [K] [L] [RS]

Fulfillment [H]
Conduct [N]
The Symbol of Deliberate Action [CC]

The Great Symbolism (大象, Da Xiang) says,

Heaven above and a Marsh below.	上天下澤. 履.
This is Lu. The superior person, according	君子以辯上下.
with this, discriminates the high and low,	定民志.
and secures the will of the people.	

Sexagenary Placement

Heavenly Stem: Wu 戊 (5th Stem, Yang)—**Earth** (土, Tu)
Earthly Branch: Zi 子 (1st Branch, Yang)—**Rat** (鼠, Shu)
Represents the *Year of the Earth Rat* (25th Year of the Sixty-Year Cycle)
Years: 1888 – 1948 – 2008 – 2068

Trigram Correlations

Upper Gua (Heaven)

Qian 乾
Represents: Heaven, Sky, Male, Father, Emperor
Actions: Creative Principle, Persisting, Forceful
Influences: Blessings, Good Fortune, Strength, Spiritual Power
Shape: Circle   **Color:** White
Body: Head   **Season:** Summer (Summer Solstice)
Moon Phase: Full Moon
Animals: Earthly Horse, Celestial Red Phoenix
Directions: South (BH), Northwest (AH)
Nine Palaces Numbers: Fu Xi: **2**
　　Yu the Great: Ho River Map, **9**—Lo River Script, **6**
Internal Alchemy: Clarity, Illumination
　　Qi Center: Ni Wan (Mud Pellet)
　　Qi Meridian: Du Mai (Control Vessel)

Lower Gua (Valley)

⚌ **Dui** 兑
Represents: Valley, River, Lake/Marsh, Youngest Daughter
Actions: Joyous, Opening, Stimulating
Influences: Family, Future, Collecting, Pleasure, Absorbing, Complacency.
Shape: Introverted Triangle   Color: Brown
Body: Mouth   Season: Beginning Spring
Moon Phase: Waning Gibbous
Animals: Earthly Goat, Celestial Great Roc
Directions: Southeast (BH), West (AH)
Nine Palaces Numbers: Fu Xi: 5
   Yu the Great: Ho River Map, 4—Lo River Script, 7
Internal Alchemy: Po (Earthly) Spirit
   Qi Center: Xuan Guan (Mysterious Pass)
   Qi Meridian: Yang Wei Mai (Yang Preserving Vessel)

Associated Developed Hexagrams of Lu

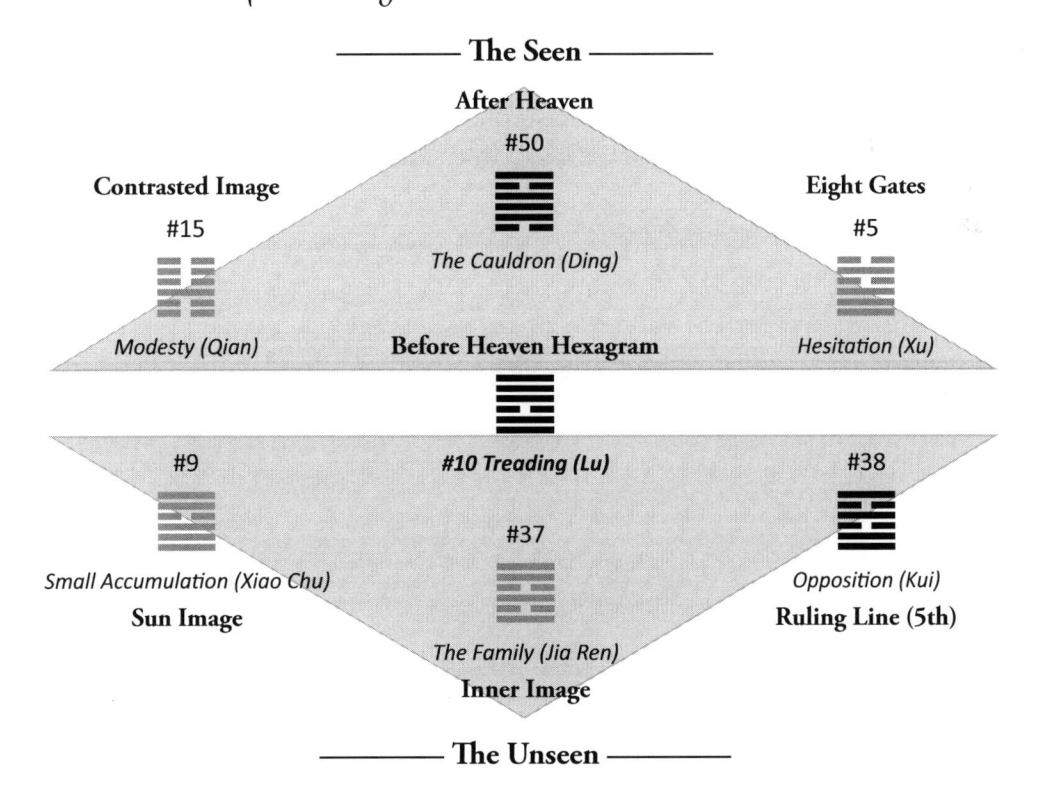

── **The Seen** ──

After Heaven
#50
The Cauldron (Ding)

Contrasted Image
#15
Modesty (Qian)

Eight Gates
#5
Hesitation (Xu)

Before Heaven Hexagram
#10 Treading (Lu)

#9
Small Accumulation (Xiao Chu)
Sun Image

#37
The Family (Jia Ren)
Inner Image

#38
Opposition (Kui)
Ruling Line (5th)

── **The Unseen** ──

Tai

泰

Peacefulness

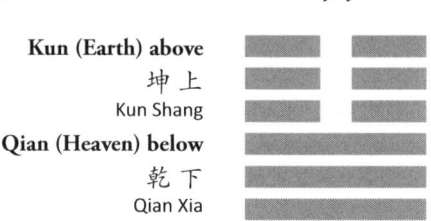

11

Kun (Earth) above
坤上
Kun Shang
Qian (Heaven) below
乾下
Qian Xia

Sun/Yang Image

The Prediction (象, Tuan)

Peacefulness:
The small departs and the great arrives.　　泰. 小往大來. 吉亨.
Auspiciousness through perseverance.

Through perseverance, health, wealth, and adoration is gained. Even though something small is lost, something big will be gained. This shows how fortunate the situation is.

The Lines (爻, Yao)

First Nine (初九, Chu Jiu)
Pulling up grass, the roots of the stalks　　拔茅茹. 以其彙. 征吉.
come with it. Bringing about one's
own kind. Advancing is auspicious.

When pulling up plants, the roots and stalks of other plants come with it, as they are all entwined. This is a good omen because it symbolizes sharing your good fortune with others.

Second Nine (九二, Jiu Er)
Bearing with the uncultivated. Using a boat　　包荒. 用馮河. 不遐遺.
to cross the river. Forgetting not about　　朋亡. 得尚于中行.
the distance. Friends vanish. Obtaining
a position by acting in the middle.

If attempting to conquer something with people of lesser resolve, do not forget the lessons learned from previous experiences and journeys. Stay with the Middle Way and take credit for it. So be independent and use your courage, but above all be tolerant of those beneath you.

#11 Peacefulness (Tai)

Third Nine (九 三, Jiu San)
Without the level, there is no slope.
Without going, there is no return.
Difficulty in being firm. This is without fault. No pity for the sincere. Nourish the existing good fortune.

无平不陂. 无往不復.
艱貞无咎. 勿恤其孚.
于食有福.

No matter how smooth something seems, there is always a slope. All good fortune can easily change to misfortune. There is no going without a coming back. There is no error of predicting within hardships. It will be auspicious to leave without thoughts of coming back. There is good fortune in nourishing yourself.

Fourth Six (六 四, Liu Si)
Fluttering downward to and fro.
No wealth through one's own neighbors.
No warning, but sincere.

翩翩. 不富以其鄰.
不戒以孚.

Unaware of coming dangers. Do not depend on neighbors or friends for acquiring wealth. No need to be wary of those who serve you. Do not act in pretense nor be intolerant of those beneath you.

Fifth Six (六 五, Liu Wu)
The Supreme Ruler gives his younger sister in marriage. This brings happiness and great auspiciousness.

帝乙歸妹. 以祉元吉.

The Supreme Ruler has married off his younger sister. There is a union of those in high and low positions, so modesty becomes the rule. From the beginning, this signals a very good and long-lasting fortune.

Topmost Six (上 六, Shang Liu)
The walls recede into the dry moat outside the city. No use for an army. Commands issued [from Heaven] to the people of the city. Even though correct, regret.

城復于隍. 勿用師.
自邑告命. 貞吝.

The walls have crumbled and collapsed into the moat. This was not the right time to send out troops from the city, as the city lost its means of defense. Orders were given from inside the camp, and more trouble is now predicted. Accepting and submitting to the inevitable, learning to let go of things, is the correct response.

Alternate English Translations for the Hexagram of Tai, 泰

The Symbol of Successfulness [S]
Peace [B] [CS] [L] [WB]
Tranquility [C]
Pervading [K]

Advance [H]
Peace—Harmony—Good Opportunity [N]
Compenetration [RS]
The Symbol of Success [CC]

The Great Symbolism (大象, Da Xiang) says,

Heaven and Earth communicate. This is Tai. The ruler, according with this, fashions and completes the Dao of Heaven and Earth. Supporting and assisting Heaven and Earth in the proper manner to benefit the people.

天地交. 泰.
后以財成天地之道.
輔相天地之宜.
以左右民.

Sexagenary Placement

Heavenly Stem: Geng 庚 (7th Stem, Yang)—**Metal** (金, Jin)
Earthly Branch: Shen 申 (9th Branch, Yang)—**Monkey** (猴, Hou)
Represents the *Year of the Metal Monkey* (57th Year of the Sixty-Year Cycle)
Years: 1860 – 1920 – 1980 – 2040

Trigram Correlations

Upper Gua (Earth)

Kun 坤
- **Represents:** Earth, Soil, Fields, Female, Mother, Empress
- **Actions:** Receptive, Expanding, Yielding
- **Influences:** Relationships, Love, Submission
- **Shape:** Square **Color:** Yellow
- **Body:** Stomach **Season:** Winter (Winter Solstice)
- **Moon Phase:** New Moon
- **Animals:** Earthly Ox, Celestial Black Tortoise
- **Directions:** North (BH), Southwest (AH)
- **Nine Palaces Numbers:** Fu Xi: **10**
    - Yu the Great: Ho River Map, **1**—Lo River Script, **2**
- **Internal Alchemy:** Tranquility, Void
    - Qi Center: Hui Yin (Returning Yin)
    - Qi Meridian: Ren Mai (Function Vessel)

Lower Gua (Heaven)

Qian 乾   **Represents:** Heaven, Sky, Male, Father, Emperor
Actions: Creative Principle, Persisting, Forceful
Influences: Blessings, Good Fortune, Strength, Spiritual Power
Shape: Circle   **Color:** White
Body: Head   **Season:** Summer (Summer Solstice)
Moon Phase: Full Moon
Animals: Earthly Horse, Celestial Red Phoenix
Directions: South (BH), Northwest (AH)
Nine Palaces Numbers: Fu Xi: 2
   Yu the Great: Ho River Map, **9**—Lo River Script, **6**
Internal Alchemy: Clarity, Illumination
   Qi Center: Ni Wan (Mud Pellet)
   Qi Meridian: Du Mai (Control Vessel)

Associated Developed Hexagrams of Tai

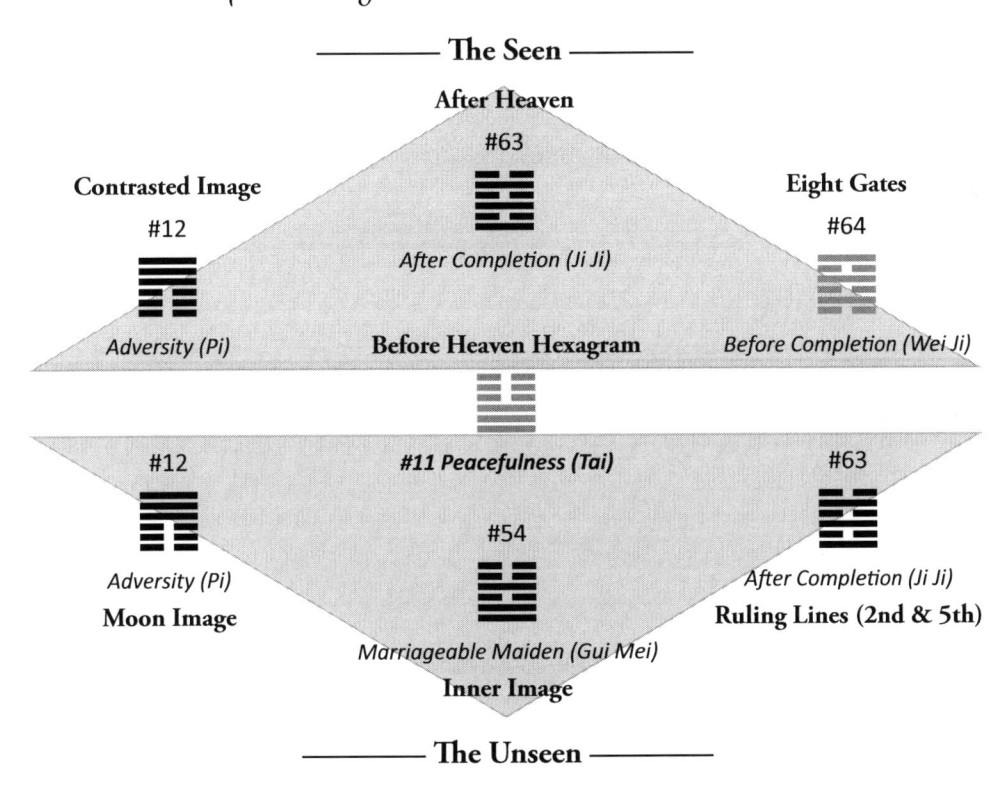

— **The Seen** —

After Heaven
#63
After Completion (Ji Ji)

Contrasted Image
#12
Adversity (Pi)

Eight Gates
#64
Before Completion (Wei Ji)

Before Heaven Hexagram

#11 Peacefulness (Tai)

#12
Adversity (Pi)
Moon Image

#54
Marriageable Maiden (Gui Mei)
Inner Image

#63
After Completion (Ji Ji)
Ruling Lines (2nd & 5th)

— **The Unseen** —

Pi

否

Adversity

12

Qian (Heaven) above
乾上
Qian Shang
Kun (Earth) below
坤下
Kun Xia

Moon/Yin Image

The Prediction (彖, Tuan)

Adversity:
Adversity with the wrong people.
The wise person is firm, yet no advantage.
The great departs and the small arrives.

否之匪人. 不利君子貞.
大往小來.

It is beneficial to have a good sense of your own moral compass. Be cautious and stand on solid ground. Conceal your true skills and wisdom, and forego situations of public praise. Do not reach for things without first securing the feet. It is good to predict prospects, but know that the big ones will be lost and only small ones gained. The wise person seeks be in the background as the common person is at the center of the situation.

The Lines (爻, Yao)

First Six (初 六, Chu Liu)
Pulling up grass, the roots of the stalks come
with it. Bringing about one's own kind.
Correct, auspicious, and persevering.

拔茅茹. 以其彙. 貞吉亨.

The roots and stalks of surrounding plants are all entwined. Use your intuition and skills to protect others. This, then, is an omen for good fortune.

Second Six (六 二, Liu Er)
Bearing with responsibility. For inferior
people it is auspicious. Adversity
for the elder. Perseverance.

包承. 小人吉. 大人否. 亨.

Accepting flattery is good for a common person, but the master finds it just a means of being ill-informed. Confused people will seek your advice. Better to just keep to yourself.

Third Six (六 三, Liu San)
Bearing shame. 包羞.

Other people's humiliation must be condoned as their confusion does nothing but stir up contention, bringing up the feeling that everything is wrong.

Fourth Nine (九 四, Jiu Si)
Possession of one's destiny is without fault. 有命无咎. 疇離祉.
Happiness comes through companions.

You are far away from the place that brings you happiness, yet you are immune from disasters if staying close to companions. Listen to your intuition about leading, and then act upon it.

Fifth Nine (九 五, Jiu Wu)
Resting in Adversity. Auspicious for the elder. 休否. 大人吉. 其亡其亡.
"They perish, they perish!" Binding one's self 繫于苞桑.
firmly to a mulberry tree.

It is fortunate for the master to be away from those who ill-informed him. They nearly caused a great disaster. Paying attention to providing food and nourishment shows wisdom and caution.

Topmost Nine (上 九, Shang Jiu)
Adversity has ended. Without Adversity, 傾否. 无否後喜.
afterwards there will be joy.

Using great effort to end stagnant conditions, misfortune reverses itself. There was a run-in with bad luck at first, but it all becomes good fortune later.

Alternate English Translations for the Hexagram of Pi, 否

The Symbol of Closing [S]
Standstill (Stagnation) [CS] [WB]
Stagnation (Obstruction) [B]
The Symbol of Failure [CC]

Obstruction [C] [K] [RS]
Hindrance [H]
Misfortune [N]
Stagnation [L]

The Great Symbolism (大象, Da Xiang) says,

Heaven and Earth do not communicate. This is Pi. Superior persons, according with this, restrain their virtue to remove the difficulties. Unable to flourish and bring prosperity.	天地不交.否. 君子以儉德辟難. 不可榮以祿.

䷋ Sexagenary Placement

Heavenly Stem: Geng 庚 (7th Stem, Yang)—**Metal** (金, Jin)
Earthly Branch: Yin 寅 (3rd Branch, Yang)—**Tiger** (虎, Hu)
Represents the *Year of the Metal Tiger* (27th Year of the Sixty-Year Cycle)
Years: 1890 – 1950 – 2010 – 2070

Trigram Correlations

Upper Gua (Heaven)

☰ **Qian** 乾   **Represents:** Heaven, Sky, Male, Father, Emperor
Actions: Creative Principle, Persisting, Forceful
Influences: Blessings, Good Fortune, Strength, Spiritual Power
Shape: Circle   **Color:** White
Body: Head   **Season:** Summer (Summer Solstice)
Moon Phase: Full Moon
Animals: Earthly Horse, Celestial Red Phoenix
Directions: South (BH), Northwest (AH)
Nine Palaces Numbers: Fu Xi: **2**
   Yu the Great: Ho River Map, **9**—Lo River Script, **6**
Internal Alchemy: Clarity, Illumination
   Qi Center: Ni Wan (Mud Pellet)
   Qi Meridian: Du Mai (Control Vessel)

#12 Adversity (Pi)

Lower Gua (Earth)

☷ **Kun** 坤   **Represents:** Earth, Soil, Fields, Female, Mother, Empress
Actions: Receptive, Expanding, Yielding
Influences: Relationships, Love, Submission
Shape: Square   **Color:** Yellow
Body: Stomach   **Season:** Winter (Winter Solstice)
Moon Phase: New Moon
Animals: Earthly Ox, Celestial Black Tortoise
Directions: North (BH), Southwest (AH)
Nine Palaces Numbers: Fu Xi: **10**
   Yu the Great: Ho River Map, **1**—Lo River Script, **2**
Internal Alchemy: Tranquility, Void
   Qi Center: Hui Yin (Returning Yin)
   Qi Meridian: Ren Mai (Function Vessel)

Associated Developed Hexagrams of Pi

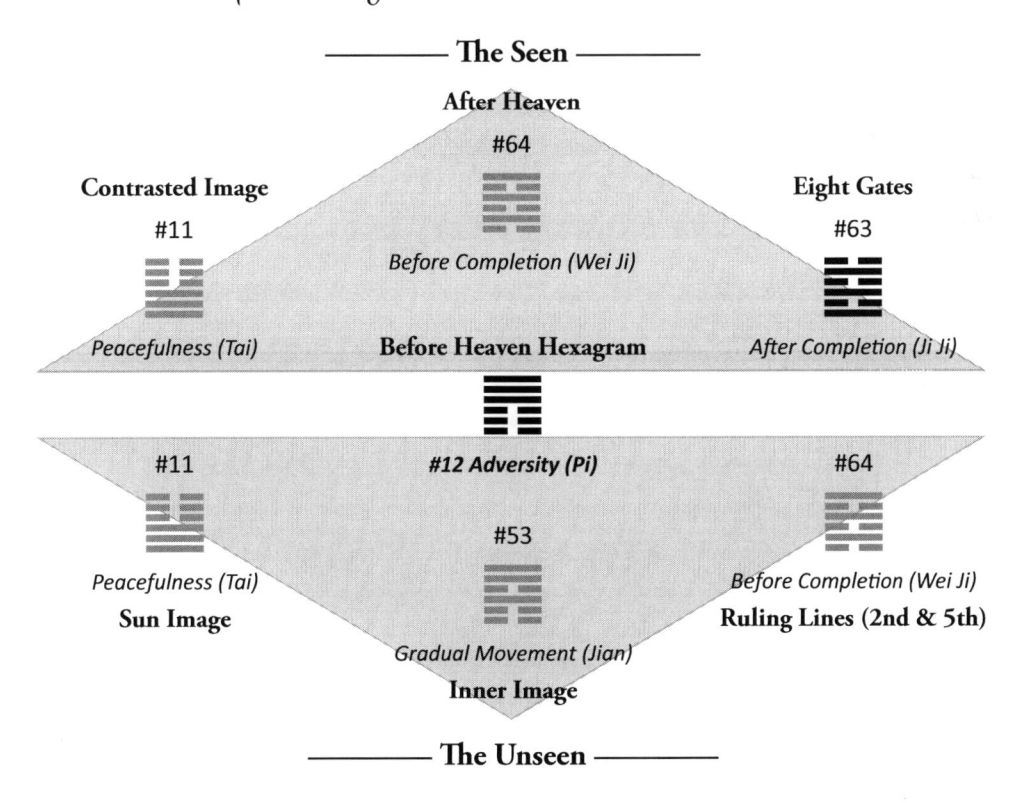

——— **The Seen** ———

After Heaven
#64
Before Completion (Wei Ji)

Contrasted Image
#11
Peacefulness (Tai)

Eight Gates
#63
After Completion (Ji Ji)

Before Heaven Hexagram

#12 Adversity (Pi)

#11
Peacefulness (Tai)
Sun Image

#53
Gradual Movement (Jian)
Inner Image

#64
Before Completion (Wei Ji)
Ruling Lines (2nd & 5th)

——— **The Unseen** ———

Tong Ren

同人

People United

13

Qian (Heaven) above
乾上
Qian Shang
Li (Fire) below
離下
Li Xia

Sun/Yang Image

The Prediction (彖, Tuan)

People United:
People United in the wilderness. Perseverance. Advantage in fording the great stream. Beneficial for the wise person to be resolute.

同人野. 亨. 利涉大川.
利君子貞.

Support those who are worthy. Attempt to stay on good terms with people in your field, as a big river needs to be crossed. Plans must be made and followed. The goal of bringing people together is not a matter of individual interests but for the common good of all. Such unification brings great rewards to everyone.

The Lines (爻, Yao)

First Nine (初 九, Chu Jiu)
People United at the gateway.
Without fault.

同人于門. 无咎.

People who share the same beliefs and ideals who gather inside the same gateway can avoid disasters and trouble. This requires equality and openness with everyone involved.

Second Six (六 二, Liu Er)
People United in the ancestral clan.
Regret.

同人于宗. 吝.

Refrain from only being close to your ancestors and family. Those from the outside will try to persuade you to make expedient actions, but doing so brings disaster.

#13 People United (Tong Ren)

Third Nine (九三, Jiu San)
Within the undergrowth lies an ambush
with weapons. Ascend to the high mound.
For three years no rising.

伏戎于莽. 升其高陵.
三歲不興.

Soldiers hiding with weapons occupy the high ground for defense, and so there's no need to send out troops for three years. The holding of troops causes factions to quarrel because they want action, but to follow their advice will bring humiliation.

Fourth Nine (九四, Jiu Si)
Ascending their city walls.
Assault is difficult, but auspicious.

乘其墉. 弗克攻. 吉.

Having ascended the city walls of the enemy does not mean the city has been captured. Continue attacking if things are to be auspicious. Do not get involved in the quarrel and position yourself to gain a good overview of the situation.

Fifth Nine (九五, Jiu Wu)
People United first call out
weeping and afterward laughing.
The great armies agree.

同人先號咷而後笑.
大師克相遇.

Those under the same banner cried first, then broke out in laughter. The victorious force has come to meet with the defeated force and everything is brought back to harmony and peace. There were disagreements, but in the end unity took place and all are now joyful.

Topmost Nine (上九, Shang Jiu)
People United at the borders.
Without regret.

同人于郊. 无悔.

Those of the same beliefs and ideals have gathered in the outlying fields. They do not regret what has been done in the past. There is no real companionship even though everyone is together, but no one is blaming past actions.

Alternate English Translations for the Hexagram of Tong Ren, 同人

The Symbol of Companionship [S]
Fellowship with Men [WB]
Seeking Harmony [H]
Concording People [K] [RS]
Lovers, Beloved, Friends, Like-Minded Persons, Universal Brotherhood [B]

Fellowship, Brotherhood [CS]
Sameness With People [C]
Uniting With People [N]
The Symbol of Community [CC]
Fellowship of Men [L]

The Great Symbolism (大象, Da Xiang) says,

Heaven together with Fire. This is Tong Ren.	天與火.同人.
The superior person, according with this, discriminates the classes of all things.	君子以類族辨物.

Sexagenary Placement

Heavenly Stem: Yi 乙 (2nd Stem, Yin)—**Wood** (木, Mu)
Earthly Branch: Hai 亥 (12th Branch, Yin)—**Pig** (猪, Zhu)
Represents the *Year of the Wood Pig* (12th Year of the Sixty-Year Cycle)
Years: 1875 – 1935 – 1995 – 2055

Trigram Correlations

Upper Gua (Heaven)

Qian 乾   **Represents:** Heaven, Sky, Male, Father, Emperor
Actions: Creative Principle, Persisting, Forceful
Influences: Blessings, Good Fortune, Strength, Spiritual Power
Shape: Circle   **Color:** White
Body: Head   **Season:** Summer (Summer Solstice)
Moon Phase: Full Moon
Animals: Earthly Horse, Celestial Red Phoenix
Directions: South (BH), Northwest (AH)
Nine Palaces Numbers: Fu Xi: **2**
    Yu the Great: Ho River Map, **9**—Lo River Script, **6**
Internal Alchemy: Clarity, Illumination
    Qi Center: Ni Wan (Mud Pellet)
    Qi Meridian: Du Mai (Control Vessel)

#13 People United (Tong Ren)

Lower Gua (Fire)

☲ **Li** 離
Represents: Fire, Lightning, Sun, Middle Daughter
Actions: Clinging, Illuminating, Congregating
Influences: Fame, Reputation, Brightness, Elegance
Shape: Triangle   **Color:** Red
Body: Eyes   **Season:** Spring (Spring Equinox)
Moon Phase: Last Quarter
Animals: Earthly Rooster, Celestial Green Dragon
Directions: East (BH), South (AH)
Nine Palaces Numbers: Fu Xi: 8
   Yu the Great: Ho River Map, 3—Lo River Script, 9
Internal Alchemy: Mercury, Qi
   Qi Center: Jiang Gong (Crimson Palace)
   Qi Meridian: Dai Mai (Belt Vessel)

Associated Developed Hexagrams of Tong Ren

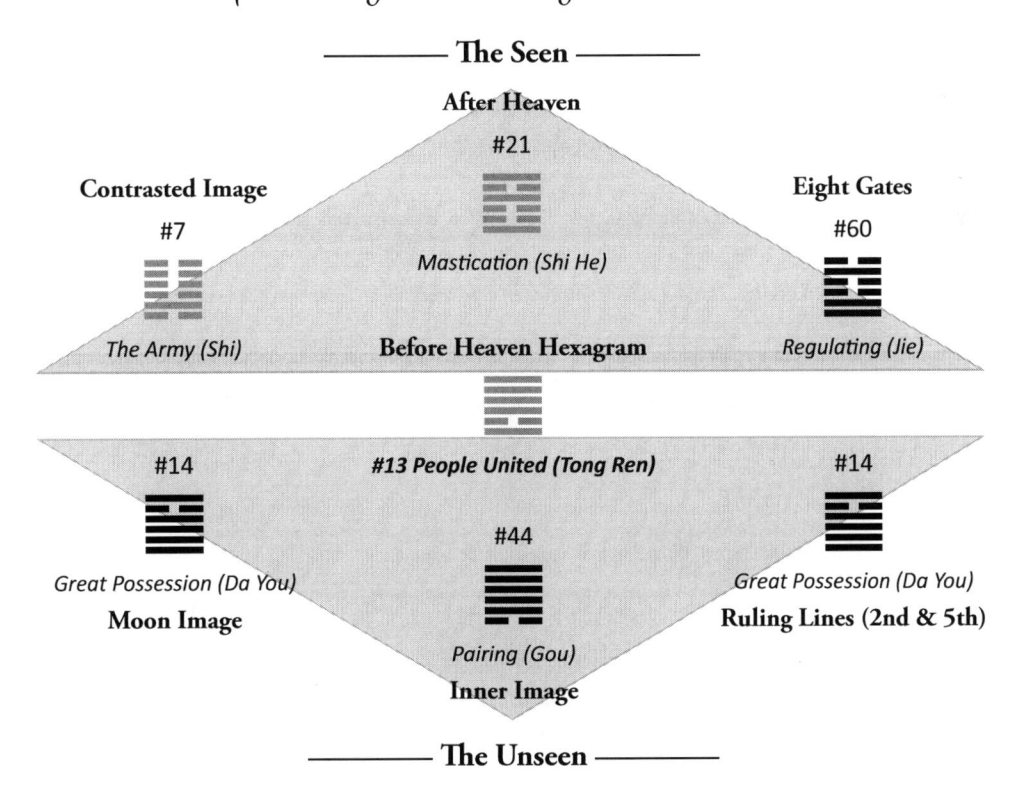

—— **The Seen** ——

After Heaven
#21
Mastication (Shi He)

Contrasted Image
#7
The Army (Shi)

Eight Gates
#60
Regulating (Jie)

Before Heaven Hexagram

#13 People United (Tong Ren)

#14
Great Possession (Da You)
Moon Image

#44
Pairing (Gou)
Inner Image

#14
Great Possession (Da You)
Ruling Lines (2nd & 5th)

—— **The Unseen** ——

53

Da You — Great Possession — 14

Li (Fire) above
離 上
Li Shang

Qian (Heaven) below
乾 下
Qian Xia

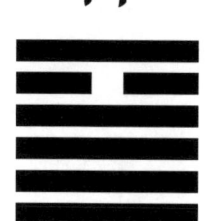

Moon/Yin Image

The Prediction (象, Tuan)

Great Possession:
Great perseverance.　　　　　　　　大有.元亨.

From great possession must come great generosity. A bumper harvest and large profits have occurred. All this shows the ease of things from the beginning. The brightness of fire brings clarity to the situation; with clarity there can be wisdom. External clarity combined with internal fortitude makes the situation very successful.

The Lines (爻, Yao)

First Nine (初 九, Chu Jiu)
No meeting with what is injurious.　　无 交 害.匪 咎.艱 則 无 咎.
There is no fault. Knowing the
difficulty is without fault.

No offenses are being made. Without the root of calamity, no fruit can derive from it. This is a good time for contemplating the temptations and distractions coming from wealth.

Second Nine (九 二, Jiu Er)
A big cart for loading. Having　　　大 車 以 載.有 攸 往.无 咎.
somewhere to go. Without fault.

The transporting of goods in large carts will be without trouble. This means there will be new and rich resources being made available. Act on this situation before it disappears.

Third Nine (九三, Jiu San)
A duke employs offerings to the Son of Heaven [Emperor]. 公用亨于天子.小人弗克.
The inferior person cannot do this.

A person of high rank or nobility can deliver goods to the emperor, but the common person cannot do this. Real wealth can only come from those of a higher position, not from those beneath you.

Fourth Nine (九四, Jiu Si)
Robbed of one's own strength. 匪其彭.无咎.
Without fault.

Drums are not beating to announce the bringing in of a bumper harvest, rather they sound the call to war. Yet, nothing has become disastrous. It is wise to stay calm and discern things clearly amidst your wealth.

Fifth Six (六五, Liu Wu)
Sincere in meeting with some. 厥孚交如.威如.吉.
Imposing to others. Auspicious.

Enemies have been bound so the victors can show off their arrogance and pride. But this is greatly auspicious if you guard your dignity and do not become insolent.

Topmost Nine (上九, Shang Jiu)
Protection from Heaven. Auspicious. 自天祐之.吉.无不利.
Everything is beneficial.

Having the blessings of Heaven is greatly auspicious. Use your wealth to help others, then even more good fortune will come to you.

Alternate English Translations for the Hexagram of Da You, 大有

The Symbol of Great Possession [S]
Possession of Great Measure [WB]
Great Possessions [B] [L]
Great Possessing (Amassing) [CS]
The Symbol of Abundance [CC]

Great Possession [C]
Great Harvest [H]
Great Provider—Great Harvest [N]
Great Possessing [K] [RS]

The Great Symbolism (大象, Da Xiang) says,

Fire dwelling in Heaven above. This is Da You. The superior person, according with this, eradicates the bad and praises the good. Obeying Heaven's blessings are decreed.

火在天上. 大有.
君子以過惡揚善.
順天休命.

Sexagenary Placement

Heavenly Stem: Ding 丁 (4th Stem, Yin)—**Fire** (火, Huo)
Earthly Branch: You 酉 (10th Branch, Yin)—**Rooster** (雞, Ji)
Represents the *Year of the Fire Rooster* (34th Year of the Sixty-Year Cycle)
Years: 1897 – 1957 – 2017 – 2077

Trigram Correlations

Upper Gua (Fire)

Li 離
- **Represents:** Fire, Lightning, Sun, Middle Daughter
- **Actions:** Clinging, Illuminating, Congregating
- **Influences:** Fame, Reputation, Brightness, Elegance
- **Shape:** Triangle **Color:** Red
- **Body:** Eyes **Season:** Spring (Spring Equinox)
- **Moon Phase:** Last Quarter
- **Animals:** Earthly Rooster, Celestial Green Dragon
- **Directions:** East (BH), South (AH)
- **Nine Palaces Numbers:** Fu Xi: **8**
   Yu the Great: Ho River Map, **3**—Lo River Script, **9**
- **Internal Alchemy:** Mercury, Qi
   Qi Center: Jiang Gong (Crimson Palace)
   Qi Meridian: Dai Mai (Belt Vessel)

Lower Gua (Heaven)

☰ **Qian** 乾   **Represents:** Heaven, Sky, Male, Father, Emperor
Actions: Creative Principle, Persisting, Forceful
Influences: Blessings, Good Fortune, Strength, Spiritual Power
Shape: Circle   **Color:** White
Body: Head   **Season:** Summer (Summer Solstice)
Moon Phase: Full Moon
Animals: Earthly Horse, Celestial Red Phoenix
Directions: South (BH), Northwest (AH)
Nine Palaces Numbers: Fu Xi: 2
  Yu the Great: Ho River Map, 9—Lo River Script, 6
Internal Alchemy: Clarity, Illumination
  Qi Center: Ni Wan (Mud Pellet)
  Qi Meridian: Du Mai (Control Vessel)

Associated Developed Hexagrams of Da You

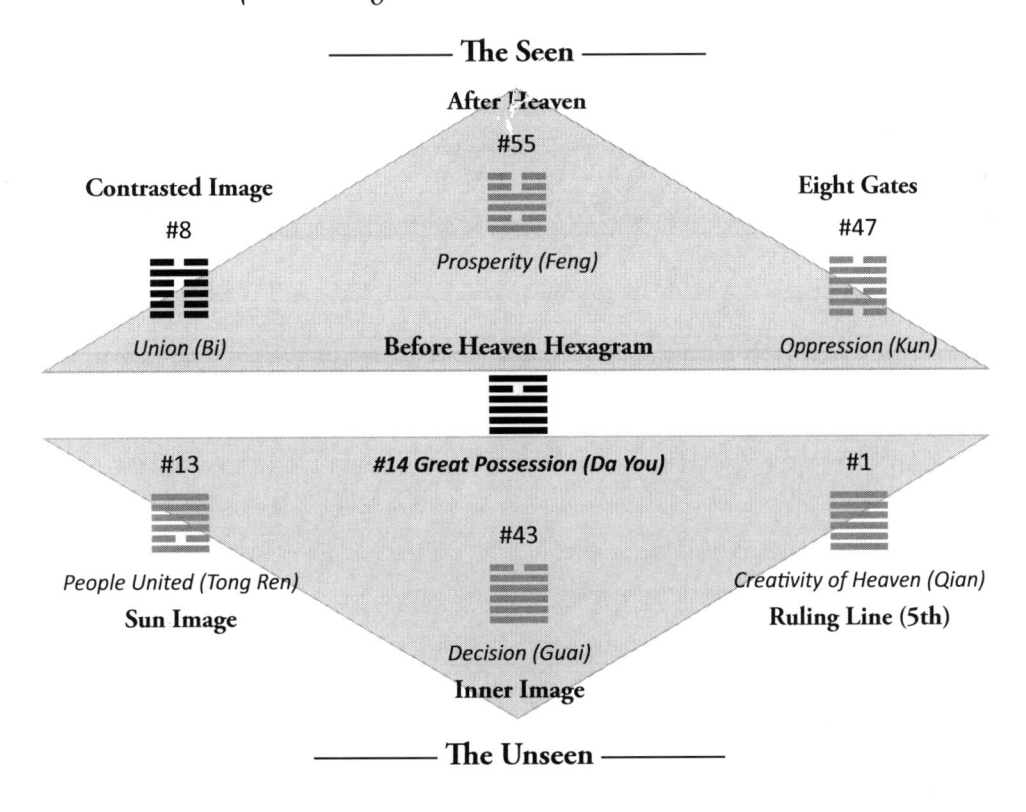

── **The Seen** ──

After Heaven
#55
Prosperity (Feng)

Contrasted Image
#8
Union (Bi)

Eight Gates
#47
Oppression (Kun)

Before Heaven Hexagram

#14 Great Possession (Da You)

#13
People United (Tong Ren)
Sun Image

#1
Creativity of Heaven (Qian)
Ruling Line (5th)

#43
Decision (Guai)
Inner Image

── **The Unseen** ──

Qian

謙

Modesty

15

Kun (Earth) above
坤上
Kun Shang
Gen (Mountain) below
艮下
Gen Xia

Sun/Yang Image

The Prediction (彖, Tuan)

Modesty:
Perseverance. The wise person is there to the end.

謙.亨.君子有終.

Do not expect or demand too much of others. A person of modesty and humility will succeed and have a good end. Modesty in all situations brings good fortune. Quietly persist in your activities and remain calm, even within the midst of a blustering storm.

The Lines (爻, Yao)

First Six (初 六, Chu Liu)
The wise person is modest about Modesty. Useful to ford the great stream. Auspicious.

謙謙君子.用涉大川.吉.

A true modest person can cross the big river because he or she has no thought of being modest. This is auspicious. True modesty does not come from the pretense of being modest.

Second Six (六 二, Liu Er)
Modesty in expression.
Correct and auspicious.

鳴謙.貞吉.

Letting modesty be seen within your persistence is auspicious.

#15 Modesty (Qian)

Third Nine (九三, Jiu San)
The wise person of Modesty and merit.　　勞謙君子.有終吉.
Auspiciousness exists to the end.

Diligent and modest persons will have a good end in whatever they do. Remain modest even when being praised for your merit and fame.

Fourth Six (六四, Liu Si)
Everything is advantageous.　　无不利.撝謙.
Humility and Modesty.

Everything goes smoothly when a person's modesty is expressed through humility.

Fifth Six (六五, Liu Wu)
No wealth from one's own neighbors.　　不富以其鄰.
Advantage in employing a raid and　　利用侵伐.
chastising. Everything is beneficial.　　无不利.

Do not depend on the wealth of neighbors and friends to attain riches, better to go off to far away places to secure wealth. Then there will be success.

Topmost Six (上六, Shang Liu)
Modesty in expression. Advantage　　鳴謙.利用行師.
in using and setting forth an army.　　征邑國.
Attack both city and country.

A person with a good reputation for modesty can be put in charge of the troops to invade other cities and states. This modesty cannot be false, however, as the just course being pursued will be hindered.

Alternate English Translations for the Hexagram of Qian, 謙

The Symbol of Humility [S]　　　　　*Humbleness* [H]
Modesty [B] [CS] [L] [WB]　　　　　*Modesty—Egolessness* [N]
Humility [C]　　　　　　　　　　　　*Humbling* [K] [RS]
The Symbol of Humility [CC]

The Great Symbolism (大象, Da Xiang) says,

Within the Earth is a Mountain. This is Qian. The superior person, according with this, reduces what is excessive and augments what is too little, and through careful determination grants equality to all things.

地中有山．謙．
君子以裒多益寡．
物平施．

Sexagenary Placement

Heavenly Stem: Wu 戊 (5th Stem, Yang)—**Earth** (土, Tu)
Earthly Branch: Wu 午 (7th Branch, Yang)—**Horse** (馬, Ma)
Represents the *Year of the Earth Horse* (55th Year of the Sixty-Year Cycle)
Years: 1858 – 1918 – 1978 – 2038

Trigram Correlations

Upper Gua (Earth)

Kun 坤
Represents: Earth, Soil, Fields, Female, Mother, Empress
Actions: Receptive, Expanding, Yielding
Influences: Relationships, Love, Submission
Shape: Square   **Color:** Yellow
Body: Stomach   **Season:** Winter (Winter Solstice)
Moon Phase: New Moon
Animals: Earthly Ox, Celestial Black Tortoise
Directions: North (BH), Southwest (AH)
Nine Palaces Numbers: Fu Xi: **10**
　　Yu the Great: Ho River Map, **1**—Lo River Script, **2**
Internal Alchemy: Tranquility, Void
　　Qi Center: Hui Yin (Returning Yin)
　　Qi Meridian: Ren Mai (Function Vessel)

#15 Modesty (Qian)

Lower Gua (Mountain)

Gen 艮
- **Represents:** Mountain, Towers, Youngest Son
- **Actions:** Stillness, Binding, Stopping
- **Influences:** Knowledge, Wisdom, Skill, Determination
- **Shape:** Vertical Column   **Color:** Blue
- **Body:** Hands and arms   **Season:** Beginning Autumn
- **Moon Phase:** Waxing Crescent
- **Animals:** Earthly Dog, Celestial Vermilion Snake
- **Directions:** Northwest (BH), Northeast (AH)
- **Nine Palaces Numbers:** Fu Xi: 7
   Yu the Great: Ho River Map, **6**— Lo River Script, **8**
- **Internal Alchemy:** Hun (Heavenly) Spirit
   Qi Center: Jing Men (Essence Gate)
   Qi Meridian: Yang Qiao Mai (Yang Heel Vessel)

Associated Developed Hexagrams of Qian

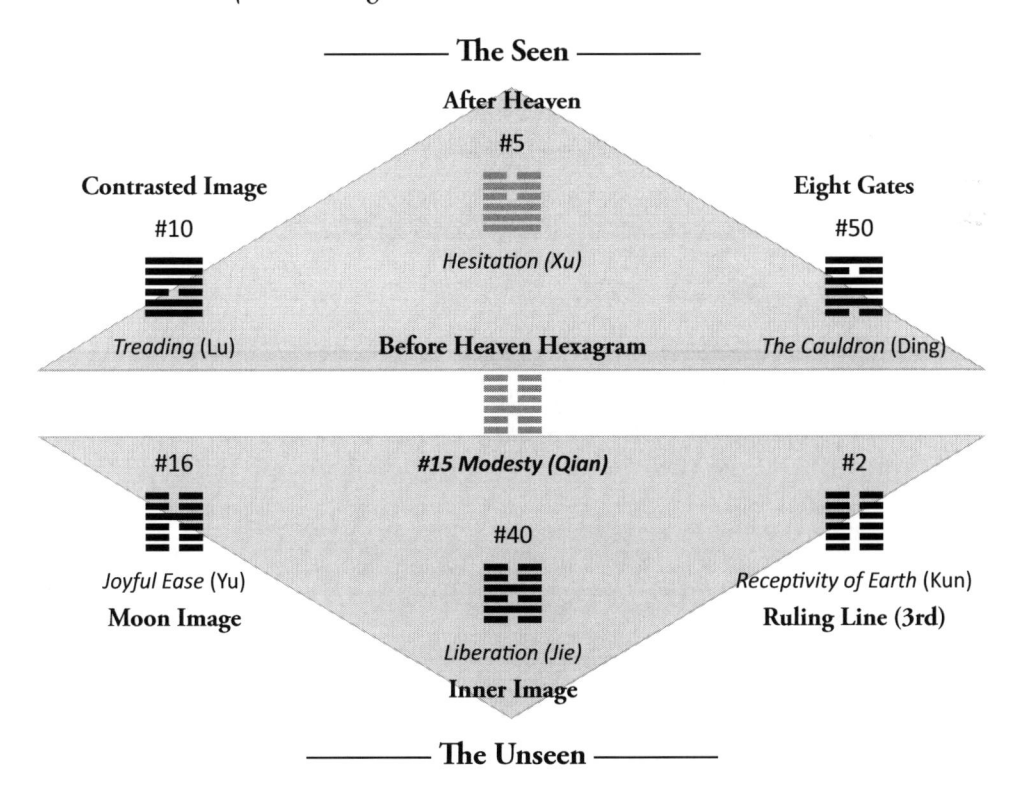

— **The Seen** —

After Heaven
#5
Hesitation (Xu)

Contrasted Image
#10
Treading (Lu)

Eight Gates
#50
The Cauldron (Ding)

Before Heaven Hexagram

#15 Modesty (Qian)

#16
Joyful Ease (Yu)
Moon Image

#40
Liberation (Jie)
Inner Image

#2
Receptivity of Earth (Kun)
Ruling Line (3rd)

— **The Unseen** —

Yu

豫

Joyful Ease

16

Zhen (Thunder) above
震上
Zhen Shang
Kun (Earth) below
坤下
Kun Xia

Moon/Yin Image

The Prediction (彖, Tuan)

Joyful Ease:
Advantage in establishing feudal princes and setting forth an army.

豫. 利建候行師.

Enjoy your good fortune, but show humility about it. Express joy with song and dance, even if beating the drums of war to establish unity. Be on guard about the joyousness so it is not abused and used for selfish ends. Conferring honors, establishing a new kingdom, and setting forth an army is auspicious provided everything is planned in advance. Being prepared leads to success.

The Lines (爻, Yao)

First Six (初六, Chu Liu)
Expressing Joyful Ease. Misfortune.

鳴豫. 凶.

If plans are divulged this will bring misfortune. Enthusiastic speech can lead others into false actions. Guard your words.

Second Six (六二, Liu Er)
Firm as a rock. Not a whole day. Correct and auspicious.

介于石. 不終日. 貞吉.

Adhere to the ideals of fair justice and good self-defense, then before the end of the day arrives there will be good fortune.

Third Six (六 三, Liu San)
Looking for Joyful Ease is regretful.　　盱豫悔.遲有悔.
Delay has regret.

If acting hesitant and moving too slowly, there will be regret.

Fourth Nine (九 四, Jiu Si)
The source of Joyful Ease.　　由豫.大有得.
Greatness is obtained. Without　　勿疑.朋盍簪.
suspicion. Friends gather about.

From a successful divination, many treasures are obtained. Opportunities were not missed, so the head may be adorned with precious objects. Many friends now appear.

Fifth Six (六 五, Liu Wu)
Correct about the illness.　　貞疾.恆不死.
Long lasting, does not die.

The illness was predicted correctly. There will be no early death.

Topmost Six (上 六, Shang Liu)
Obscurity about Joyful Ease. Having　　冥豫.成有渝.无咎.
completed the changes. Without fault.

Sit in meditation during the night and changes will occur. There will be no trouble in doing this.

Alternate English Translations for the Hexagram of Yu, 豫

The Symbol of Harmonious Joy [S]　　*Joy* [C]
Enthusiasm [WB]　　*Delight* [H]
Repose [B]　　*Comfort* [N]
Broadcasting [CS]　　*Providing* [RS]
Providing For/Provision [K]　　*The Symbol of Enthusiasm* [CC]
Happiness [L]

The Great Symbolism (大象, Da Xiang) says,

From the Earth comes the rousing of Thunder. This is Yu. The ancient kings, according with this, composed music to honor the virtuous. They made abundant offerings to the Supreme Ruler so they might be worthy of their ancestors and fathers.	雷出地奮.豫. 先王以作樂崇德. 殷薦之上帝. 以配祖考.

☷ Sexagenary Placement

Heavenly Stem: Wu 戊 (5th Stem, Yang)—**Earth** (土, Tu)
Earthly Branch: Yin 寅 (3rd Branch, Yang)—**Tiger** (虎, Hu)
Represents the *Year of the Earth Tiger* (15th Year of the Sixty-Year Cycle)
Years: 1878 – 1938 – 1998 – 2058

Trigram Correlations

Upper Gua (Thunder)

☳ **Zhen** 震
- **Represents:** Thunder, Earthquake, Eldest Son
- **Actions:** Arousing, Shaking, Initiating
- **Influences:** Foundations, Past Actions, Excitement.
- **Shape:** Vertical Column   **Color:** Green
- **Body:** Feet and legs   **Season:** Beginning Winter
- **Moon Phase:** Waning Crescent
- **Animals:** Earthly Dragons, Celestial Dragon-Horse
- **Directions:** Northeast (BH), East (AH)
- **Nine Palaces Numbers:** Fu Xi: 3
    Yu the Great: Ho River Map, 8—Lo River Script, 3
- **Internal Alchemy:** Mind-Intention
    Qi Center: Dan Tian (Elixir Field)
    Qi Meridian: Yin Qiao Mai (Yin Heel Vessel)

#16 Joyful Ease (Yu)

Lower Gua (Earth)

☷ **Kun** 坤   **Represents:** Earth, Soil, Fields, Female, Mother, Empress
Actions: Receptive, Expanding, Yielding
Influences: Relationships, Love, Submission
Shape: Square   **Color:** Yellow
Body: Stomach   **Season:** Winter (Winter Solstice)
Moon Phase: New Moon
Animals: Earthly Ox, Celestial Black Tortoise
Directions: North (BH), Southwest (AH)
Nine Palaces Numbers: Fu Xi: **10**
   Yu the Great: Ho River Map, **1**—Lo River Script, **2**
Internal Alchemy: Tranquility, Void
   Qi Center: Hui Yin (Returning Yin)
   Qi Meridian: Ren Mai (Function Vessel)

Associated Developed Hexagrams of Yu

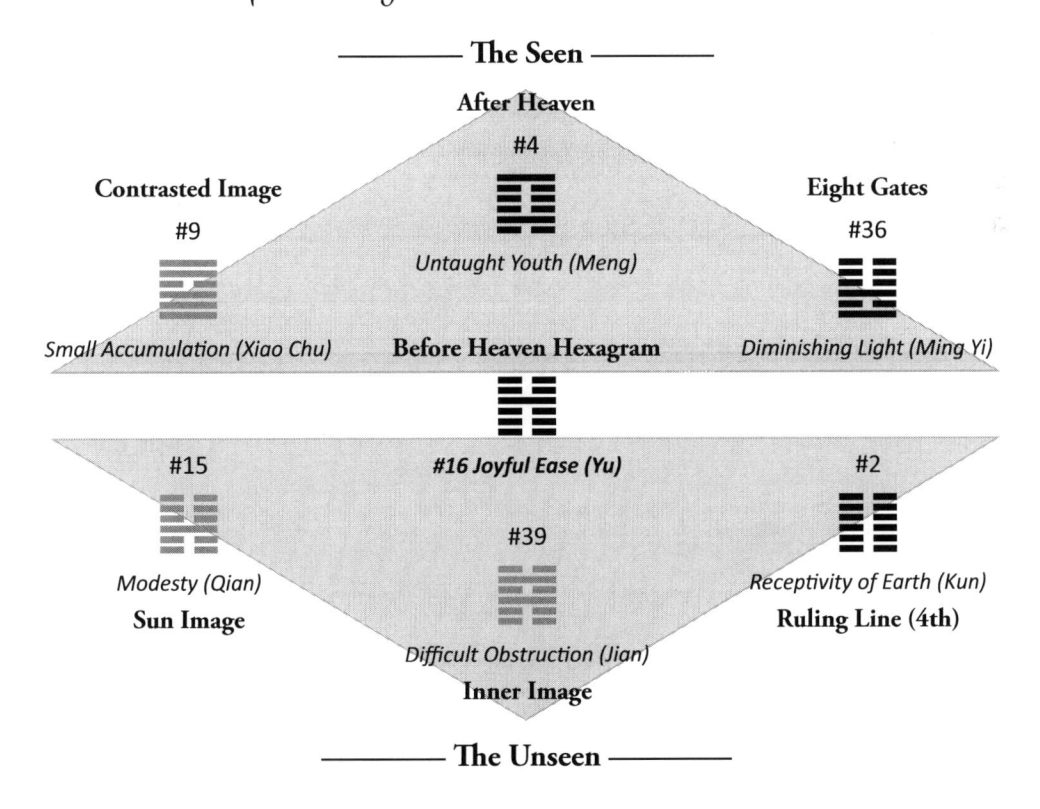

——— **The Seen** ———

After Heaven
#4
Untaught Youth (Meng)

Contrasted Image
#9
Small Accumulation (Xiao Chu)

Eight Gates
#36
Diminishing Light (Ming Yi)

Before Heaven Hexagram

#16 Joyful Ease (Yu)

#15
Modesty (Qian)
Sun Image

#39
Difficult Obstruction (Jian)
Inner Image

#2
Receptivity of Earth (Kun)
Ruling Line (4th)

——— **The Unseen** ———

Sui 隨

Following

17

Dui (Valley) above
兌 上
Dui Shang
Zhen (Thunder) below
震 下
Zhen Xia

Sun/Yang Image

The Prediction (彖, Tuan)

Following:
Great perseverance. Advantage in firmness. Without fault.

隨. 元 亨. 利 貞. 无 咎.

When people are true to themselves and to others there will be no calamities. Be content in wherever you go or what you do and everything can be harmonious from beginning to end. Leaders should follow and adjust their actions according to what is right to show great perseverance. Followers must determine what course of action to follow and be resolute in following. It is correct to use the stalks for divination during this time.

The Lines (爻, Yao)

First Nine (初 九, Chu Jiu)
Having sensed the change. Resoluteness is auspicious. Going beyond the gateway to meet has merit.

官 有 渝. 貞 吉. 出 門 交 有 功.

A person in charge has been replaced. Wisdom should determine who leads and who follows. The prediction on the future shows it will be auspicious. Now is a good time to go out and make connections with people who will be fruitful.

Second Six (六 二, Liu Er)
Clinging to the small boy. The elder is lost.

係 小 子. 失 丈 夫.

The young boy is tied up and unable to move; the able-bodied man is now escaping. The young boy cannot follow the able-bodied man.

Third Six (六三, Liu San)

Clinging to the elder. The small boy is lost. Following obtains what is sought. Advantage in remaining resolute.

係丈夫. 失小子.
隨有求得. 利居貞.

The able-bodied man is tied up and unable to move; the young boy is now escaping. The boy must be chased and found if something is to be gained. Mature actions should be applied; immature actions must be discarded. This is a good time to stay at home quietly in meditation and to divine the future.

Fourth Nine (九四, Jiu Si)

In Following, there is capture. Firmness will be unfortunate. Possessing sincerity in the Way [Dao] brings about wisdom. What fault could this be?

隨有獲. 貞凶.
有孚在道以明.
尚咎.

Enemies are captured. In following you, they forebode danger. The situation is of the blind leading the blind. While guarding them along the road, question them on coming calamities. To be sincere shows wisdom and that you are a person of the Dao.

Fifth Nine (九五, Jiu Wu)

Sincere in the good. Auspicious.

孚于嘉. 吉.

In subduing enemies it is auspicious to use deception, but only if the intent is sincere and for the good.

Topmost Six (上六, Shang Liu)

Grasping and clinging. Obeying and holding fast. The king makes use of perseverance on the Western Mountains.

拘係之. 從維之.
王用亨于西山.

The enemies have each been tied up, and so they grasp and cling to any possibility of escape. The king is using them as bargaining pawns on the Western Mountains, hoping it will create a greater alliance with his western neighbors. His guards obey and hold fast, but want it to end.

Alternate English Translations for the Hexagram of Sui, 隨

The Symbol of Following [S]
Following [C] [CS] [H] [K] [L] [RS] [WB]
The Symbol of Succession [CC]

Following, According With [B]
Compliance—Following [N]

The Great Symbolism (大象, Da Xiang) says,

Within a Marsh there is Thunder. 澤中有雷.
This is Sui. Superior persons, according 隨. 君子以嚮
with this, enter their dwellings for rest 晦入宴息.
as evening approaches.

Sexagenary Placement

Heavenly Stem: Ji 己 (6th Stem, Yin)—**Earth** (土, Tu)
Earthly Branch: Chou 丑 (2nd Branch, Yin)—**Ox** (牛, Niu)
Represents the *Year of the Earth Ox* (26th Year of the Sixty-Year Cycle)
Years: 1889 – 1949 – 2009 – 2069

Trigram Correlations

Upper Gua (Valley)

Dui 兌　　**Represents:** Valley, River, Lake/Marsh, Youngest Daughter
Actions: Joyous, Opening, Stimulating
Influences: Family, Future, Collecting, Pleasure, Absorbing, Complacency.
Shape: Introverted Triangle　　**Color:** Brown
Body: Mouth　　**Season:** Beginning Spring
Moon Phase: Waning Gibbous
Animals: Earthly Goat, Celestial Great Roc
Directions: Southeast (BH), West (AH)
Nine Palaces Numbers: Fu Xi: 5
　　Yu the Great: Ho River Map, 4—Lo River Script, 7
Internal Alchemy: Po (Earthly) Spirit
　　Qi Center: Xuan Guan (Mysterious Pass)
　　Qi Meridian: Yang Wei Mai (Yang Preserving Vessel)

#17 Following (Sui)

Lower Gua (Thunder)

Zhen 震

Represents: Thunder, Earthquake, Eldest Son
Actions: Arousing, Shaking, Initiating
Influences: Foundations, Past Actions, Excitement.
Shape: Vertical Column   **Color:** Green
Body: Feet and legs   **Season:** Beginning Winter
Moon Phase: Waning Crescent
Animals: Earthly Dragons, Celestial Dragon-Horse
Directions: Northeast (BH), East (AH)
Nine Palaces Numbers: Fu Xi: 3
    Yu the Great: Ho River Map, **8**—Lo River Script, **3**
Internal Alchemy: Mind-Intention
    Qi Center: Dan Tian (Elixir Field)
    Qi Meridian: Yin Qiao Mai (Yin Heel Vessel)

Associated Developed Hexagrams of Sui

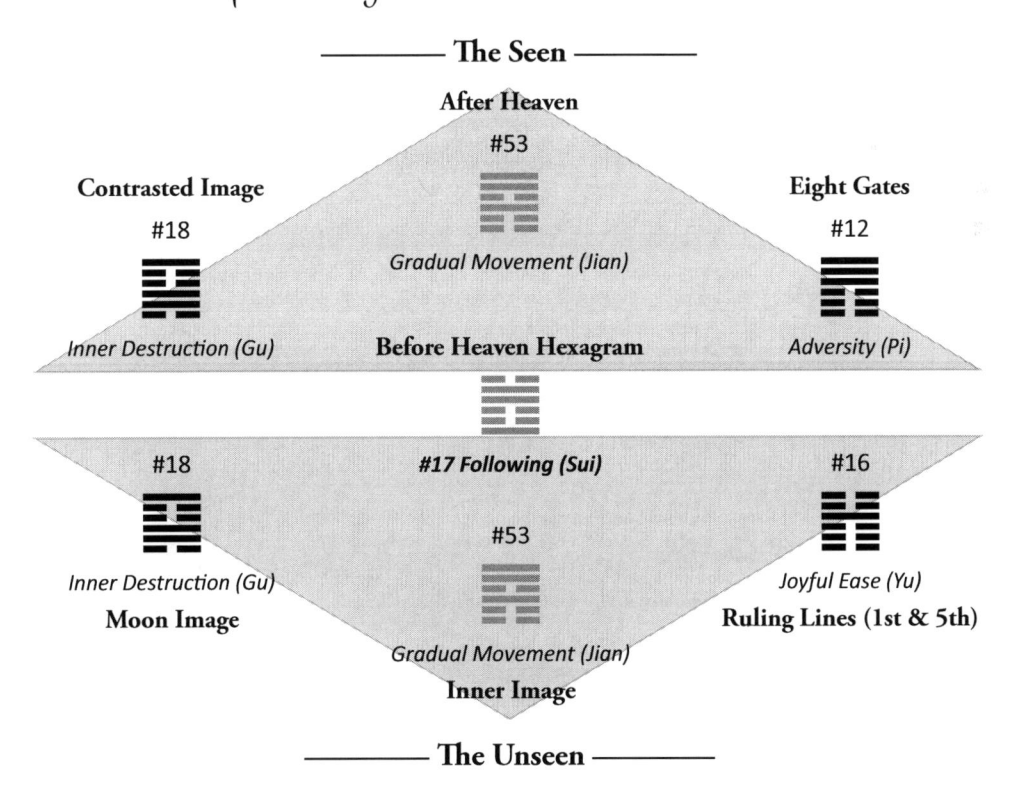

— **The Seen** —

After Heaven

#53

Gradual Movement (Jian)

Contrasted Image
#18

Inner Destruction (Gu)

Eight Gates
#12

Adversity (Pi)

Before Heaven Hexagram

#17 Following (Sui)

#18

Inner Destruction (Gu)
Moon Image

#53

Gradual Movement (Jian)
Inner Image

#16

Joyful Ease (Yu)
Ruling Lines (1st & 5th)

— **The Unseen** —

Gu

蠱

Inner Destruction

Gen (Mountain) above
艮上
Gen Shang
Xun (Wind) below
巽下
Xun Xia

18

Moon/Yin Image

The Prediction (象, Tuan)

Inner Destruction:

Great perseverance. Advantage in fording
the great stream. Before the first three days.
After the first three days.

蠱.元亨.利涉大川.
先甲三日.後甲三日.

People must think for themselves. What has been damaged through a person's errors or circumstances can be repaired through good efforts and deeds. It is beneficial to cross the great river, but the period for doing so is limited to three days before the day of Jia (Xin, Ren, and Gui) and the three days after Jia (Yi, Bing, and Ding).[3] Three days of examination and three days of restoration is the correct way, then it will be as if you had crossed a great river.

The Lines (爻, Yao)

First Six (初 六, Chu Liu)
Attending to the Inner Destruction
caused by the father. Having a son.
The father is without fault.
Sternness. The end is auspicious.

幹父之蠱.
有子.考无咎.
厲.終吉.

The son should intervene in the errors of the father's affairs. This kind of filial son will prevent calamities and ward-off dangers from occurring. In the end it will all be auspicious, but if the reform carried out by the son is too harsh, misfortune will follow.

Second Nine (九 二, Jiu Er)
Attending to the Inner Destruction caused
by the mother. Not able to be correct.

幹母之蠱.不可貞.

---

[3] See *Book of Sun and Moon,* volume I, for calendar correlations of the Ten Heavenly Stems.

A husband should intervene in the wrongful affairs of his wife, but he must use gentle guidance in reforming her. There is difficulty in predicting what the future will hold.

Third Nine (九 三, Jiu San)
Attending to the Inner Destruction caused by the father. Smallness has regret. No great fault.   幹父之蠱. 小有悔. 无大咎.

Intervening in the wrongful errors of the father, seldom does he feel regret, which proves harmful to the general affairs of the family. Small efforts bring remorse; great effort stabilizes the situation.

Fourth Six (六 四, Liu Si)
Tolerant of the Inner Destruction caused by the father. Going forward, regret is seen.   裕父之蠱. 往見吝.

Difficulties will be encountered if the father's errors are tolerated. When condoning the errors, you only enable him to further the damage.

Fifth Six (六 五, Liu Wu)
Attending to the Inner Destruction caused by the father. Praise is useful.   幹父之蠱. 用譽.

Highlight past honors when intervening in the errors of the father. Praise his good points and avoid mentioning the bad ones.

Topmost Nine (上 九, Shang Jiu)
Does not serve to the affairs of kings and feudal lords. Serve the affairs of one's own noble position.   不事王侯. 高尚其事.

Do not work for kings and those of high position and you will feel proud in your own ambitions and successes. Sage seek their highest goals without the aid of those in high positions.

Alternate English Translations for the Hexagram of Gu, 蠱

The Symbol of Destruction [S]
Work on What Has Been Spoiled (Decay) [WB]
Decay [B] [RS]
Decay (Correcting) [CS]
Corruption/Renovation [K]

Degeneration [C]
Remedying [H]
Correcting the Corruption [N]
Work After Spoiling [L]
The Symbol of Major Power [CC]

The Great Symbolism (大象, Da Xiang) says,

A Mountain and beneath it the Wind. This is Gu. The superior person, according with this, moves the people and nourishes them with virtue.

山有風．蠱．
君子以振民育德．

Sexagenary Placement

Heavenly Stem: Ji 己 (6th Stem, Yin)—**Earth** (土, Tu)
Earthly Branch: Wei 未 (8th Branch, Yin)—**Goat** (羊, Yang)
Represents the *Year of the Earth Goat* (56th Year of the Sixty-Year Cycle)
Years: 1859 – 1919 – 1979 – 2039

Trigram Correlations

Upper Gua (Mountain)

Gen 艮
- **Represents:** Mountain, Towers, Youngest Son
- **Actions:** Stillness, Binding, Stopping
- **Influences:** Knowledge, Wisdom, Skill, Determination
- **Shape:** Vertical Column   **Color:** Blue
- **Body:** Hands and arms   **Season:** Beginning Autumn
- **Moon Phase:** Waxing Crescent
- **Animals:** Earthly Dog, Celestial Vermilion Snake
- **Directions:** Northwest (BH), Northeast (AH)
- **Nine Palaces Numbers:** Fu Xi: 7
    Yu the Great: Ho River Map, **6**— Lo River Script, **8**
- **Internal Alchemy:** Hun (Heavenly) Spirit
    Qi Center: Jing Men (Essence Gate)
    Qi Meridian: Yang Qiao Mai (Yang Heel Vessel)

Lower Gua (Wind)

☴ **Xun** 巽　**Represents:** Wind, Wood, Eldest Daughter
　　　　　Actions: Gentleness, Grounding, Penetrating, Spreading
　　　　　Influences: Prosperity, Abundance, Wealth
　　　　　Shape: Rectangle　　**Color:** Purple
　　　　　Body: Waist and hips　**Season:** Beginning Summer
　　　　　Moon Phase: Waxing Gibbous
　　　　　Animals: Earthly Fowl, Celestial Golden Rooster
　　　　　Directions: Southwest (BH), Southeast (AH)
　　　　　Nine Palaces Numbers: Fu Xi: 9
　　　　　　　Yu the Great: Ho River Map, 2—Lo River Script, 4
　　　　　Internal Alchemy: Breath and Mobilizing Qi
　　　　　　　Qi Center: Yu Zhen (Jade Pillow)
　　　　　　　Qi Meridian: Yin Wei Mai (Yin Preserving Vessel)

Associated Developed Hexagrams of Gu

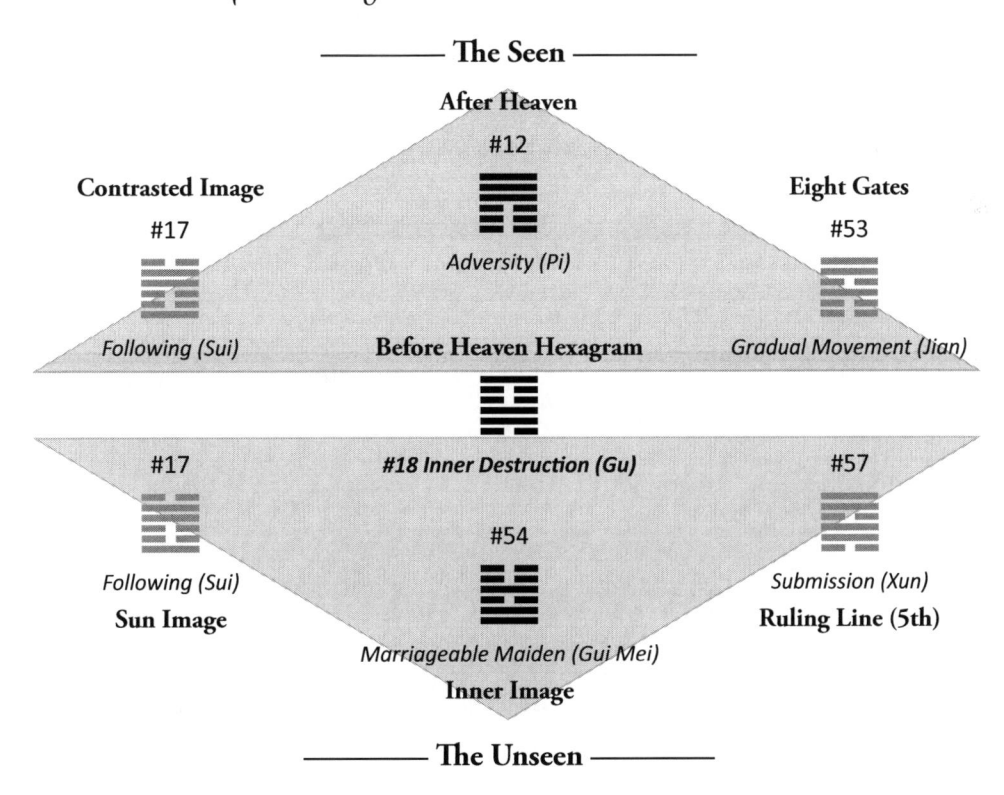

——— **The Seen** ———

After Heaven
#12
Adversity (Pi)

Contrasted Image
#17
Following (Sui)

Eight Gates
#53
Gradual Movement (Jian)

Before Heaven Hexagram
#18 Inner Destruction (Gu)

#17
Following (Sui)
Sun Image

#54
Marriageable Maiden (Gui Mei)
Inner Image

#57
Submission (Xun)
Ruling Line (5th)

——— **The Unseen** ———

Lin 臨

Approaching

19

Kun (Earth) above
坤上
Kun Shang
Dui (Valley) below
兌下
Dui Xia

Sun/Yang Image

The Prediction (彖, Tuan)

Approaching:
Great, persevering, advantageous, and resolute.
In the eighth month misfortune arrives.

臨. 元 亨 利 貞. 至 于 八 月 有 凶.

In Approaching, there is success as the Four Meritorious symbols have appeared.[4] In setting about your work, the path is smooth from the very beginning. This is an auspicious time for calculating the future, but there will be trouble in the eighth lunar month.

The Lines (爻, Yao)

First Nine (初 九, Chu Jiu)
Someone is Approaching.
Resoluteness is auspicious.

或 臨. 貞 吉.

Everyone has arrived and there is an overwhelming sense that all will go well. Others seek to join you, but it's best to stay independent.

Second Nine (九 二, Jiu Er)
Someone is Approaching. Auspicious.
Everything is beneficial.

或 臨. 吉. 无 不 利.

Join with this person. Everything is good and no misfortune will occur.

---

4   *Yuan Heng Li Zhen* (元 亨 利 貞, Great, Persevering, Advantageous, and Resolute). These four characters, first mentioned in hexagram #1 *Creativity of Heaven,* are considered extremely auspicious and descriptive of the Dao itself.

Third Six (六 三, Liu San)
Voluntary Approaching. There is no advantage. Grief at the finish. Without fault.

甘臨. 无攸利.
既憂之. 无咎.

Volunteering for a task, unexpected events happen so there is a feeling of being upset. Do not worry, as no calamity occurs. It is wise to guard against arrogance and overconfidence, and avoid indulging in too much comfort.

Fourth Six (六 四, Liu Si)
Approaching arrives and is without fault.

至臨无咎.

Do not be lax, keep yourself busy, and let others do the approaching. Doing so causes no harm.

Fifth Six (六 五, Liu Wu)
Awareness of Approaching. Befit of the great prince. Auspicious.

知臨. 大君之宜. 吉.

This is a most auspicious and appropriate time for great persons to undertake a task alone and to use their wisdom in doing so.

Topmost Six (上 六, Shang Liu)
Sincere and honest Approaching. Auspicious. Without fault.

敦臨. 吉. 无咎.

Use kindness and a heart of tolerance in all affairs. This will produce many good fortunes and ward-off calamities.

Alternate English Translations for the Hexagram of Lin, 臨

The Symbol of Advance and Arrival [S]
Approach [B] [CS] [L] [WB]
Overseeing [C]
The Symbol of Advance [CC]

Approaching [H]
Advancing [N]
Nearing [K] [RS]

The Great Symbolism (大象, Da Xiang) says,

A Marsh and above it there is Earth. This is Lin. The superior person, according with this, teaches contemplation tirelessly. Forgiving and protecting the people endlessly.	澤上有地.臨. 君子以教思无窮. 容保民无疆.

Sexagenary Placement

Heavenly Stem: Gui 癸 (10th Stem, Yin)—**Water** (水, Shui)
Earthly Branch: Mao 卯 (4th Branch, Yin)—**Rabbit** (兔, Tu)
Represents the *Year of the Water Rabbit* (40th Year of the Sixty-Year Cycle)
Years: 1843 – 1903 – 1963 – 2023

Trigram Correlations

Upper Gua (Earth)

Kun 坤
Represents: Earth, Soil, Fields, Female, Mother, Empress
Actions: Receptive, Expanding, Yielding
Influences: Relationships, Love, Submission
Shape: Square **Color:** Yellow
Body: Stomach **Season:** Winter (Winter Solstice)
Moon Phase: New Moon
Animals: Earthly Ox, Celestial Black Tortoise
Directions: North (BH), Southwest (AH)
Nine Palaces Numbers: Fu Xi: **10**
  Yu the Great: Ho River Map, **1**—Lo River Script, **2**
Internal Alchemy: Tranquility, Void
  Qi Center: Hui Yin (Returning Yin)
  Qi Meridian: Ren Mai (Function Vessel)

Lower Gua (Valley)

☱ **Dui** 兌   **Represents:** Valley, River, Lake/Marsh, Youngest Daughter
Actions: Joyous, Opening, Stimulating
Influences: Family, Future, Collecting, Pleasure, Absorbing, Complacency.
Shape: Introverted Triangle   **Color:** Brown
Body: Mouth   **Season:** Beginning Spring
Moon Phase: Waning Gibbous
Animals: Earthly Goat, Celestial Great Roc
Directions: Southeast (BH), West (AH)
Nine Palaces Numbers: Fu Xi: 5
    Yu the Great: Ho River Map, 4—Lo River Script, 7
Internal Alchemy: Po (Earthly) Spirit
    Qi Center: Xuan Guan (Mysterious Pass)
    Qi Meridian: Yang Wei Mai (Yang Preserving Vessel)

Associated Developed Hexagrams of Lin

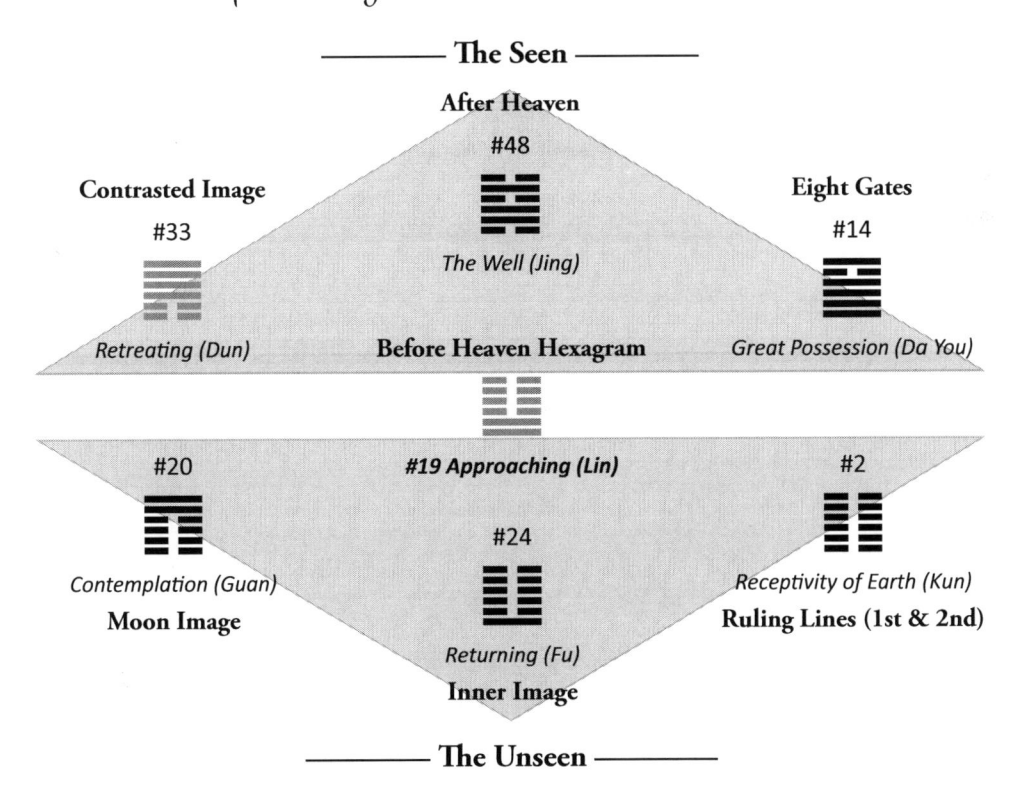

——— **The Seen** ———

After Heaven
#48
The Well (Jing)

Contrasted Image
#33
Retreating (Dun)

Eight Gates
#14
Great Possession (Da You)

Before Heaven Hexagram
#19 Approaching (Lin)

#20
Contemplation (Guan)
Moon Image

#24
Returning (Fu)
Inner Image

#2
Receptivity of Earth (Kun)
Ruling Lines (1st & 2nd)

——— **The Unseen** ———

77

Guan

觀

Contemplation

20

Xun (Wind) above
巽 上
Xun Shang
Kun (Earth) below
坤 下
Kun Xia

Moon/Yin Image

The Prediction (彖, Tuan)

Contemplation:
Cleansing of hands, but no offering of worship. Possessing sincerity and dignity is to be in accord.

觀. 盥而不薦. 有孚顒若.

All actions must be pondered and thought through carefully beforehand. The official of ceremonies has washed his hands before making offerings of wine and food in preparation of making a sacrifice. Opponents are frightened by this because the procedures are done correctly and so they cannot find fault. Examine yourself carefully and let others examine you carefully as well. Meditate on the workings of Dao and mirror your actions accordingly.

The Lines (爻, Yao)

First Six (初 六, Chu Liu)
Pure Contemplation. Inferior people are without fault. The wise person has regret.

童觀. 小人无咎. 君子吝.

Observing the world through the perspective of a child does the common person no harm. This will not work for the master, however, as he or she needs to understand everything clearly or there will be humiliation.

Second Six (六 二, Liu Er)
Contemplation by stealing a glance. Advantageous for the woman to be resolute.

闚觀. 利女貞.

Stealing glances and peeking through a small opening has great benefit for the female, because it means her prediction by the stalks came true. If the female is to be the center of attention and to lead she must have a wide and open perspective.

Third Six (六 三, Liu San)
Contemplation of my life when advancing and withdrawing.　　觀我生進退.

Observe everyone who stands by your side before deciding to advance or retreat. Contemplate the question, "Should I advance or retreat?"

Fourth Six (六 四, Liu Si)
Contemplation of the country's light. Advantage in being a guest of the king.　　觀國之光. 利用賓于王.

The ruler will invite you as his guest of honor while reviewing the troops. Offer your insights and advice but do not join the cause—stay independent.

Fifth Nine (九 五, Jiu Wu)
Contemplation of my life. The wise person is without fault.　　觀我生. 君子无咎.

Understanding clearly your effect and influence on others is wise and good.

Topmost Nine (上 九, Shang Jiu)
Contemplation of their life. The wise person is without fault.　　觀其生. 君子无咎.

It is fortunate if the ruler visits the common people and observes their conditions from their perspective.

Alternate English Translations for the Hexagram of Guan, 觀

The Symbol of Steady Observation [S]　　*Watching* [H]
Contemplation (View) [WB]　　*Contemplation—Point of View* [N]
Looking Down [B]　　*Overseeing* [RS]
Overseeing [C]　　*Observation* [L]
Contemplation [CS]　　*Viewing* [K]
The Symbol of Contemplation [CC]

The Great Symbolism (大象, Da Xiang) says,

The Wind moves above the Earth.	風行地上. 觀.
This is Guan. The ancient kings accordingly examined the regions, contemplated the people, and so established loyalty.	先王以省方觀民設教.

Sexagenary Placement

Heavenly Stem: Yi 乙 (2nd Stem, Yin)— 木 **Wood** (Mu)
Earthly Branch: Mao 卯 (4th Branch, Yin)— 兔 **Rabbit** (Tu)
Represents the *Year of the Wood Rabbit* (52nd Year of the Sixty-Year Cycle)
Years: 1855 – 1915 – 1975 – 2035

Trigram Correlations

Upper Gua (Wind)

Xun 巽

Represents: Wind, Wood, Eldest Daughter
Actions: Gentleness, Grounding, Penetrating, Spreading
Influences: Prosperity, Abundance, Wealth
Shape: Rectangle   **Color:** Purple
Body: Waist and hips   **Season:** Beginning Summer
Moon Phase: Waxing Gibbous
Animals: Earthly Fowl, Celestial Golden Rooster
Directions: Southwest (BH), Southeast (AH)
Nine Palaces Numbers: Fu Xi: 9
  Yu the Great: Ho River Map, 2—Lo River Script, 4
Internal Alchemy: Breath and Mobilizing Qi
  Qi Center: Yu Zhen (Jade Pillow)
  Qi Meridian: Yin Wei Mai (Yin Preserving Vessel)

#20 Contemplation (Guan)

Lower Gua (Earth)

☷ **Kun** 坤   **Represents:** Earth, Soil, Fields, Female, Mother, Empress
Actions: Receptive, Expanding, Yielding
Influences: Relationships, Love, Submission
Shape: Square   **Color:** Yellow
Body: Stomach   **Season:** Winter (Winter Solstice)
Moon Phase: New Moon
Animals: Earthly Ox, Celestial Black Tortoise
Directions: North (BH), Southwest (AH)
Nine Palaces Numbers: Fu Xi: **10**
  Yu the Great: Ho River Map, **1**—Lo River Script, **2**
Internal Alchemy: Tranquility, Void
  Qi Center: Hui Yin (Returning Yin)
  Qi Meridian: Ren Mai (Function Vessel)

Associated Developed Hexagrams of Guan

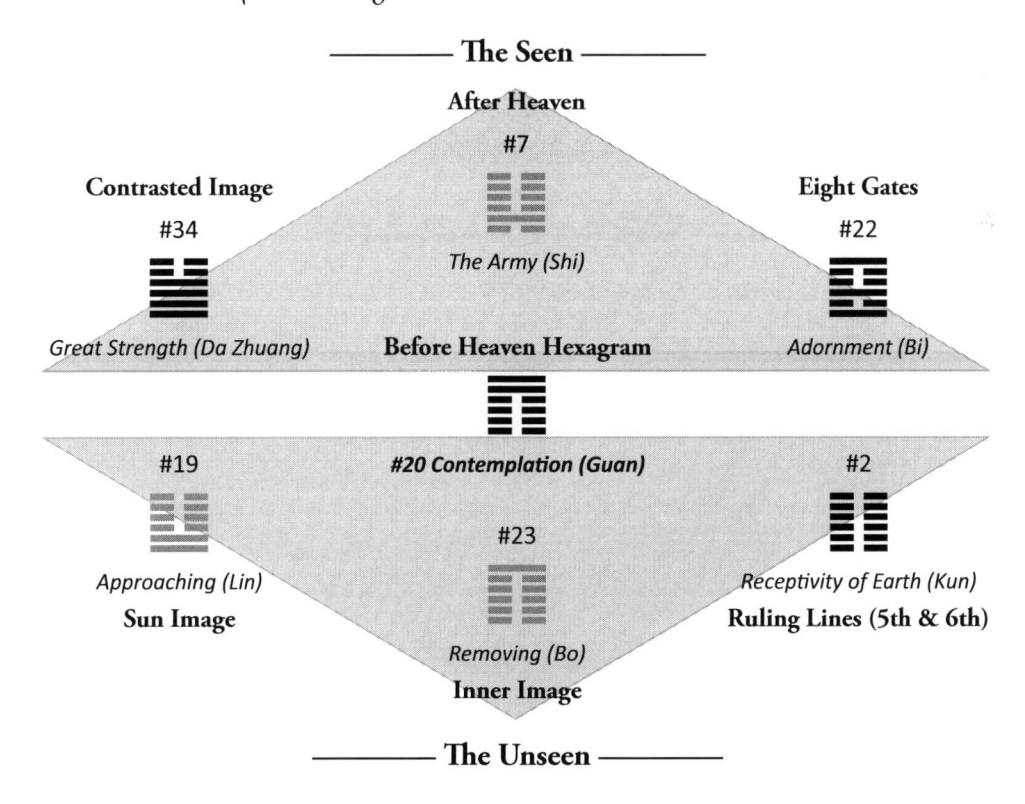

——— **The Seen** ———

After Heaven
#7
The Army (Shi)

Contrasted Image
#34
Great Strength (Da Zhuang)

Eight Gates
#22
Adornment (Bi)

Before Heaven Hexagram

#20 Contemplation (Guan)

#19
Approaching (Lin)
Sun Image

#23
Removing (Bo)
Inner Image

#2
Receptivity of Earth (Kun)
Ruling Lines (5th & 6th)

——— **The Unseen** ———

Shi He — *Mastication* — 21

Li (Fire) above
離 上
Li Shang
Zhen (Thunder) below
震 下
Zhen Xia

Sun/Yang Image

The Prediction (象, Tuan)

Mastication:
Perseverance. Advantage in employing legal constraints.

噬嗑. 亨. 利用獄.

Peace of mind will most certainly arrive if good laws and rules are presented with clarity. If having enough to eat and drink, litigations can be handled smoothly. If, however, an obstacle has to be moved by force, apply just measures and restraints.

The Lines (爻, Yao)

First Nine (初九, Chu Jiu)
The feet are in stocks and he is deprived of toes. Without fault.

履校滅趾. 无咎.

The prisoner sits in his cell with shackled feet. Hopefully, he learns from this light punishment. There is no great danger yet.

Second Six (六二, Liu Er)
Biting and gnawing, deprived of the nose. Without fault.

噬盧滅鼻. 无咎.

Eating a large piece of meat that is pressed up against the nose. This shows greed has brought forth the punishment, but nothing is really bad at this point.

#21 Mastication (Shi He)

Third Six (六 三, Liu San)
Biting on dried fleshy meat.
Poison is found. Small regret.
Without fault.

噬腊肉. 遇毒. 小吝. 无咎.

Feeling ill, one has been poisoned by eating preserved meat, but it is not serious. This is the result of a brazen and foolish demeanor, resulting in embarrassment.

Fourth Nine (九 四, Jiu Si)
Biting dried meat on pieces of bone,
golden arrows are received. Advantage in
what is hard and resolute. Auspicious.

噬乾胏. 得金矢. 利艱貞. 吉.

When eating the meat you find a gold arrowhead near the bones. This is auspicious, yet you must predict your prospects. This shows that your persistence has won the litigation.

Fifth Six (六 五, Liu Wu)
Biting on dried meat. Receives yellow gold.
Firm discipline. Without fault.

噬乾肉. 得黃金. 貞厲. 无咎.

You bite down hard on a piece of gold when eating the meat. This forebodes danger but no calamities will result from it. Seek the Middle Way and don't be too lenient nor too harsh in your dealings with others.

Topmost Nine (上 九, Shang Jiu)
Enduring the stocks and deprived of ears.
Misfortune.

何校滅耳. 凶.

It is very bad luck to be confined by a cangue that hides and obstructs the ears. This shows you have been deaf to all good advice and now things have turned bad and you are constrained.

Alternate English Translations for the Hexagram of Shi He, 噬嗑

Biting Through [C] [WB]
Gnawing [B]
Gnawing Through [CS]
*The Symbol of Mastication and Punishment
    by Pressing and Squeezing* [S]
The Symbol of Criminal Proceedings [CC]

Biting Through Hardships [N]
Gnawing and Biting [RS]
Chewing [L]
Eradicating [H]
Gnawing Bite [K]

The Great Symbolism (大象, Da Xiang) says,

Thunder and Lightning are Shi He.	雷電噬嗑.
The ancient kings, according with this, punished through wisdom and through imperial law.	先王以明罰敕法.

Sexagenary Placement

Heavenly Stem: Ren 壬 (9th Stem, Yang)—**Water** (水, Shui)
Earthly Branch: Zi 子 (1st Branch, Yang)—**Rat** (鼠, Shu)
Represents the *Year of the Water Rat* (49th Year of the Sixty-Year Cycle)
Years: 1852 – 1912 – 1972 – 2032

Trigram Correlations

Upper Gua (Fire)

Li 離
- **Represents:** Fire, Lightning, Sun, Middle Daughter
- **Actions:** Clinging, Illuminating, Congregating
- **Influences:** Fame, Reputation, Brightness, Elegance
- **Shape:** Triangle   **Color:** Red
- **Body:** Eyes   **Season:** Spring (Spring Equinox)
- **Moon Phase:** Last Quarter
- **Animals:** Earthly Rooster, Celestial Green Dragon
- **Directions:** East (BH), South (AH)
- **Nine Palaces Numbers:** Fu Xi: **8**
    Yu the Great: Ho River Map, **3**—Lo River Script, **9**
- **Internal Alchemy:** Mercury, Qi
    Qi Center: Jiang Gong (Crimson Palace)
    Qi Meridian: Dai Mai (Belt Vessel)

Lower Gua (Thunder)

Zhen 震 **Represents:** Thunder, Earthquake, Eldest Son
Actions: Arousing, Shaking, Initiating
Influences: Foundations, Past Actions, Excitement.
Shape: Vertical Column   **Color:** Green
Body: Feet and legs   **Season:** Beginning Winter
Moon Phase: Waning Crescent
Animals: Earthly Dragons, Celestial Dragon-Horse
Directions: Northeast (BH), East (AH)
Nine Palaces Numbers: Fu Xi: 3
   Yu the Great: Ho River Map, **8**—Lo River Script, **3**
Internal Alchemy: Mind-Intention
   Qi Center: Dan Tian (Elixir Field)
   Qi Meridian: Yin Qiao Mai (Yin Heel Vessel)

Associated Developed Hexagrams of Shi He

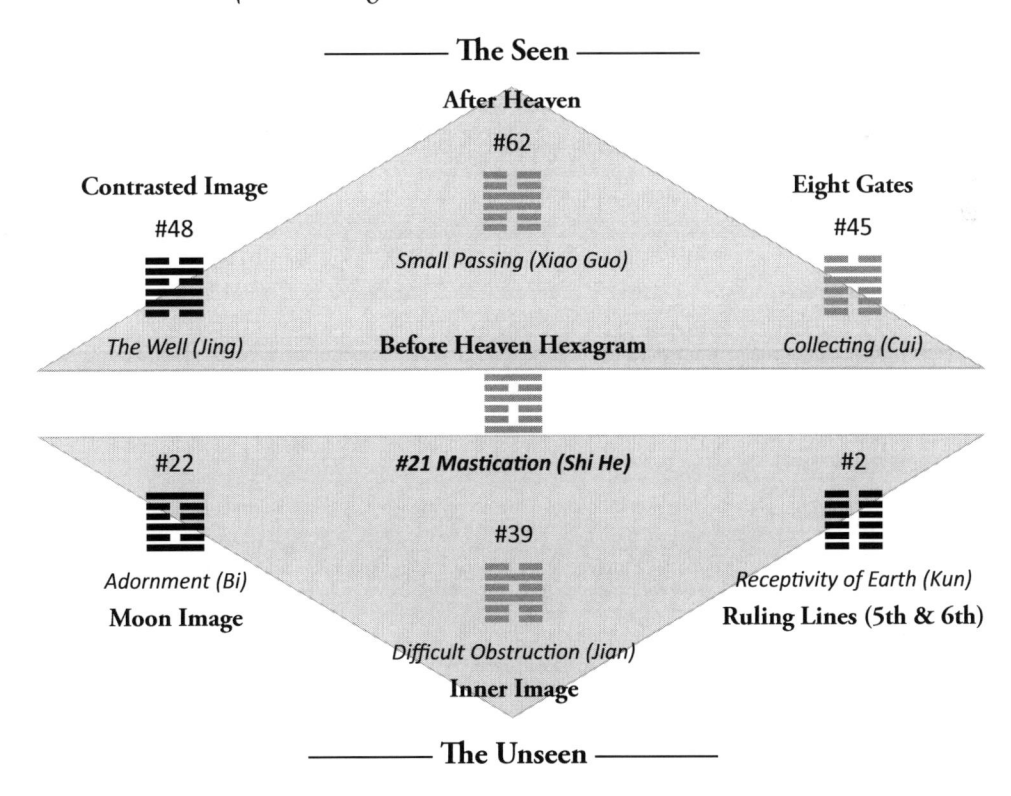

——— **The Seen** ———

After Heaven
#62
Small Passing (Xiao Guo)

Contrasted Image
#48
The Well (Jing)

Eight Gates
#45
Collecting (Cui)

Before Heaven Hexagram

#21 Mastication (Shi He)

#22
Adornment (Bi)
Moon Image

#39
Difficult Obstruction (Jian)
Inner Image

#2
Receptivity of Earth (Kun)
Ruling Lines (5th & 6th)

——— **The Unseen** ———

Bi

賁

Adornment

22

Gen (Mountain) above
艮 上
Gen Shang
Li (Fire) below
離 下
Li Xia

Moon/Yin Image

The Prediction (彖, Tuan)

Adornment:
Perseverance. Little advantage in having somewhere to go.

賁. 亨. 小利有攸往.

Right action and right thought prevail in all matters. Adornment is the image of clarity, possessing both the inner and outer beauty of tranquility. It shows no struggles in daily life and reflects the model of Heaven. Within adornment, life goes smoothly. Conditions are favorable, and it is good to move forward.

The Lines (爻, Yao)

First Nine (初 九, Chu Jiu)
Adornment of the toes. Discards the carriage and goes on foot.

賁其趾. 舍車而徒.

The toes are tattooed, colored, and bejeweled with rings. It's best to get out of the cart and walk on foot so to reveal the adornments.

Second Six (六 二, Liu Er)
Adornment of the beard.

賁其須.

The beard is decorated, but the head is insecure. Vanity overrides inner contentment.

Third Nine (九 三, Jiu San)
Immersed in Adornment. Long lasting resoluteness is auspicious.

賁如濡如. 永貞吉.

The adorning design is so bright it forebodes a long-lasting auspiciousness, so keep to perseverance to maintain good fortune.

Fourth Six (六 四, Liu Si)
Adornment in white. As if flying 賁如皤如. 白馬翰如.
on a white horse. Not a thief, 匪寇婚媾.
but a marriageable maiden.

The white cloth is well trimmed and fitted. A white horse gallops with its head raised high. No bandits are about, just suitors looking for marriage. A female adorned in sheer white clothing galloping upon a white stallion symbolizes her purity. Her seductive adorned appearance upon the stallion makes some think she is a thief, but she is only seeking a husband.

Fifth Six (六 五, Liu Wu)
Adornment of the hills and gardens. 賁于丘園. 束帛戔戔.
A roll of silk small and slight. Regret. 吝. 終吉.
The end is auspicious.

Rolls of fine and beautiful silk are laid out to adorn the surrounding hills and gardens. Some of the silk is damaged, but everything is still auspicious. A poor person attempting to adorn him or herself suffers some humiliation, but in the end there is good fortune.

Topmost Nine (上 九, Shang Jiu)
Adornment in white. 白賁. 无咎.
Without fault.

There is no error in wearing sheer white clothing in front of males (symbolized by the top Yang line). The adornment is sublime and no remorse will be experienced.

Alternate English Translations for the Hexagram of Bi, 賁

The Symbol of Decoration [S]   *Adornment* [C]
Grace [WB]   *Adorning* [H] [K] [RS]
Elegance [B]   *Adornment—Beautification* [N]
Ornamentation [CS]   *Gracefulness (Decoration)* [L]
The Symbol of Model [CC]

The Great Symbolism (大象, Da Xiang) says,

A Mountain and beneath there is Fire.	山下有火. 賁.
This is Bi. The superior person, according	君子以明庶政.
with this, makes clear the governing	无敢折獄.
of the people, but does not venture	
into deciding on criminal litigations.	

Sexagenary Placement

Heavenly Stem: Jia 甲 (1st Stem, Yang)—**Wood** (木, Mu)
Earthly Branch: Wu 午 (7th Branch, Yang)—**Horse** (馬, Ma)
Represents the *Year of the Wood Horse* (31st Year of the Sixty-Year Cycle)
Years: 1894 – 1954 – 2014 – 2074

Trigram Correlations

Upper Gua (Mountain)

Gen 艮
- **Represents:** Mountain, Towers, Youngest Son
- **Actions:** Stillness, Binding, Stopping
- **Influences:** Knowledge, Wisdom, Skill, Determination
- **Shape:** Vertical Column   **Color:** Blue
- **Body:** Hands and arms   **Season:** Beginning Autumn
- **Moon Phase:** Waxing Crescent
- **Animals:** Earthly Dog, Celestial Vermilion Snake
- **Directions:** Northwest (BH), Northeast (AH)
- **Nine Palaces Numbers:** Fu Xi: 7
    Yu the Great: Ho River Map, **6**— Lo River Script, **8**
- **Internal Alchemy:** Hun (Heavenly) Spirit
    Qi Center: Jing Men (Essence Gate)
    Qi Meridian: Yang Qiao Mai (Yang Heel Vessel)

Lower Gua (Fire)

☲ Li 離

Represents: Fire, Lightning, Sun, Middle Daughter
Actions: Clinging, Illuminating, Congregating
Influences: Fame, Reputation, Brightness, Elegance
Shape: Triangle **Color:** Red
Body: Eyes **Season:** Spring (Spring Equinox)
Moon Phase: Last Quarter
Animals: Earthly Rooster, Celestial Green Dragon
Directions: East (BH), South (AH)
Nine Palaces Numbers: Fu Xi: **8**
  Yu the Great: Ho River Map, **3**—Lo River Script, **9**
Internal Alchemy: Mercury, Qi
  Qi Center: Jiang Gong (Crimson Palace)
  Qi Meridian: Dai Mai (Belt Vessel)

Associated Developed Hexagrams of Bi

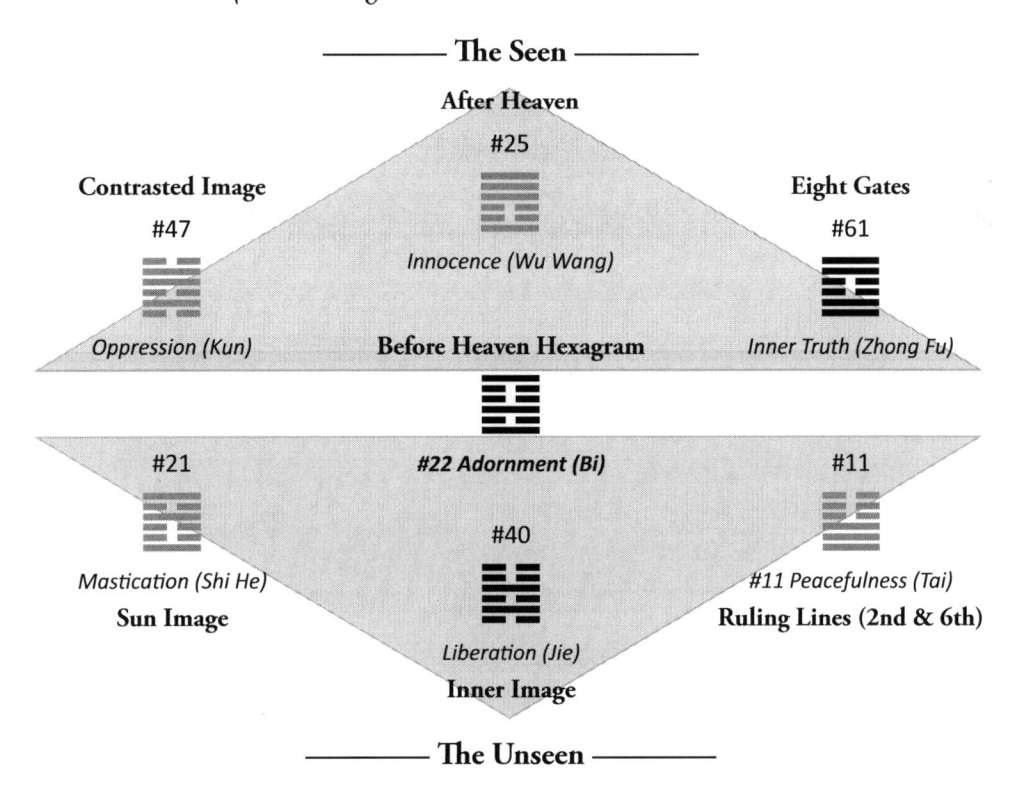

——— **The Seen** ———

After Heaven
#25
Innocence (Wu Wang)

Contrasted Image
#47
Oppression (Kun)

Eight Gates
#61
Inner Truth (Zhong Fu)

Before Heaven Hexagram

#22 Adornment (Bi)

#21
Mastication (Shi He)
Sun Image

#40
Liberation (Jie)
Inner Image

#11
#11 Peacefulness (Tai)
Ruling Lines (2nd & 6th)

——— **The Unseen** ———

Bo 剥 — *Removing* — 23

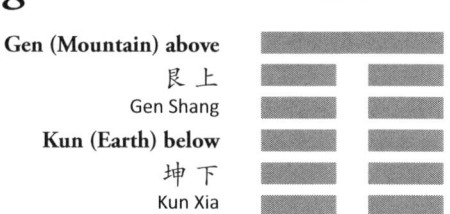

Gen (Mountain) above
艮 上
Gen Shang
Kun (Earth) below
坤 下
Kun Xia

Sun/Yang Image

The Prediction (彖, Tuan)

Removing:
Advantage in having somewhere to go.　　剝. 不利有攸往.

Misfortune occurs to those who are arrogant or insincere. Corrosion is occurring, so there is no benefit in moving without first making repairs. The common people are pushing an agenda forward and have somewhere to go, but the wise person knows that the ebb and flow of society changes, and so does not move, rather observes the flow of change.

The Lines (爻, Yao)

First Six (初 六, Chu Liu)
The legs at the foot of the bed are removed.　　剝牀以足. 蔑貞凶.
Disregarding resoluteness is unfortunate.

The legs of the bed are broken. This portends an ominous situation that cannot be ignored. Failing to remain persistent will bring about misfortune.

Second Six (六 二, Liu Er)
The entire bed frame is removed.　　剝牀以辨. 蔑貞凶.
Disregarding resoluteness is unfortunate.

The bed is beginning to fall apart. Attend to this situation immediately.

Third Six (六 三, Liu San)
The entire bed is removed.
Without fault.

剝之. 无咎.

The bed has been removed and the deterioration discovered. The problem is not that serious, but it's best if all connections with friends and enemies be discontinued.

Fourth Six (六 四, Liu Si)
The frame of the bed is removed
up to the skin. Misfortune.

剝牀以膚. 凶.

There is misfortune if you lie upon a broken bed, as there will be injury to the skin.

Fifth Six (六 五, Liu Wu)
A string of fish brings favor
through the people of the palace.
Everything is beneficial.

貫魚以宮人寵. 无不利.

You have numerous servants and friends walking about you like fish calmly swimming in a pond. There is success in whatever you do and wherever you go. The problems of the bed are over and things will go your way now.

Topmost Nine (上 九, Shang Jiu)
Large fruits are not eaten. The wise person
acquires a carriage. Inferior people are
removed from their dwellings.

頂果不食. 君子得輿.
小人剝廬.

The larger fruits are left aside and not consumed. The master has acquired a cart for hauling and the common people have to build new dwellings.

Alternate English Translations for the Hexagram of Bo, 剝

The Symbol of Falling or Flaying [S]
Splitting Apart [WB]
Peeling Off [B]
Cleavage [CS]
Stripping Away [C]

Falling Away [H]
Erosion—Decline [N]
Stripping [K] [RS]
Decay [L]
The Symbol of Dispersion [CC]

The Great Symbolism (大象, Da Xiang) says,

A Mountain depending upon the Earth. 山附於地.剝.
This is Bo. Those above, according with this, 上以厚下安宅.
are generous to those below, bringing
comfort and rest.

Sexagenary Placement

Heavenly Stem: Ren 壬 (9th Stem, Yang)—**Water** (水, Shui)
Earthly Branch: Chen 辰 (5th Branch, Yang)—**Dragon** (龍, Long)
Represents the *Year of the Water Dragon* (29th Year of the Sixty-Year Cycle)
Years: 1892 – 1952 – 2012 – 2072

Trigram Correlations

Upper Gua (Mountain)

Gen 艮
- **Represents:** Mountain, Towers, Youngest Son
- **Actions:** Stillness, Binding, Stopping
- **Influences:** Knowledge, Wisdom, Skill, Determination
- **Shape:** Vertical Column **Color:** Blue
- **Body:** Hands and arms **Season:** Beginning Autumn
- **Moon Phase:** Waxing Crescent
- **Animals:** Earthly Dog, Celestial Vermilion Snake
- **Directions:** Northwest (BH), Northeast (AH)
- **Nine Palaces Numbers:** Fu Xi: 7
    Yu the Great: Ho River Map, **6**— Lo River Script, **8**
- **Internal Alchemy:** Hun (Heavenly) Spirit
    Qi Center: Jing Men (Essence Gate)
    Qi Meridian: Yang Qiao Mai (Yang Heel Vessel)

#23 Removing (Bo)

Lower Gua (Earth)

☷ **Kun** 坤　**Represents:** Earth, Soil, Fields, Female, Mother, Empress
Actions: Receptive, Expanding, Yielding
Influences: Relationships, Love, Submission
Shape: Square　　**Color:** Yellow
Body: Stomach　　**Season:** Winter (Winter Solstice)
Moon Phase: New Moon
Animals: Earthly Ox, Celestial Black Tortoise
Directions: North (BH), Southwest (AH)
Nine Palaces Numbers: Fu Xi: **10**
　Yu the Great: Ho River Map, **1**—Lo River Script, **2**
Internal Alchemy: Tranquility, Void
　Qi Center: Hui Yin (Returning Yin)
　Qi Meridian: Ren Mai (Function Vessel)

Associated Developed Hexagrams of Bo

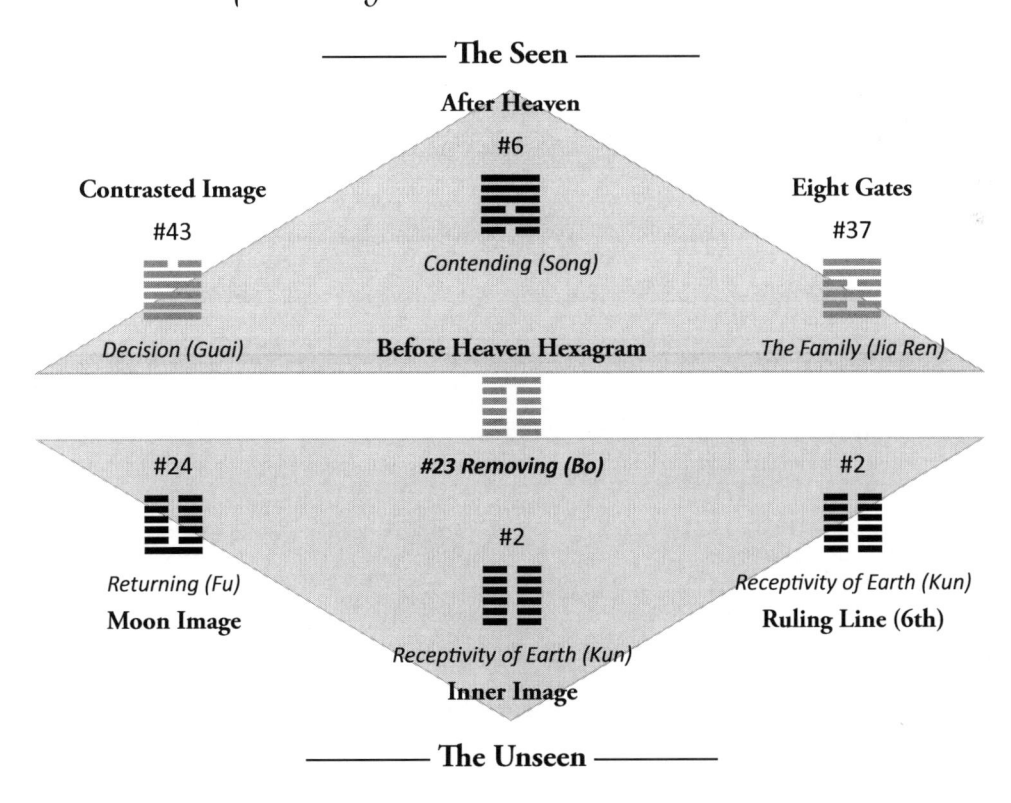

— **The Seen** —

After Heaven
#6

Contending (Song)

Contrasted Image
#43

Decision (Guai)

Before Heaven Hexagram

Eight Gates
#37

The Family (Jia Ren)

#23 Removing (Bo)

#24

Returning (Fu)
Moon Image

#2

Receptivity of Earth (Kun)
Inner Image

#2

Receptivity of Earth (Kun)
Ruling Line (6th)

— **The Unseen** —

93

Fu 復

Returning 24

Kun (Earth) above
坤上
Kun Shang
Zhen (Thunder) below
震下
Zhen Xia

Moon/Yin Image

The Prediction (象, Tuan)

Returning:
Perseverance. Leaving and entering is
without illness. Friends arrive, without fault.
Returning with friends to the Way [Dao].
On the seventh day comes Returning.
Advantage in having somewhere to go.

復. 亨. 出入无疾.
朋來无咎. 友復其道.
七日來復. 利有攸往.

Within Returning, ambitions are fulfilled. Departing and returning occur easily, and no illness occurs. Treasures are obtained without any trouble. Use the same road you left upon when coming back. Return once every seven days. It is good to function in this manner.

The Lines (爻, Yao)

First Nine (初 九, Chu Jiu)
Returning from not far away.
Without respect there is regret.
Great auspiciousness.

不遠復. 无祇悔. 元吉.

Walking short distances and then returning is very auspicious and without regret.

Second Six (六 二, Liu Er)
Returning after abstaining
is auspicious.

休復吉.

When reaching the end of the abstention period it is auspicious to return to normalcy.

Third Six (六 三, Liu San)
Hurried Returning is burdensome. 　　頻 復. 厲. 无 咎.
Without fault.

Going back and forth hurriedly, and too many times, will cause problems. Fortunately, nothing bad occurs.

Fourth Six (六 四, Liu Si)
Walking in the middle, 　　中 行 獨 復.
the Returning is alone.

Traversing on the Middle Way with others means you have to return alone.

Fifth Six (六 五, Liu Wu)
Noble Returning. 　　敦 復. 无 悔.
Without regret.

Returning with your integrity and your noble heart is without any regret.

Topmost Six (上 六, Shang Liu)
Returning gone astray. Misfortune. 　　迷 復. 凶. 有 災 眚. 用 行 師.
Disasters [from Heaven] bring calamity. 　　終 有 大 敗. 以 其 國 君 凶.
Setting forth an army. In the end there is 　　至 于 十 年. 不 克 征.
great defeat. This is unfortunate for the
nation's prince. Even in ten years
there can be no attack.

It is very dangerous to lose your way back and miss your Returning. If you lead people like this you will suffer humiliation and loss of respect. Heaven itself will bring down calamities. Nothing can make up for this mistake. Even ten years will not be long enough to repair the damage.

Alternate English Translations for the Hexagram of Fu, 復

The Symbol of Returning [S] 　　*Turning Back* [H]
Return (The Turning Point) [WB] 　　*Revival—Renew* [N]
Return [B] [C] [CS] [RS] 　　*Return (Revival)* [L]
Returning [K] 　　*The Symbol of Reversal* [CC]

The Great Symbolism (大象, Da Xiang) says,

Lightning in the middle of the Earth. This is Fu. The ancient kings, according with this, on the day of the solstice closed the passes on the frontiers so the traveling merchants could not just journey about, nor the princes examine their borders.

雷在地中.復.
先王以至日閉關.
商旅不行.后不省方.

Sexagenary Placement

Heavenly Stem: Geng 庚 (7th Stem, Yang)—**Metal** (金, Jin)
Earthly Branch: Chen 辰 (5th Branch, Yang)—**Dragon** (龍, Long)
Represents the *Year of the Metal Dragon* (17th Year of the Sixty-Year Cycle)
Years: 1880 – 1940 – 2000 – 2060

Trigram Correlations

Upper Gua (Earth)

Kun 坤
- **Represents:** Earth, Soil, Fields, Female, Mother, Empress
- **Actions:** Receptive, Expanding, Yielding
- **Influences:** Relationships, Love, Submission
- **Shape:** Square   **Color:** Yellow
- **Body:** Stomach   **Season:** Winter (Winter Solstice)
- **Moon Phase:** New Moon
- **Animals:** Earthly Ox, Celestial Black Tortoise
- **Directions:** North (BH), Southwest (AH)
- **Nine Palaces Numbers:** Fu Xi: **10**
    Yu the Great: Ho River Map, **1**—Lo River Script, **2**
- **Internal Alchemy:** Tranquility, Void
    Qi Center: Hui Yin (Returning Yin)
    Qi Meridian: Ren Mai (Function Vessel)

#24 Returning (Fu)

Lower Gua (Thunder)

☷ Zhen 震
Represents: Thunder, Earthquake, Eldest Son
Actions: Arousing, Shaking, Initiating
Influences: Foundations, Past Actions, Excitement.
Shape: Vertical Column   **Color:** Green
Body: Feet and legs   **Season:** Beginning Winter
Moon Phase: Waning Crescent
Animals: Earthly Dragons, Celestial Dragon-Horse
Directions: Northeast (BH), East (AH)
Nine Palaces Numbers: Fu Xi: 3
  Yu the Great: Ho River Map, 8—Lo River Script, 3
Internal Alchemy: Mind-Intention
  Qi Center: Dan Tian (Elixir Field)
  Qi Meridian: Yin Qiao Mai (Yin Heel Vessel)

Associated Developed Hexagrams of Fu

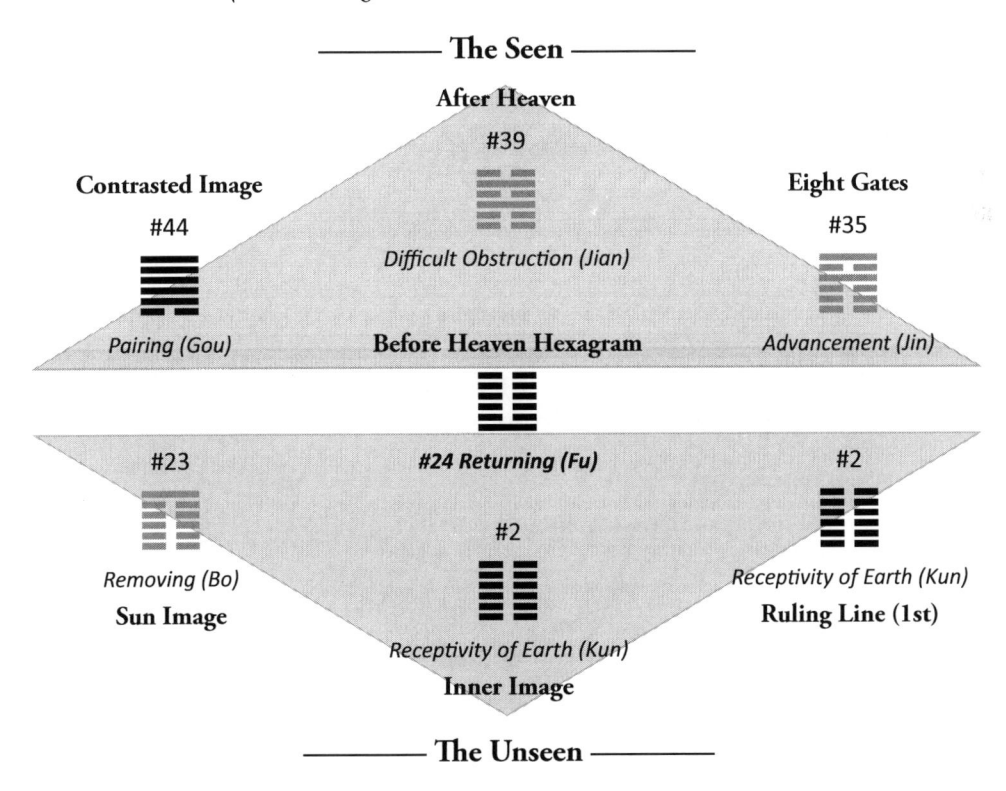

——— **The Seen** ———

After Heaven
#39

Difficult Obstruction (Jian)

Contrasted Image
#44

Pairing (Gou)

Eight Gates
#35

Advancement (Jin)

Before Heaven Hexagram

#24 Returning (Fu)

#2

#23

Removing (Bo)
Sun Image

#2

Receptivity of Earth (Kun)
Ruling Line (1st)

Receptivity of Earth (Kun)
Inner Image

——— **The Unseen** ———

97

Wu Wang

无妄

Innocence

25

Qian (Heaven) above
乾上
Qian Shang
Zhen (Thunder) below
震下
Zhen Xia

Sun/Yang Image

The Prediction (象, Tuan)

Not False:
Great perseverance. Advantage in being resolute. If untrue there is injury.
No advantage in having somewhere to go.

无妄.元亨.利贞.
其匪正有眚.
不利有攸往.

This image shows there must be a listening to one's own heart to protect innocence. Regulate your passions and things will go smoothly right from the start. Choose the right road or there will be trouble, and moving forward will be unfavorable.

The Lines (爻, Yao)

First Nine (初 九, Chu Jiu)
Innocence. To go is auspicious.

无妄.往吉.

Right conduct and following your heart make it possible to move forward and produce good fortune.

Second Six (六 二, Liu Er)
No plowing until harvesting. For three years the fields have not been cultivated. Hence, having some place to go.

不耕穫.不菑畬.
則有攸往.

Uncultivated land has been harvested, and the cultivated land has not been used for three years. In this situation it is the right time to examine future prospects and to not make premature decisions, then you can move forward.

#25 Innocence (Wu Wang)

Third Six (六 三, Liu San)
Innocence leads to disaster. Like a tied-up ox, a passing person takes it. This brings calamity to the people of the city.

无妄之灾. 或繫之牛.
行人之得. 邑人之灾.

An unexpected calamity occurs. An ox tied to a post has been led away by a stranger. This will bring trouble to those living nearby, if they are blamed. Do not be foolish and careless. These are not the qualities or actions of innocence.

Fourth Nine (九 四, Jiu Si)
Able to be resolute. Without fault.

可贞. 无咎.

This is a good time to consult the stalks and plan for the future. In doing so, there will be no calamity.

Fifth Nine (九 五, Jiu Wu)
Innocence leads to illness.
No medicine, but there is joy.

无妄之疾. 勿藥有喜.

An unexpected illness occurs, but things turn better because no medicine is taken. This is a result of allowing nature to heal the problem.

Topmost Nine (上 九, Shang Jiu)
Innocence. Action has injury.
Nowhere is there advantage.

无妄. 行有眚. 无攸利.

Regulate your emotions, do not oppose yourself, and be tranquil. Failing to be calm will bring disaster and there will be no benefit whatsoever.

Alternate English Translations for the Hexagram of Wu Wang, 无忘

The Symbol of Freedom From Error [S]
Innocence (The Unexpected) [WB]
Integrity, The Unexpected [B]
Circumspection (The Unexpected) [CS]
Fidelity (No Error) [C]
The Symbol of Innocence [CC]

Without Falsehood [H]
Innocence—Unexpected Happening [N]
Without Entanglement [RS]
The Unexpected (Innocence) [L]
Disentangling [K]

The Great Symbolism (大象, Da Xiang) says,

Beneath Heaven, Thunder is moving, and everything is Wu Wang. The ancient kings, according with this, actively responded to the seasons and so nourished the myriad of things.

天下雷行.物與无忘.
先王以茂對時育萬物.

䷘ Sexagenary Placement

Heavenly Stem: Bing 丙 (3rd Stem, Yang)—**Fire** (火, Huo)
Earthly Branch: Zi 子 (1st Branch, Yang)—**Rat** (鼠, Shu)
Represents the *Year of the Fire Rat* (13th Year of the Sixty-Year Cycle)
Years: 1876 – 1936 – 1996 – 2056

Trigram Correlations

Upper Gua (Heaven)

☰ **Qian** 乾
Represents: Heaven, Sky, Male, Father, Emperor
Actions: Creative Principle, Persisting, Forceful
Influences: Blessings, Good Fortune, Strength, Spiritual Power
Shape: Circle **Color:** White
Body: Head **Season:** Summer (Summer Solstice)
Moon Phase: Full Moon
Animals: Earthly Horse, Celestial Red Phoenix
Directions: South (BH), Northwest (AH)
Nine Palaces Numbers: Fu Xi: **2**
  Yu the Great: Ho River Map, **9**—Lo River Script, **6**
Internal Alchemy: Clarity, Illumination
  Qi Center: Ni Wan (Mud Pellet)
  Qi Meridian: Du Mai (Control Vessel)

Lower Gua (Thunder)

Zhen 震 **Represents:** Thunder, Earthquake, Eldest Son
Actions: Arousing, Shaking, Initiating
Influences: Foundations, Past Actions, Excitement.
Shape: Vertical Column   **Color:** Green
Body: Feet and legs   **Season:** Beginning Winter
Moon Phase: Waning Crescent
Animals: Earthly Dragons, Celestial Dragon-Horse
Directions: Northeast (BH), East (AH)
Nine Palaces Numbers: Fu Xi: 3
   Yu the Great: Ho River Map, 8—Lo River Script, 3
Internal Alchemy: Mind-Intention
   Qi Center: Dan Tian (Elixir Field)
   Qi Meridian: Yin Qiao Mai (Yin Heel Vessel)

Associated Developed Hexagrams of Wu Wang

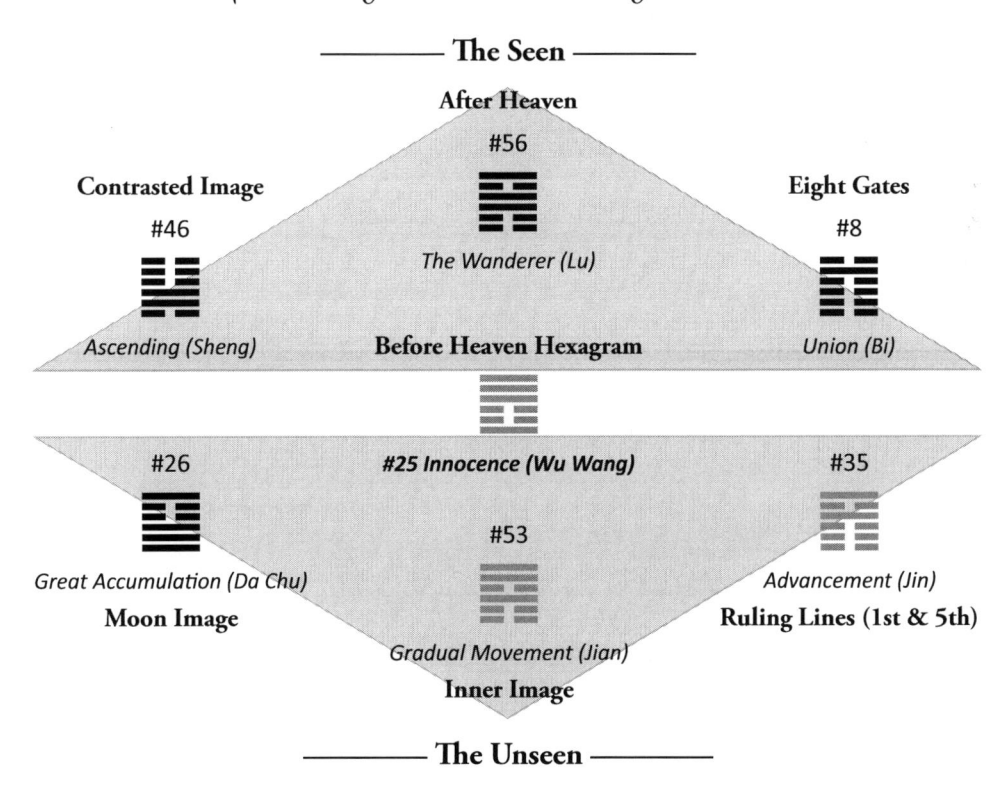

——— **The Seen** ———

After Heaven
#56
The Wanderer (Lu)

Contrasted Image
#46
Ascending (Sheng)

Eight Gates
#8
Union (Bi)

Before Heaven Hexagram

#26
Great Accumulation (Da Chu)
Moon Image

#25 Innocence (Wu Wang)

#35
Advancement (Jin)
Ruling Lines (1st & 5th)

#53
Gradual Movement (Jian)
Inner Image

——— **The Unseen** ———

Da Chu *Great Accumulation* 26

Gen (Mountain) above
艮上
Gen Shang
Qian (Heaven) below
乾下
Qian Xia

Moon/Yin Image

The Prediction (象, Tuan)

Great Accumulation:
Advantage in being resolute. Not eating at home is auspicious. Advantage in fording the great stream.

大畜. 利貞. 不家食.
吉. 利涉大川.

Do away with shallow conduct and unprofitable pursuits. Much has been saved and so this is a suitable time to plan future projects and pursuits. You are experiencing high energy, so keep your mind clear. It is wise to know when to hold back on your heightened sense of power. This is also an auspicious time to eat away from home and to cross a big river.

The Lines (爻, Yao)

First Nine (初 九, Chu Jiu)
Severity exists and so advantage in finishing.

有厲利已.

Do not go further. Stop immediately. Be patient as the time is not right for moving forward. There is a danger looming. Finish the task at hand, but go no further.

Second Nine (九 二, Jiu Er)
The wood axle supports are removed from the carriage.

輿說輹.

The axle is broken and so there can be no advancement. You must be patient and wait for the repair to be finished.

Third Nine (九 三, Jiu San)
A good horse follows. Advantage
in honest resoluteness. Train daily
in charioteering and defense.
Advantage in having somewhere to go.

良馬逐. 利艱貞. 日閑輿衛.
利有攸往.

Horses in pursuit of each other is a good omen to plan for the future. With daily training in defense, it is suitable to move forward.

Fourth Six (六 四, Liu Si)
A young ox is yoked. Great auspiciousness.

童牛之牿. 元吉.

The ox's horns are yoked and fastened so they can cause no injury to people. Anticipate what can go wrong before taking action. This is auspicious from the outset.

Fifth Six (六 五, liu Wu)
A pig shackled for castration
shows his teeth. Auspicious.

豶豕之牙. 吉.

It is auspicious that the young pig's teeth are starting to emerge, so it is not castrated. Look to your creative side to find ways to avoid misfortune.

Topmost Nine (上 九, Shang Jiu)
Commanding the roads to Heaven.
Perseverance.

何天之衢. 亨.

Adhere to spiritual ways and all will be auspicious.

Alternate English Translations for the Hexagram of Da Chu, 大畜

The Symbol of Great Accumulation [S]
Taming Power of the Great [WB]
The Great Nourisher [B]
The Great Restraining [CS]
Nurturance of the Great [C]
The Symbol of Great Taming Force [CC]

Great Accumulation [H]
Great Amassment [N]
The Great Accumulating [RS]
Taming the Great Powers [L]
Great Accumulating [K]

The Great Symbolism (大象, Da Xiang) says,

Heaven dwelling within the Mountain.   天在山中. 大畜.
This is Da Chu. Superior persons, according   君子以多識前言
with this, record the numerous sayings [of sages]   往行. 以畜其德.
from the past, moving and acting upon them.
Thus, accumulating their virtue.

Sexagenary Placement

Heavenly Stem: Ren 壬 (9th Stem, Yang)—**Water** (水, Shui)
Earthly Branch: Shen 申 (9th Branch, Yang)—**Monkey** (猴, Hou)
Represents the *Year of the Water Monkey* (9th Year of the Sixty-Year Cycle)
Years: 1872 – 1932 – 1992 – 2052

Trigram Correlations

Upper Gua (Mountain)

Gen 艮   **Represents:** Mountain, Towers, Youngest Son
           Actions: Stillness, Binding, Stopping
           Influences: Knowledge, Wisdom, Skill, Determination
           Shape: Vertical Column   **Color:** Blue
           Body: Hands and arms   **Season:** Beginning Autumn
           Moon Phase: Waxing Crescent
           Animals: Earthly Dog, Celestial Vermilion Snake
           Directions: Northwest (BH), Northeast (AH)
           Nine Palaces Numbers: Fu Xi: 7
               Yu the Great: Ho River Map, **6**— Lo River Script, **8**
           Internal Alchemy: Hun (Heavenly) Spirit
               Qi Center: Jing Men (Essence Gate)
               Qi Meridian: Yang Qiao Mai (Yang Heel Vessel)

Lower Gua (Heaven)

☰ **Qian** 乾   **Represents:** Heaven, Sky, Male, Father, Emperor
Actions: Creative Principle, Persisting, Forceful
Influences: Blessings, Good Fortune, Strength, Spiritual Power
Shape: Circle   **Color:** White
Body: Head   **Season:** Summer (Summer Solstice)
Moon Phase: Full Moon
Animals: Earthly Horse, Celestial Red Phoenix
Directions: South (BH), Northwest (AH)
Nine Palaces Numbers: Fu Xi: 2
   Yu the Great: Ho River Map, 9—Lo River Script, 6
Internal Alchemy: Clarity, Illumination
   Qi Center: Ni Wan (Mud Pellet)
   Qi Meridian: Du Mai (Control Vessel)

Associated Developed Hexagrams of Da Chu

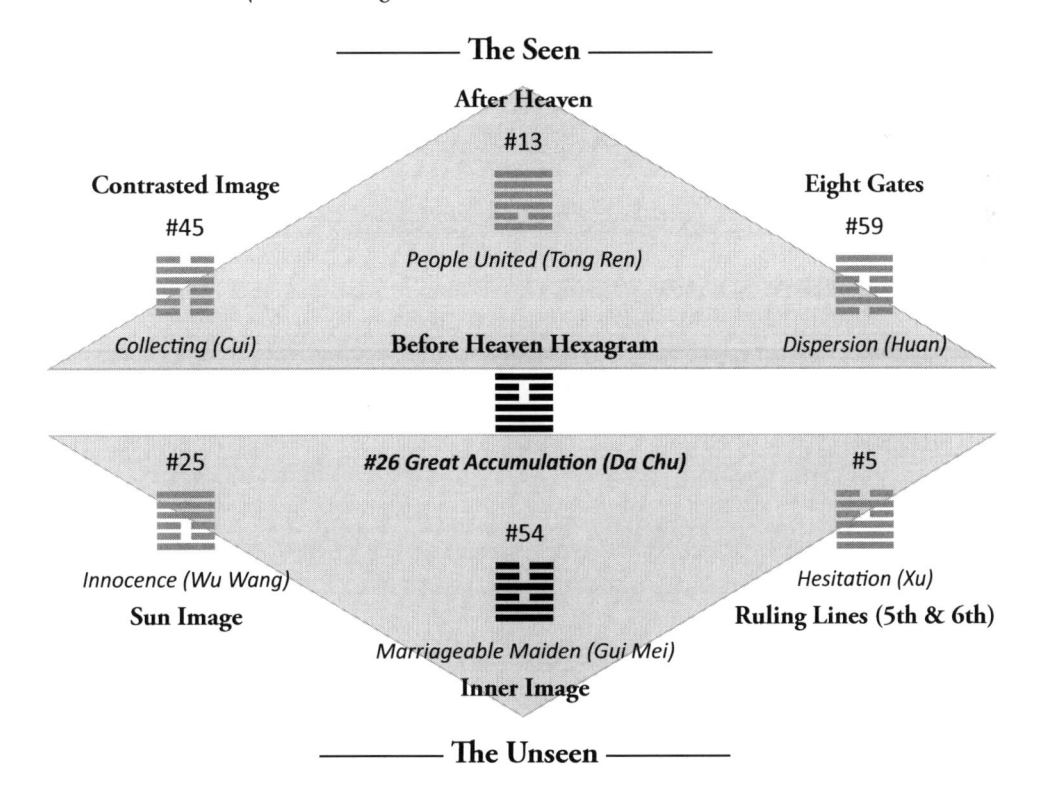

——— **The Seen** ———

After Heaven
#13
People United (Tong Ren)

Contrasted Image
#45
Collecting (Cui)

Eight Gates
#59
Dispersion (Huan)

Before Heaven Hexagram
#26 Great Accumulation (Da Chu)

#25
Innocence (Wu Wang)
Sun Image

#54
Marriageable Maiden (Gui Mei)
Inner Image

#5
Hesitation (Xu)
Ruling Lines (5th & 6th)

——— **The Unseen** ———

Yi

頤

Nourishment

Gen (Mountain) above
艮上
Gen Shang
Zhen (Thunder) below
震下
Zhen Xia

27

Moon Eclipse/Yin Image

The Prediction (彖, Tuan)

Nourishment:
Firmness is auspicious. Contemplation of Nourishment. Seeks small fruits for the mouth.

頤. 貞 吉. 觀 頤. 自 求 口 實.

This image shows envy should never be expressed against others. A round and robust face is an omen of auspiciousness. To see such a face shows the person has enough food to spare and to share. Nature provides nourishment to all things, so the wise person seeks to provide the proper nourishment to others as well as oneself through moderation, in both the physical and mental sense. Choosing small fruits instead of large ones shows moderation in behavior.

The Lines (爻, Yao)

First Nine (初 九, Chu Jiu)
Releasing the spiritual tortoise. Contemplating me while your jaws move in eating. Misfortune.

舍 爾 靈 龜. 觀 我 朵 頤. 凶.

Setting aside the tortoise shell for divination, reading another's face while finishing a meal, this shows greed and arrogance toward others and brings misfortune.

Second Six (六 二, Liu Er)
Nourishment on the summit. Opposing proper conduct. Going to the mound for Nourishment. Misfortune.

顛 頤 拂 經. 于 丘 頤 征. 凶.

The face is trembling and distorted, so the cheeks are rubbed with the hands. First going to the high place and then to the low to get nourishment. This shows a person who is exploiting others. If this behavior continues, there will be misfortune.

Third Six (六三, Liu San)

Rejects Nourishment. Firmness is unfortunate. Ten years without activity, no advantage in any way.

拂頤. 貞凶. 十年勿用. 无攸利.

Rubbing the face indicates misfortune. Your skills cannot be drawn upon for ten years, therefore success is out of reach. You are only nourishing your own self-destruction and defeat.

Fourth Six (六四, Liu Si)

Nourishment at the summit. Auspicious. Like a tiger stalking prey, one's own desire causes eagerness. Without auspiciousness.

顛頤. 吉. 虎視耽耽.
其欲逐逐. 无吉.

The face still trembles, but there is good fortune at hand. The expression is like a tiger ready to ponce upon its prey. No mistakes are made.

Fifth Six (六五, Liu Wu)

Rejecting proper conduct. Remaining resolute is auspicious. Unable to ford the great stream.

拂經. 居貞吉. 不可涉大川.

The cheeks are lightly brushed with the hands. Remain at home in meditation and contemplate your future plans and all will be auspicious. Do not attempt to cross a big river.

Topmost Nine (上九, Shang Jiu)

The source of Nourishment is stern discipline and is auspicious. Advantage in fording the great stream.

由頤厲吉. 利涉大川.

The crisis is over and misfortune has been avoided. This is auspicious and the big river can be crossed over easily, but you must nourish your spirit beforehand.

Alternate English Translations for the Hexagram of Yi, 頤

The Symbol of the Cheeks and of Nourishment [S]
Nourishment (literally Jaws) [B]
Jaws (Nourishment) [CS]
Lower Jaw (Nourishment) [C]
Jaws/Swallowing [K]
*The Corners of the Mouth
   (Providing Nourishment)* [WB]

Nourishing [H]
Providing Nourishment [N]
The Jaws [RS]
Nourishment [L]
The Symbol of Sustenance [CC]

The Great Symbolism (大象, Da Xiang) says,

Beneath the Mountain there is Thunder.　　山下有雷. 頤. 君子
This is Yi. Superior persons, according with this,　以愼言語節飮食.
are cautious of their words in conversation,
and in regulating their eating and drinking.

Sexagenary Placement

Heavenly Stem: Ding 丁 (4th Stem, Yin)—**Fire** (火, Huo)
Earthly Branch: Si 巳 (6th Branch, Yin)—**Snake** (蛇, She)
Represents the *Year of the Fire Snake* (54th Year of the Sixty-Year Cycle)
Years: 1857 – 1917 – 1977 – 2037

Trigram Correlations

Upper Gua (Mountain)

Gen 艮　　**Represents:** Mountain, Towers, Youngest Son
Actions: Stillness, Binding, Stopping
Influences: Knowledge, Wisdom, Skill, Determination
Shape: Vertical Column　　**Color:** Blue
Body: Hands and arms　　**Season:** Beginning Autumn
Moon Phase: Waxing Crescent
Animals: Earthly Dog, Celestial Vermilion Snake
Directions: Northwest (BH), Northeast (AH)
Nine Palaces Numbers: Fu Xi: 7
　　Yu the Great: Ho River Map, **6**— Lo River Script, **8**
Internal Alchemy: Hun (Heavenly) Spirit
　　Qi Center: Jing Men (Essence Gate)
　　Qi Meridian: Yang Qiao Mai (Yang Heel Vessel)

Lower Gua (Thunder)

☳ **Zhen** 震   **Represents:** Thunder, Earthquake, Eldest Son
Actions: Arousing, Shaking, Initiating
Influences: Foundations, Past Actions, Excitement.
Shape: Vertical Column   **Color:** Green
Body: Feet and legs   **Season:** Beginning Winter
Moon Phase: Waning Crescent
Animals: Earthly Dragons, Celestial Dragon-Horse
Directions: Northeast (BH), East (AH)
Nine Palaces Numbers: Fu Xi: **3**
   Yu the Great: Ho River Map, **8**—Lo River Script, **3**
Internal Alchemy: Mind-Intention
   Qi Center: Dan Tian (Elixir Field)
   Qi Meridian: Yin Qiao Mai (Yin Heel Vessel)

Associated Developed Hexagrams of Yi

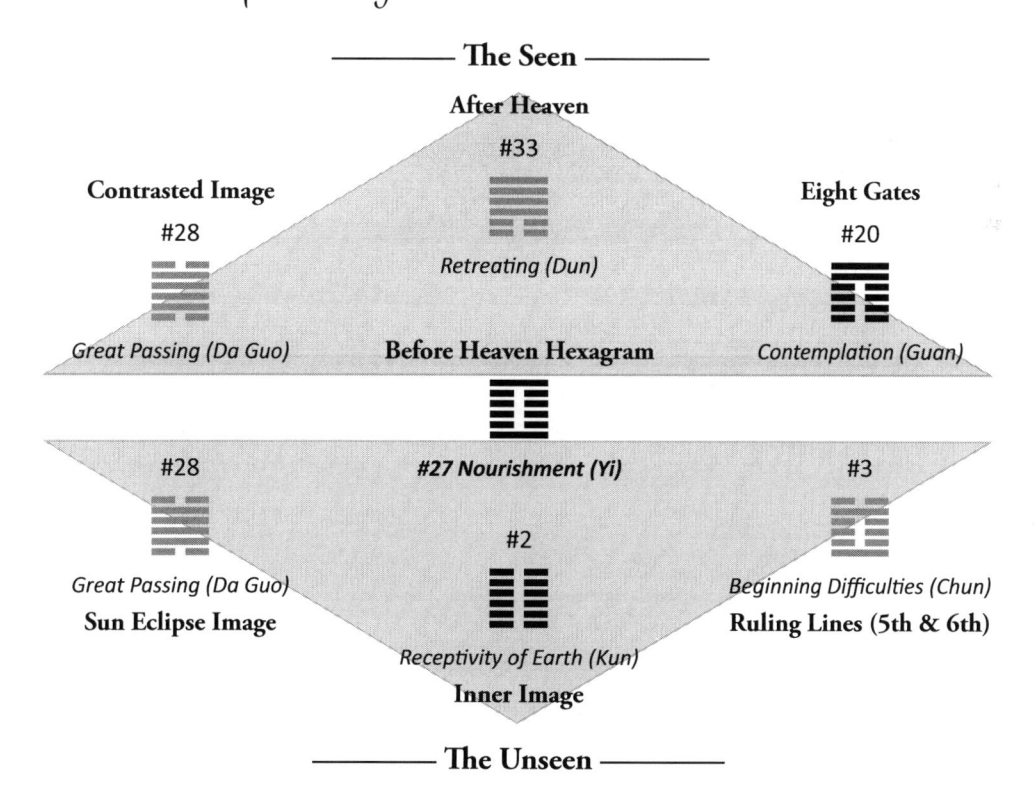

——— **The Seen** ———

After Heaven
#33
Retreating (Dun)

Contrasted Image
#28
Great Passing (Da Guo)

Eight Gates
#20
Contemplation (Guan)

Before Heaven Hexagram

#28
Great Passing (Da Guo)
Sun Eclipse Image

#27 Nourishment (Yi)
#2
Receptivity of Earth (Kun)
Inner Image

#3
Beginning Difficulties (Chun)
Ruling Lines (5th & 6th)

——— **The Unseen** ———

Da Guo *Great Passing* 28

Dui (Valley) above
兑上
Dui Shang
Xun (Wind) below
巽下
Xun Xia

Sun Eclipse/Yang Image

The Prediction (彖, Tuan)

Great Passing:
The ridgepole is weak. Advantage in having somewhere to go. Perseverance.

大過.棟橈.利有攸往.亨.

This image indicates that one should save money and preserve one's position and status. The support beams of the house have been weakened and bent by the excessive weight put upon them. You are carrying an exceptional weight at this time and you need to act quickly and with a clear head. Extreme situations call for extreme action. Contemplate the inner meaning of the situation. This is an auspicious time to travel. All things will work out well.

The Lines (爻, Yao)

First Six (初 六, Chu Liu)
Laying down mats of white rushes.
Without fault.

藉用白茅.无咎.

Spreading out a soft white mat upon the ground and sitting in meditation upon it will prevent injury and ward-off negative influences. Take action, but do not cause damage.

Second Nine (九 二, Jiu Er)
A withering willow sprouts shoots from dried roots. An old man acquires a young wife. Everything is beneficial.

枯楊生梯.老夫得
其女妻.无不利.

New buds shoot forth from an old withered tree, and a young woman becomes a wife of an older man. All benefit from this and there is no misfortune.

Third Nine (九三, Jiu San)
The ridgepole sags. Misfortune.   棟橈. 凶.

Danger is looming from above. Use your strength to hold things up, but depart quickly if your strength is not enough.

Fourth Nine (九四, Jiu Si)
The ridgepole is strengthened. Auspicious.   棟隆. 吉. 有它. 吝.
Possession of another. Regret.

The beam is arched for more strength. This is auspicious, but take caution if a snake creeps onto the beam, as it is an omen of ill-fortune. The snake reveals your selfishness and so humiliates you by causing a fright. Do not attempt to move others in front of the snake, as this will also result in humiliation.

Fifth Nine (九五, Jiu Wu)
A withering willow sprouts flowers.   枯楊生華. 老婦得士夫. 无譽.
An old woman acquires a gentlemen.
Without praise.

Flowers have bloomed on a withering willow tree. There is a miracle occurring, but do not speak of it to others. An older woman acquires a younger man. No harm will come to her, but she is not honored or praised by other women, rather she is envied.

Topmost Six (上六, Shang Liu)
Crossing through the stream and the head   過涉滅頂. 无咎.
is submerged. Misfortune. Without fault.

There is danger in crossing a river deeper than your height. This is an error in judgement, yet still shows courage. In the end no harm is done.

Alternate English Translations for the Hexagram of Da Guo, 大過

The Symbol of Great Passing [S]   *Excess of the Great* [C]
Preponderance of the Great [WB]   *Great Exceeding* [H]
Excess [B]   *Great Excess* [L] [N]
Inner Preponderance [CS]   *The Great Exceeding* [RS]
Great Traversing [K]   *The Symbol of Major Preponderance* [CC]

The Great Symbolism (大象, Da Xiang) says,

A Marsh destroys Wood. This is Da Guo. Superior persons, according with this, stand alone without fear, and conceal themselves from the world without any sorrow.	澤滅木. 大過. 君子以獨立不懼. 遯世无悶.

䷛ Sexagenary Placement

Heavenly Stem: Ding 丁 (4th Stem, Yin)—**Fire** (火, Huo)
Earthly Branch: Hai 亥 (12th Branch, Yin)—**Pig** (猪, Zhu)
Represents the *Year of the Fire Pig* (24th Year of the Sixty-Year Cycle)
Years: 1887 – 1947 – 2007 – 2067

Trigram Correlations

Upper Gua (Valley)

☱ **Dui** 兑   **Represents:** Valley, River, Lake/Marsh, Youngest Daughter
    Actions: Joyous, Opening, Stimulating
    Influences: Family, Future, Collecting, Pleasure, Absorbing, Complacency.
    Shape: Introverted Triangle   **Color:** Brown
    Body: Mouth   **Season:** Beginning Spring
    Moon Phase: Waning Gibbous
    Animals: Earthly Goat, Celestial Great Roc
    Directions: Southeast (BH), West (AH)
    Nine Palaces Numbers: Fu Xi: 5
        Yu the Great: Ho River Map, 4—Lo River Script, 7
    Internal Alchemy: Po (Earthly) Spirit
        Qi Center: Xuan Guan (Mysterious Pass)
        Qi Meridian: Yang Wei Mai (Yang Preserving Vessel)

Lower Gua (Wind)

Xun 巽

Represents: Wind, Wood, Eldest Daughter
Actions: Gentleness, Grounding, Penetrating, Spreading
Influences: Prosperity, Abundance, Wealth
Shape: Rectangle   **Color:** Purple
Body: Waist and hips   **Season:** Beginning Summer
Moon Phase: Waxing Gibbous
Animals: Earthly Fowl, Celestial Golden Rooster
Directions: Southwest (BH), Southeast (AH)
Nine Palaces Numbers: Fu Xi: **9**
   Yu the Great: Ho River Map, **2**—Lo River Script, **4**
Internal Alchemy: Breath and Mobilizing Qi
   Qi Center: Yu Zhen (Jade Pillow)
   Qi Meridian: Yin Wei Mai (Yin Preserving Vessel)

Associated Developed Hexagrams of Da Guo

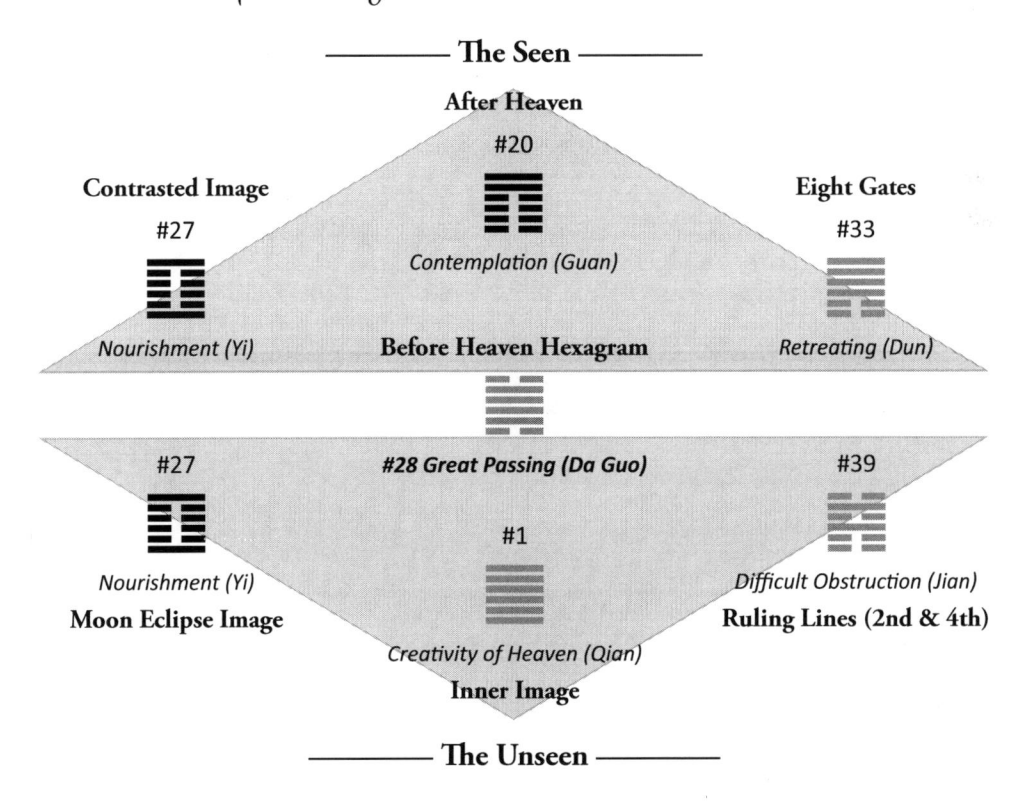

——— **The Seen** ———

After Heaven

#20
Contemplation (Guan)

Contrasted Image
#27
Nourishment (Yi)

Eight Gates
#33
Retreating (Dun)

Before Heaven Hexagram

#28 Great Passing (Da Guo)

#27
Nourishment (Yi)
Moon Eclipse Image

#1
Creativity of Heaven (Qian)
Inner Image

#39
Difficult Obstruction (Jian)
Ruling Lines (2nd & 4th)

——— **The Unseen** ———

Kan 坎

The Abyss   29

Kan (Water) above
坎上
Kan Shang
Kan (Water) below
坎下
Kan Xia

Moon/Yin Image

The Prediction (象, Tuan)

The Abyss repeated:
Possessing sincerity. Holding together the heart with perseverance. To act has honor.

習坎. 有孚. 維心亨. 行有尚.

This is an image indicating how the imagination can breed fear, bringing you to the edge of an abyss. However, by maintaining your principles and ideals in a dangerous situation, and from capturing others' hearts, actions can result in success and be rewarded. Just stay true to yourself and do not betray your own sense of what is right.

The Lines (爻, Yao)

First Six (初 六, Chu Liu)
The Abyss repeated. Someone has entered into the pit of The Abyss. Misfortune.

習坎. 入于坎窞. 凶.

Having fallen into a trap under dangerous conditions. This is very ominous. Do not become complacent.

Second Nine (九 二, Jiu Er)
The Abyss possesses danger.
Seeking has little gain.

坎有險. 求小得.

The situation is not going well and is dangerous. Better to be satisfied with just a little success, so take small steps to relieve the situation.

Third Six (六 三, Liu San)
Multiple waters are arriving. Danger in further resting. Entering into a water pit. Do not employ.

來之坎坎. 險且枕.
入于坎窞. 勿用.

A bad place has been found. It is deep and dangerous, and misfortune prevails. It's like a trap one can't escape. No movement is possible even if struggling to do so.

Fourth Six (六 四, Liu Si)
Goblets of wine and two bamboo baskets of grain are placed into earthenware. Alliances are received through a window. The end is without fault.

樽酒簋. 貳用缶.
納約自牖.
終无咎.

Friends pass cups of wine, two baskets of grains, and fine tableware through a window. No disasters can happen until the sacrifices of the ceremony have ended. Everything feels unconventional, but relief is on the way.

Fifth Nine (九 五, Jiu Wu)
The Abyss does not overflow.
Only at the finish is there peace.
Without fault.

坎不盈. 祇既平. 无咎.

The pits are not filled and the small hills nearby are flattened. Take the path of least resistance, then there is no misfortune.

Topmost Six (上 六, Shang Liu)
Bound by a three-stranded cord.
Placed inside a clump of thorny bushes.
For three years no gain. Misfortune.

係用徽纆. 置于叢棘.
三歲不得. 凶.

A person is bound in ropes and placed in a jail surrounded by thorns and brambles. For three years there can be no pardon. This situation is very ominous.

Alternate English Translations for the Hexagram of Kan, 坎

The Symbol of Sinking [S]
The Abysmal (Water) [WB]
The Abyss [B] [CS] [N]
Mastering Pitfalls (Double Pitfalls) [C]
The Symbol of Sinking [CC]

Darkness [H]
The Gorge [RS]
Water [L]
Gorge [K]

The Great Symbolism (大象, Da Xiang) says,

Water flowing continuously, this is Kan repeated. Superior persons, according with this, maintain constant virtue in all their actions, and repeat the instructions of their affairs.	水洊至. 習坎. 君子以常德行. 習教事.

Sexagenary Placement

Heavenly Stem: Xin 辛 (8th Stem, Yin)—**Metal** (金, Jin)
Earthly Branch: Si 巳 (6th Branch, Yin)—**Snake** (蛇, She)
Represents the *Year of the Metal Snake* (18th Year of the Sixty-Year Cycle)
Years: 1881 – 1941 – 2001 – 2061

Trigram Correlations

Upper Gua (Water)

Kan 坎　　**Represents:** Water, Moon, Springs/Streams, Middle Son
Actions: Peril, Danger, and Difficulty.
Influences: Abysmal Life Path and Vocation
Shape: Wave　　**Color:** Black
Body: Ears　　**Season:** Autumn (Autumn Equinox)
Moon Phase: First Quarter
Animals: Earthly Pig, Celestial White Tiger
Directions: West (BH), North (AH)
Nine Palaces Numbers: Fu Xi: 4
　　Yu the Great: Ho River Map, 7—Lo River Script, **1**
Internal Alchemy: Essence, Jing, Lead
　　Qi Center: Shuang Guan (Double Pass)
　　Qi Meridian: Chong Mai (Penetrating Vessel)

#29 The Abyss (Kan)

Lower Gua (Water)

☵ **Kan** 坎   **Represents:** Water, Moon, Springs/Streams, Middle Son
Actions: Peril, Danger, and Difficulty.
Influences: Abysmal Life Path and Vocation
Shape: Wave   **Color:** Black
Body: Ears   **Season:** Autumn (Autumn Equinox)
Moon Phase: First Quarter
Animals: Earthly Pig, Celestial White Tiger
Directions: West (BH), North (AH)
Nine Palaces Numbers: Fu Xi: 4
   Yu the Great: Ho River Map, 7—Lo River Script, 1
Internal Alchemy: Essence, Jing, Lead
   Qi Center: Shuang Guan (Double Pass)
   Qi Meridian: Chong Mai (Penetrating Vessel)

Associated Developed Hexagrams of Kan

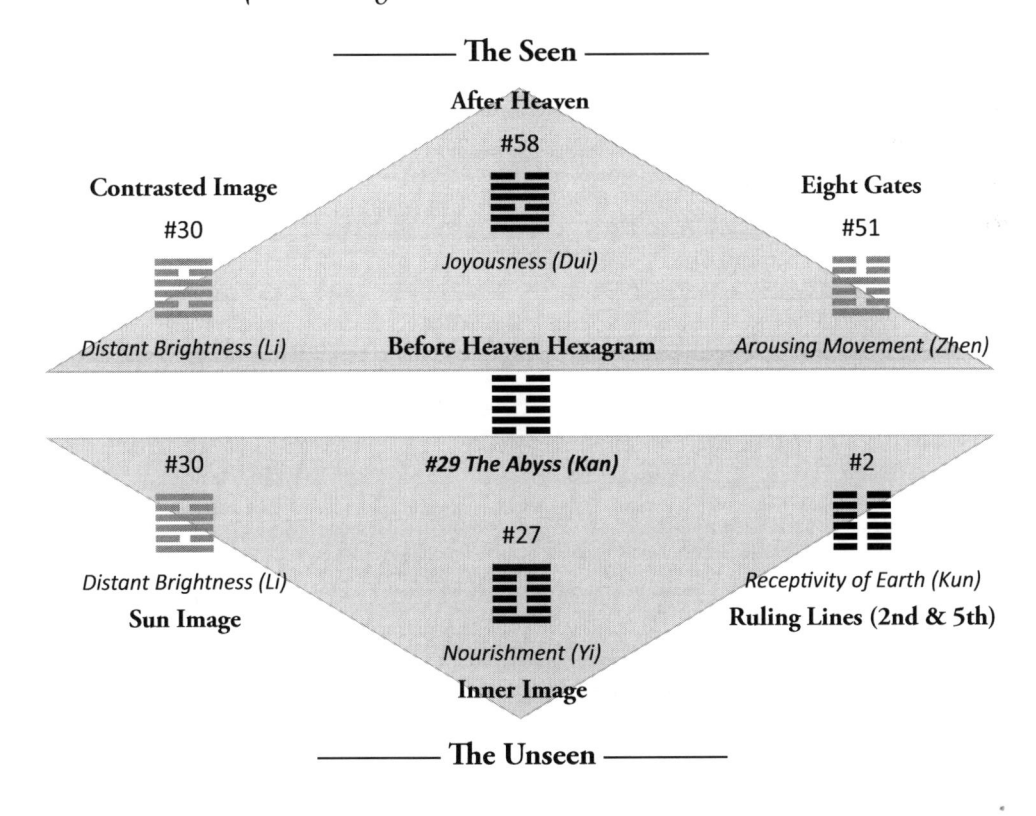

——— **The Seen** ———

After Heaven
#58
Joyousness (Dui)

Contrasted Image
#30
Distant Brightness (Li)

Eight Gates
#51
Arousing Movement (Zhen)

Before Heaven Hexagram

#29 The Abyss (Kan)

#30
Distant Brightness (Li)
Sun Image

#27
Nourishment (Yi)
Inner Image

#2
Receptivity of Earth (Kun)
Ruling Lines (2nd & 5th)

——— **The Unseen** ———

Li

離

Distant Brightness

30

Li (Fire) above
離 上
Li Shang
Li (Fire) below
離 下
Li Xia

Sun/Yang Image

The Prediction (象, Tuan)

Distant Brightness:
Advantage in being resolute. Perseverance.
Nourishing the female ox. Auspicious.

離. 利 貞. 亨. 畜 牝 牛. 吉.

This image shows it is better to be a realist than an idealist because of the brightness and fire. This is a good time to plan for the future, and it is auspicious to nourish the female ox. This image shows fire burning in the Heavens, as do the Sun and Moon. Cling to the forces of nature and accept whatever comes to you.

The Lines (爻, Yao)

First Nine (初 九, Chu Jiu)
Treading in error and confusion.
Mindfulness. Without fault.

履 錯 然. 敬 之. 无 咎.

Even when making mistakes and being confused about a situation, be respectful because no one will blame the person who is polite and trying to be mindful. Like being active in the early morning sun, be calm and get all your affairs in order.

Second Six (六 二, Liu Er)
The Distant Brightness of yellow.
Great auspiciousness.

黃 離. 元 吉.

The yellow sunshine of the midday light is auspicious.

Third Nine (九 三, Jiu San)
In the afternoon the Distant Brightness
of the sun. There is no drumming

日 昃 之 離. 不 鼓 缶
而 歌. 則 大 耋 之 嗟. 凶.

on the pot, but there is singing.
An old person of eighty arrives sighing.
Misfortune.

There is celebration during the afternoon sun. The pots are not used for drumming as everyone is singing offbeat. An elder person warns of danger. The warning is unclear, as the elder is speaking from intuition, but the news is very ominous.

Fourth Nine (九四, Jiu Si)
Their arrival is abrupt. Catching fire. 　　突如其來如. 死如. 棄如.
Death. Casting things aside.

Strangers appear out of nowhere, like a flash of fire, and create a sudden disaster. People die in a fire and many things are lost or discarded.

Fifth Six (六五, Liu Wu)
Tears flow forth. Streams of 　　出涕沱若. 戚嗟若. 吉.
sighs and sorrow. Auspicious.

Tears flow down like rain from the survivors and they cry out in great sadness. This signals good fortune, however, because the heart-stricken always win in matters of attaining justice.

Topmost Nine (上九, Shang Jiu)
The king puts forth an attack. 　　王用出征. 有嘉折首.
Victory is attained and leaders are 　　獲匪其醜. 无咎.
destroyed. Punishment of those
not of their own kind. Without fault.

The leader sets forth an attack and declares that whoever captures the enemy leader will be rewarded. Many who are apprehended are not really the enemy, they are just different. No great problems result from this because punishments are moderate and justice prevails for the innocent.

Alternate English Translations for the Hexagram of Li, 離

The Symbol of Brightness and of Separateness [S]
The Clinging, Fire [WB]
Flaming Beauty [B]
Clinging Light (Fire) [CS]
*The Symbol of Adherence,
　or of Fire and Light* [CC]

Fire [C] [L]
Brightness [H]
Radiance [K] [N]
The Radiance [RS]

The Great Symbolism (大象, Da Xiang) says,

The workings of Illumination. This is Li.　　明兩作.離.大人以繼明
The elders, according with this,　　　　　　照于四方.
adopt the illumination and reflect it
to the four directions.

Sexagenary Placement

Heavenly Stem: Xin 辛 (8th Stem, Yin)—**Metal** (金, Jin)
Earthly Branch: Hai 亥 (12th Branch, Yin)—**Pig** (猪, Zhu)
Represents the *Year of the Metal Pig* (48th Year of the Sixty-Year Cycle)
Years: 1851 – 1911 – 1971 – 2031

Trigram Correlations

Upper Gua (Fire)

Li 離
- **Represents:** Fire, Lightning, Sun, Middle Daughter
- **Actions:** Clinging, Illuminating, Congregating
- **Influences:** Fame, Reputation, Brightness, Elegance
- **Shape:** Triangle　　**Color:** Red
- **Body:** Eyes　　**Season:** Spring (Spring Equinox)
- **Moon Phase:** Last Quarter
- **Animals:** Earthly Rooster, Celestial Green Dragon
- **Directions:** East (BH), South (AH)
- **Nine Palaces Numbers:** Fu Xi: **8**
   Yu the Great: Ho River Map, **3**—Lo River Script, **9**
- **Internal Alchemy:** Mercury, Qi
   Qi Center: Jiang Gong (Crimson Palace)
   Qi Meridian: Dai Mai (Belt Vessel)

Lower Gua (Fire)

☲ **Li** 離 **Represents:** Fire, Lightning, Sun, Middle Daughter
Actions: Clinging, Illuminating, Congregating
Influences: Fame, Reputation, Brightness, Elegance
Shape: Triangle   **Color:** Red
Body: Eyes   **Season:** Spring (Spring Equinox)
Moon Phase: Last Quarter
Animals: Earthly Rooster, Celestial Green Dragon
Directions: East (BH), South (AH)
Nine Palaces Numbers: Fu Xi: **8**
  Yu the Great: Ho River Map, **3**—Lo River Script, **9**
Internal Alchemy: Mercury, Qi
  Qi Center: Jiang Gong (Crimson Palace)
  Qi Meridian: Dai Mai (Belt Vessel)

Associated Developed Hexagrams of Li

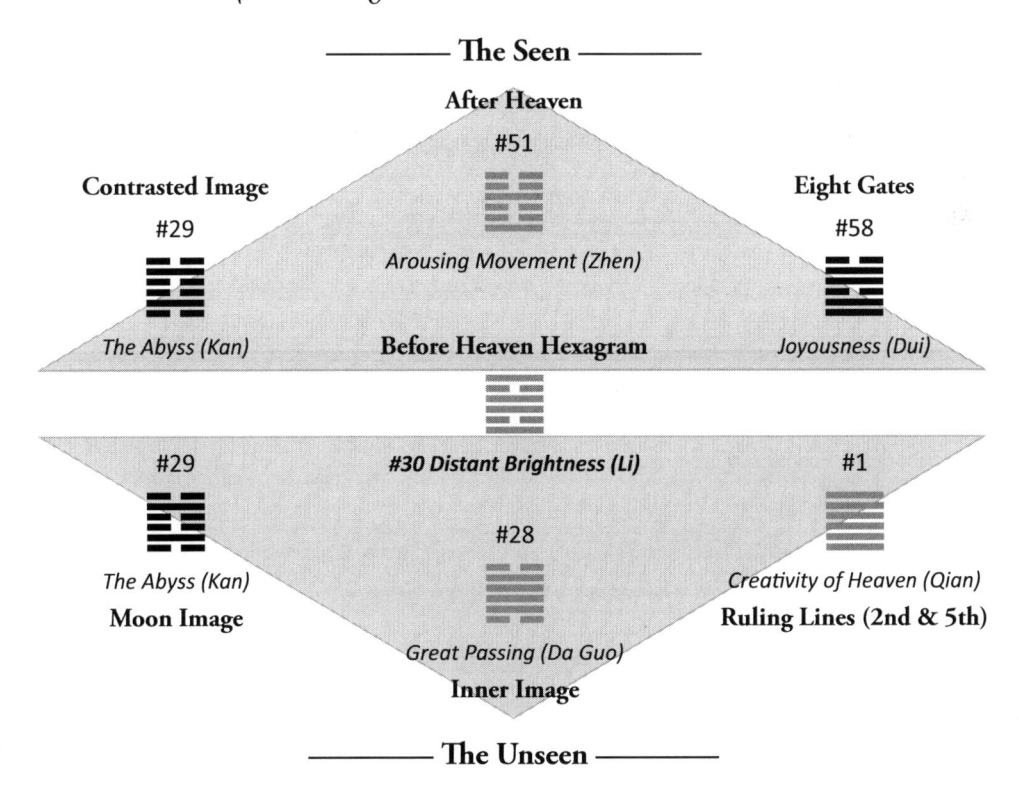

——— **The Seen** ———

After Heaven
#51
Arousing Movement (Zhen)

Contrasted Image
#29
The Abyss (Kan)

Eight Gates
#58
Joyousness (Dui)

Before Heaven Hexagram
#30 Distant Brightness (Li)

#29
The Abyss (Kan)
Moon Image

#28
Great Passing (Da Guo)
Inner Image

#1
Creativity of Heaven (Qian)
Ruling Lines (2nd & 5th)

——— **The Unseen** ———

Book of Sun and Moon

Lower Book

下經
Xia Jing

[Images #31 thru #64]

Xian

咸

Attraction — 31

Dui (Valley) above
兌 上
Dui Shang
Gen (Mountain) below
艮 下
Gen Xia

Sun/Yang Image

The Prediction (象, Tuan)

Attraction:
Perseverance. There is advantage in being resolute. Choosing a female is auspicious.

咸. 亨. 利 貞. 取 女 吉.

This image shows that clear judgement brings benefit to all those concerned. The contact made between a man and woman is enjoyed by both. It is good to plan for the future from this encounter, and it would be auspicious to enter into marriage. This is an image showing the inner workings of being attracted because of a strong affinity with the other person. Be open-minded and humble while seeking good counsel and when giving counsel.

The Lines (爻, Yao)

First Six (初 六, Chu Liu)
Attraction in the big toes.

咸 其 拇.

Her toes have been touched, but things feel indifferent because the attraction is hardly noticeable.

Second Six (六 二, Liu Er)
Attraction in the calf of the leg.
Misfortune. Abiding is auspicious.

咸 其 腓. 凶. 居 吉.

Her calf has been touched. This is not good as it is too hasty. It is better to stop and simply dwell alongside her. The attraction is too sudden and so feels blinded.

Third Nine (九 三, Jiu San)
Attraction in the thighs. Following   咸其股. 執其隨. 往吝.
their grasping brings regret.

The thighs have been touched and the movements toward intimacy are very capricious. To continue only brings humiliation.

Fourth Nine (九 四, Jiu Si)
Resoluteness is auspicious. Regret vanishes.   貞吉. 悔亡. 憧憧
Unsettled and irresolute, going "to and fro."   往來. 朋從爾思.
Friends follow the plan.

There is a feeling of auspiciousness and all regrets are ending. Even though there are some feelings of hesitancy, be assured that your partner wants and will do whatever is desired. However, the intimacy is inconsistent, yet friends think all is going according to plan.

Fifth Nine (九 五, Jiu Wu)
Attraction in the middle of the back.   咸其脢. 无悔.
No repentance.

There is no reason to regret touching the middle of her back. The action is intuitive and so there will be no regret.

Topmost Six (上 六, Shang Jiu)
Attraction in one's own jaws and tongue.   咸其輔頰舌.

The cheeks and tongues have touched through kissing, showing a persuasive measure to further the attraction.

Alternate English Translations for the Hexagram of Xian, 咸

The Symbol of Exerting Influence [S]   *Sensitivity* [C]
Influence (Wooing) [WB]   *Mutual Influence* [H] [N]
Attraction, Sensation [B]   *Conjunction* [RS]
Stimulation (Compelling) [CS]   *Attraction (Stimulation)* [L]
Conjoining [K]   *The Symbol of Mutual Influence* [CC]

The Great Symbolism (大象, Da Xiang) says,

Above the Mountain there is a Marsh. 山上有澤. 咸.
This is Xian. The superior person, 君子以虛受人.
according with this, is unprejudiced
and receptive to others.

Sexagenary Placement

Heavenly Stem: Xin 辛 (8th Stem, Yin)—**Metal** (金, Jin)
Earthly Branch: You 酉 (10th Branch, Yin)—**Rooster** (雞, Ji)
Represents the *Year of the Metal Rooster* (58th Year of the Sixty-Year Cycle)
Years: 1861 – 1921 – 1981 – 2041

Trigram Correlations

Upper Gua (Valley)

Dui 兑
Represents: Valley, River, Lake/Marsh, Youngest Daughter
Actions: Joyous, Opening, Stimulating
Influences: Family, Future, Collecting, Pleasure, Absorbing, Complacency.
Shape: Introverted Triangle   **Color:** Brown
Body: Mouth   **Season:** Beginning Spring
Moon Phase: Waning Gibbous
Animals: Earthly Goat, Celestial Great Roc
Directions: Southeast (BH), West (AH)
Nine Palaces Numbers: Fu Xi: 5
     Yu the Great: Ho River Map, 4—Lo River Script, 7
Internal Alchemy: Po (Earthly) Spirit
     Qi Center: Xuan Guan (Mysterious Pass)
     Qi Meridian: Yang Wei Mai (Yang Preserving Vessel)

Lower Gua (Mountain)

Gen 艮
- **Represents:** Mountain, Towers, Youngest Son
- **Actions:** Stillness, Binding, Stopping
- **Influences:** Knowledge, Wisdom, Skill, Determination
- **Shape:** Vertical Column   **Color:** Blue
- **Body:** Hands and arms   **Season:** Beginning Autumn
- **Moon Phase:** Waxing Crescent
- **Animals:** Earthly Dog, Celestial Vermilion Snake
- **Directions:** Northwest (BH), Northeast (AH)
- **Nine Palaces Numbers:** Fu Xi: 7
  Yu the Great: Ho River Map, 6— Lo River Script, 8
- **Internal Alchemy:** Hun (Heavenly) Spirit
  Qi Center: Jing Men (Essence Gate)
  Qi Meridian: Yang Qiao Mai (Yang Heel Vessel)

Associated Developed Hexagrams of Xian

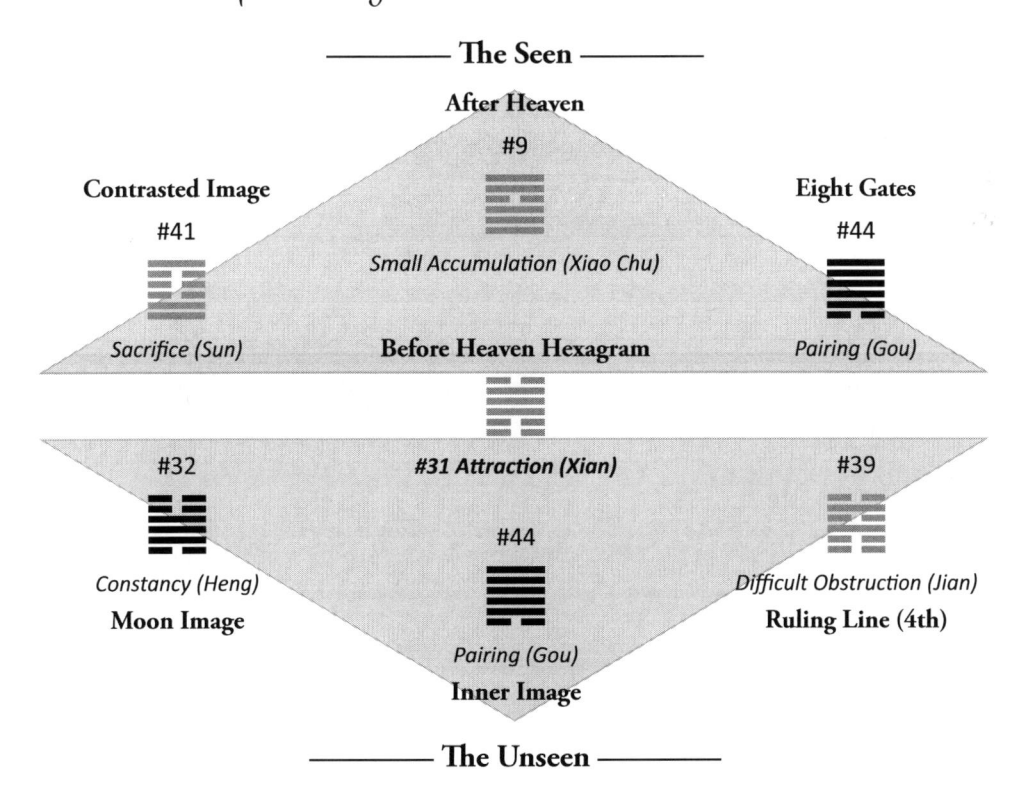

——— **The Seen** ———

After Heaven
#9
Small Accumulation (Xiao Chu)

Contrasted Image
#41
Sacrifice (Sun)

Before Heaven Hexagram

Eight Gates
#44
Pairing (Gou)

#31 Attraction (Xian)

#32
Constancy (Heng)
Moon Image

#44
Pairing (Gou)
Inner Image

#39
Difficult Obstruction (Jian)
Ruling Line (4th)

——— **The Unseen** ———

Heng
恆

Constancy

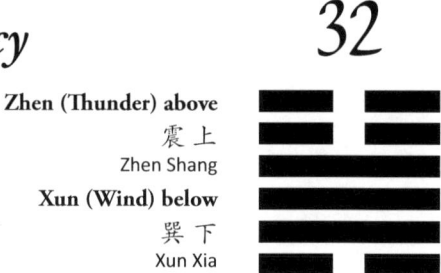

32

Zhen (Thunder) above
震上
Zhen Shang
Xun (Wind) below
巽下
Xun Xia

Moon/Yin Image

The Prediction (彖, Tuan)

Constancy:
Perseverance. Without fault.
There is advantage in being resolute.
There is advantage in having
somewhere to go.

恆. 亨. 无咎. 利貞.
利有攸往.

This image indicates maintaining harmony between nature and society. In Constancy, affairs move smoothly without making any errors. This is a good situation in which to move forward on plans for the future. The laws of nature remain constant, but nature itself is in constant change. So remain flexible and adapt to changing times, yet stay unchanging with your inner sense of truth.

The Lines (爻, Yao)

First Six (初 六, Chu Liu)
With deep Constancy, even resoluteness
is unfortunate. To be unconcerned
is advantageous.

浚恆. 貞凶. 无攸利.

Constant extortion brings misfortune and has no benefit. Ignore extortionists for they will fall into ruin.

Second Nine (九 二, Jiu Er)
Regret vanishes.

悔亡.

No need to hide, all regrets are gone.

Third Nine (九 三, Jiu San)
No Constancy about one's own virtue.　　不恆其德. 或承之羞. 貞吝.
Some acknowledge their shame.
Even if resolute, regret.

Maintain modesty. If not, others will bring humiliation, and all things will go awry. Be like the wind when it comes to changing your view of things.

Fourth Nine (九 四, Jiu Si)
The fields are without birds and animals.　　田无禽.

The fields are empty and no hunting for food can be undertaken. This is like trying to search for something within an empty field. Nothing is there for you.

Fifth Six (六 五, Liu Wu)
Constancy about one's own virtue.　　恆其德. 貞. 婦人吉. 夫子凶.
Resoluteness. The wife is auspicious.
The husband, unfortunate.

Maintain modesty so virtue comes forth. Be resolute in actions and affairs. It is auspicious to predict the actions of a female, but not auspicious to predict the actions of a man. Those of strength find no constancy in the weak.

Topmost Six (上 六, Shang Liu)
Excitement about Constancy.　　振恆. 凶.
Misfortune.

Constant demands of others brings misfortune. Do not put others in danger. There is a restlessness about things and it is difficult to be constant and enduring.

Alternate English Translations for the Hexagram of Heng, 恒

The Symbol of Constancy [S]　　　　　　*Constancy* [C] [N]
Duration [WB]　　　　　　　　　　　　*Long Lasting* [H]
The Long Enduring [B]　　　　　　　　*Persevering* [K] [RS]
Constancy (Enduring) [CS]　　　　　　*Duration* [L]
The Symbol of Perseverance [CC]

Book of Sun and Moon

The Great Symbolism (大象, Da Xiang) says,

Thunder and Wind. This is Heng. The superior person, according with this, stands firm and does not change methods.

雷風. 恒. 君子
以立不易方.

Sexagenary Placement

Heavenly Stem: Gui 癸 (10th Stem, Yin)—**Water** (水, Shui)
Earthly Branch: Hai 亥 (12th Branch, Yin)—**Pig** (猪, Zhu)
Represents the *Year of the Water Pig* (60th Year of the Sixty-Year Cycle)
Years: 1863 – 1923 – 1983 – 2043

Trigram Correlations

Upper Gua (Thunder)

Zhen 震
- **Represents:** Thunder, Earthquake, Eldest Son
- **Actions:** Arousing, Shaking, Initiating
- **Influences:** Foundations, Past Actions, Excitement.
- **Shape:** Vertical Column   **Color:** Green
- **Body:** Feet and legs   **Season:** Beginning Winter
- **Moon Phase:** Waning Crescent
- **Animals:** Earthly Dragons, Celestial Dragon-Horse
- **Directions:** Northeast (BH), East (AH)
- **Nine Palaces Numbers:** Fu Xi: **3**
    - Yu the Great: Ho River Map, **8**—Lo River Script, **3**
- **Internal Alchemy:** Mind-Intention
    - Qi Center: Dan Tian (Elixir Field)
    - Qi Meridian: Yin Qiao Mai (Yin Heel Vessel)

#32 Constancy (Heng)

Lower Gua (Wind)

☴ **Xun** 巽   **Represents:** Wind, Wood, Eldest Daughter
Actions: Gentleness, Grounding, Penetrating, Spreading
Influences: Prosperity, Abundance, Wealth
Shape: Rectangle   **Color:** Purple
Body: Waist and hips   **Season:** Beginning Summer
Moon Phase: Waxing Gibbous
Animals: Earthly Fowl, Celestial Golden Rooster
Directions: Southwest (BH), Southeast (AH)
Nine Palaces Numbers: Fu Xi: **9**
  Yu the Great: Ho River Map, **2**—Lo River Script, **4**
Internal Alchemy: Breath and Mobilizing Qi
  Qi Center: Yu Zhen (Jade Pillow)
  Qi Meridian: Yin Wei Mai (Yin Preserving Vessel)

Associated Developed Hexagrams of Heng

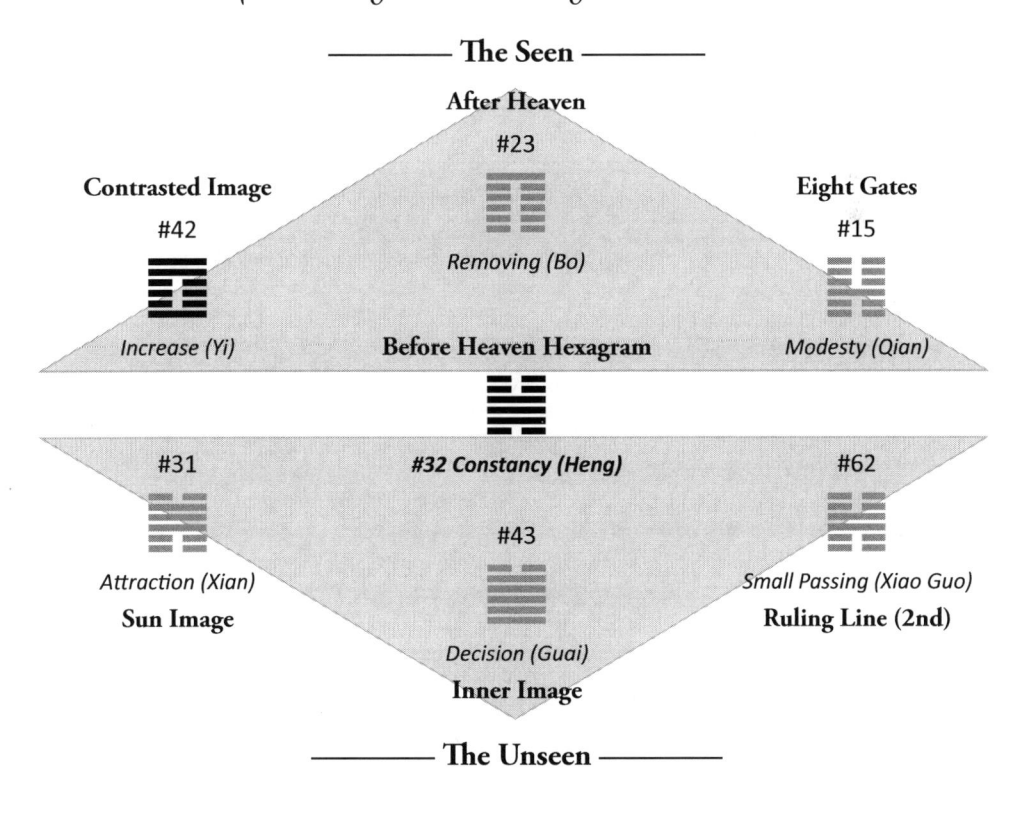

───── **The Seen** ─────

After Heaven
#23
Removing (Bo)

Contrasted Image
#42
Increase (Yi)

Eight Gates
#15
Modesty (Qian)

Before Heaven Hexagram

#32 Constancy (Heng)

#31
Attraction (Xian)
Sun Image

#43
Decision (Guai)
Inner Image

#62
Small Passing (Xiao Guo)
Ruling Line (2nd)

───── **The Unseen** ─────

Dun 遯

Retreating   33

Qian (Heaven) above
乾上
Qian Shang
Gen (Mountain) below
艮下
Gen Xia

Sun/Yang Image

The Prediction (彖, Tuan)

Retreating:
Perseverance. There is small advantage in being resolute.

遯.亨.小利貞.

This image is saying to head to safer ground and to conceal yourself with grace. It is within the law of nature for light to retreat from darkness. Raising pigs and cows is auspicious and creates a good situation in which to plan for the future, especially concerning retirement. Retreating to basics is the only way success can be obtained.

The Lines (爻, Yao)

First Six (初六, Chu Liu)
Retreating, the tail is in peril.
No use in having somewhere to go.

遯尾厲.勿用有攸往.

The animal's tail has been severed, so make no plans to go anywhere. Being at a disadvantage, neither retreat nor advance. Remain still.

Second Six (六二, Liu Er)
Grasp onto the use of a yellow ox's hide.
No persuasion can overcome him.

執之用黃牛之革.莫之勝說.

Use the hide of an ox to bind the pig so it will be unable to set itself free. This shows that the use of something discarded (an old yellowed ox hide) can bring protection to something in use (the pig who is stubbornly trying to escape). The pig cannot be called back. It must be bound.

Third Nine (九三, Jiu San)
Retreating in bondage. There is a severe illness. Nourish servants and concubines. Auspicious.

係遯. 有疾厲. 畜臣妾. 吉.

The bound pig falls ill and its condition grows more serious. It is auspicious to nourish and be kind to male servants and female concubines. It is wise not to retreat and so abandon friends. Rather, stay and cure the illness.

Fourth Nine (九四, Jiu Si)
Voluntary Retreating. Auspicious for the wise person, not for the inferior person.

好遯. 君子吉. 小人否.

The pig is fat and beautiful. This is an auspicious time for the superior person, not for the inferior one. Superior persons retreat from inferior people in this situation.

Fifth Nine (九五, Jiu Wu)
Admirable Retreating. To be resolute is auspicious.

嘉遯. 貞吉.

Giving praise to the pigs brings good fortune because it shows resoluteness in retreating.

Topmost Nine (上九, Shang Jiu)
Noble Retreating. Everything is of advantage.

肥遯. 无不利.

Nourishing is noble, and so only healthy and fat pigs will be raised. To do so, the heart will be light and good fortune will come.

Alternate English Translations for the Hexagram of Dun, 遯

The Symbol of Retirement [S]
Retreat [H] [N] [WB]
Yielding, Withdrawal [B]
Retiring (Withdrawal) [CS]
Withdrawal [C]
Retiring [K] [RS]
Retreat (Withdrawal) [L]
The Symbol of Regression [CC]

The Great Symbolism (大象, Da Xiang) says,

Heaven is above a Mountain. This is Dun. The superior person, according with this, keeps distant from inferior people. Not because they are evil, but to maintain dignity.

天上有山．遯．君子以遠小人．不惡而嚴．

Sexagenary Placement

Heavenly Stem: Gui 癸 (10th Stem, Yin)—**Water** (水, Shui)
Earthly Branch: You 酉 (10th Branch, Yin)—**Rooster** (雞, Ji)
Represents the *Year of the Water Rooster* (10th Year of the Sixty-Year Cycle)
Years: 1873 – 1933 – 1993 – 2053

Trigram Correlations

Upper Gua (Heaven)

Qian 乾
Represents: Heaven, Sky, Male, Father, Emperor
Actions: Creative Principle, Persisting, Forceful
Influences: Blessings, Good Fortune, Strength, Spiritual Power
Shape: Circle **Color:** White
Body: Head **Season:** Summer (Summer Solstice)
Moon Phase: Full Moon
Animals: Earthly Horse, Celestial Red Phoenix
Directions: South (BH), Northwest (AH)
Nine Palaces Numbers: Fu Xi: **2**
  Yu the Great: Ho River Map, **9**—Lo River Script, **6**
Internal Alchemy: Clarity, Illumination
  Qi Center: Ni Wan (Mud Pellet)
  Qi Meridian: Du Mai (Control Vessel)

#33 Retreating (Dun)

Lower Gua (Mountain)

Gen 艮

Represents: Mountain, Towers, Youngest Son
Actions: Stillness, Binding, Stopping
Influences: Knowledge, Wisdom, Skill, Determination
Shape: Vertical Column **Color:** Blue
Body: Hands and arms **Season:** Beginning Autumn
Moon Phase: Waxing Crescent
Animals: Earthly Dog, Celestial Vermilion Snake
Directions: Northwest (BH), Northeast (AH)
Nine Palaces Numbers: Fu Xi: 7
  Yu the Great: Ho River Map, 6— Lo River Script, 8
Internal Alchemy: Hun (Heavenly) Spirit
  Qi Center: Jing Men (Essence Gate)
  Qi Meridian: Yang Qiao Mai (Yang Heel Vessel)

Associated Developed Hexagrams of Dun

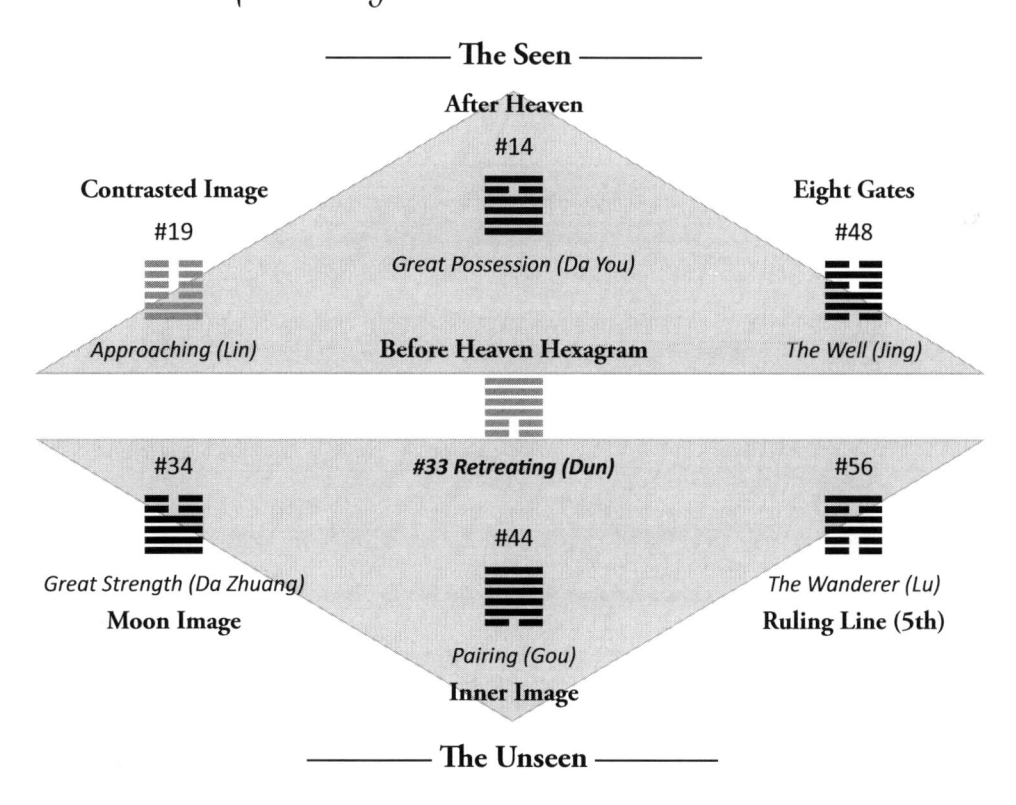

——— **The Seen** ———

After Heaven
#14
Great Possession (Da You)

Contrasted Image
#19
Approaching (Lin)

Eight Gates
#48
The Well (Jing)

Before Heaven Hexagram

#33 Retreating (Dun)

#34
Great Strength (Da Zhuang)
Moon Image

#44
Pairing (Gou)
Inner Image

#56
The Wanderer (Lu)
Ruling Line (5th)

——— **The Unseen** ———

Da Zhuang   *Great Strength*   34

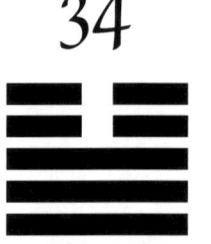

大壯

Zhen (Thunder) above
震上
Zhen Shang

Qian (Heaven) below
乾下
Qian Xia

Moon/Yin Image

The Prediction (象, Tuan)

Great Strength:
There is advantage in being resolute.   大壯. 利貞.

Prove you are honorable by meeting obligations to friends. With this strength, it is good to plan for the future. This is a time of great power and influence wherein the very power of nature is being reflected, so to maintain greatness you must strive to be incorruptible in your actions.

The Lines (爻, Yao)

First Nine (初 九, Chu Jiu)
Strength within the toes. Misfortune   壯于趾. 征凶. 有孚.
if aggressive. Possessing truth.

There is strength in the feet, but still it is dangerous to go on expeditions or travels. Even so, many things will be seized and acquired. This shows there is brawn but little brain. Refrain from forcing things, rather think through actions first.

Second Nine (九 二, Jiu Er)
Auspicious to be resolute.   貞吉.

Planning for the future is auspicious. Strength should be used but without excess.

Third Nine (九 三, Jiu San)
The inferior person uses strength.   小人用壯. 君子用罔.
The wise person uses none. Resolute   貞厲. 羝羊觸藩.
discipline. The goat butts the hedge   羸其角.
and entangles his horns.

There is danger and misfortune for a common person to act as if from a high position. It is equally unfortunate for the person of high position to be confused over a situation. Both actions are like a goat running straight into a fence made of brambles, where it gets stuck and is vulnerable. This represents an empty show of strength, and only leads to danger.

Fourth Nine (九 四, Jiu Si)
Resoluteness is auspicious. Regret vanishes. 　　貞吉. 悔亡. 藩決不羸.
The hedge opens and there are no 　　　　　　壯于大輿之輹.
entanglements. As powerful as an axel
supporting a large carriage.

Good fortune has been predicted and all regrets have vanished. True strength is showing calmness in the face of danger. The fence has been broken so the goat escapes, but then collides with the wheel of a large cart. In its excitement, it could not slow down and navigate its movements properly.

Fifth Six (六 五, Liu Wu)
The goat is easily lost. 　　　　　　　　喪羊于易. 无悔.
There is no regret.

During an interaction with others, the goat wanders off and gets lost. No need to worry, however, so you can relax.

Topmost Six (上 六, Shang Liu)
The goat butts the hedge. Unable 　　　　羝羊觸藩. 不能退.
to withdraw and unable to advance. 　　　不能遂. 无攸利.
Nothing is advantageous. 　　　　　　　艱則吉.
Seeing the difficulty is auspicious.

The goat breaks open the hedge only to discover it is an entrapment. It cannot move backward or forward, so there's no advantage. However, even if the goat is left stranded, the situation is still auspicious. This is like a stalemate, so there's no need to struggle needlessly.

Alternate English Translations for the Hexagram of Da Zhuang, 大壯

The Symbol of Great Vigor [S]　　　　　*Great Strength* [H] [N]
The Power of the Great [B] [CS] [WB]　*The Great's Vigor* [RS]
Great Power [C] [L]　　　　　　　　　*Great Invigorating* [K]
The Symbol of Major Power [CC]

The Great Symbolism (大象, Da Xiang) says,

Thunder within Heaven above. 　雷在天上.大壯.
This is Da Zhuang. The superior person, 　君子以非禮不履.
according with this, treads not one step
out of propriety.

☳ Sexagenary Placement

Heavenly Stem: Yi 乙 (2nd Stem, Yin)—**Wood** (木, Mu)
Earthly Branch: You 酉 (10th Branch, Yin)—**Rooster** (雞, Ji)
Represents the *Year of the Wood Rooster* (22nd Year of the Sixty-Year Cycle)
Years: 1885 – 1945 – 2005 – 2065

Trigram Correlations

Upper Gua (Thunder)

☳ **Zhen** 震
Represents: Thunder, Earthquake, Eldest Son
Actions: Arousing, Shaking, Initiating
Influences: Foundations, Past Actions, Excitement.
Shape: Vertical Column   **Color:** Green
Body: Feet and legs   **Season:** Beginning Winter
Moon Phase: Waning Crescent
Animals: Earthly Dragons, Celestial Dragon-Horse
Directions: Northeast (BH), East (AH)
Nine Palaces Numbers: Fu Xi: **3**
　　Yu the Great: *Ho River Map,* **8**—*Lo River Script,* **3**
Internal Alchemy: Mind-Intention
　　Qi Center: Dan Tian (Elixir Field)
　　Qi Meridian: Yin Qiao Mai (Yin Heel Vessel)

#34 Great Strength (Da Zhuang)

Lower Gua (Heaven)

☰ **Qian** 乾   **Represents:** Heaven, Sky, Male, Father, Emperor
Actions: Creative Principle, Persisting, Forceful
Influences: Blessings, Good Fortune, Strength, Spiritual Power
Shape: Circle   **Color:** White
Body: Head   **Season:** Summer (Summer Solstice)
Moon Phase: Full Moon
Animals: Earthly Horse, Celestial Red Phoenix
Directions: South (BH), Northwest (AH)
Nine Palaces Numbers: Fu Xi: 2
  Yu the Great: Ho River Map, 9—Lo River Script, 6
Internal Alchemy: Clarity, Illumination
  Qi Center: Ni Wan (Mud Pellet)
  Qi Meridian: Du Mai (Control Vessel)

Associated Developed Hexagrams of Da Zhuang

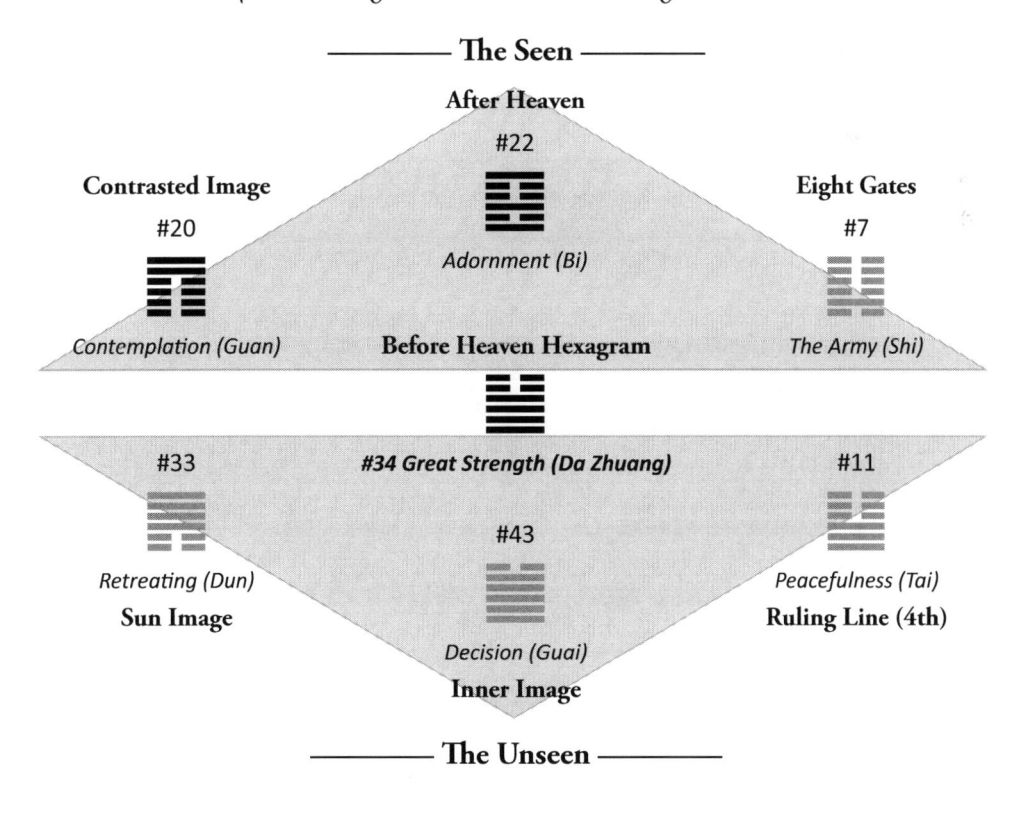

——— **The Seen** ———

After Heaven
#22
Adornment (Bi)

Contrasted Image
#20
Contemplation (Guan)

Eight Gates
#7
The Army (Shi)

Before Heaven Hexagram

#33
Retreating (Dun)
Sun Image

#34 Great Strength (Da Zhuang)

#43
Decision (Guai)
Inner Image

#11
Peacefulness (Tai)
Ruling Line (4th)

——— **The Unseen** ———

Jin

Advancement

35

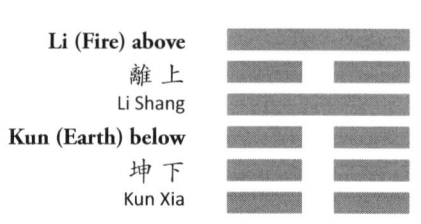

晋

Li (Fire) above
離上
Li Shang
Kun (Earth) below
坤下
Kun Xia

Sun/Yang Image

The Prediction (彖, Tuan)

Advancement:
The prince finds peace as a great many horses are bestowed to him by the king. Three times in a day he is received [by the king].

晋.康侯用錫馬
蕃庶.晝日三接.

This image shows advancement of returning generosity in kind. A king gives a prince many horses of a very good breed. The prince, in turn, breeds the horses, and so repays the favor by delivering the offspring to the king. It takes the prince three times in one day to deliver the three colts to the king.

The Lines (爻, Yao)

First Six (初 六, Chu Liu)
Advancement meets with obstacles. Resoluteness is auspicious. Even though untrustworthy, his generosity is without fault.

晋如如.貞吉.罔孚.
裕无咎.

Making a bold and sweeping advance is auspicious. Even though promised items of value were not acquired, no mistakes were made that could bring harm later. Persist in this matter whether feeling confident or not.

Second Six (六 二, Liu Er)
Advancement meets with sorrow. To be resolute is auspicious. Receives a great blessing from one's own grandmother.

晋如愁如.貞吉.
受茲介福于其王母.

There is good fortune in those who feel concern and sorrow about advancing because they know that others can be hurt. The grandmother gives good advice and blessings. Persist whether recognition is given or not.

Third Six (六三, Liu san)
All are loyal. Regret vanishes.　　　眾允. 悔亡.

All worries vanish when those around you are loyal and trusting.

Fourth Nine (九四, Jiu Si)
Advancement like a squirrel.　　　晉如鼫鼠. 貞厲.
Use firm discipline.

Do not advance like a scurrying squirrel as this brings danger. Do not misuse the situation just to amass things.

Fifth Six (六五, Liu Wu)
Regret vanishes. No emotions about　　　悔亡. 失得勿恤.
loss or gain. To act is auspicious.　　　往吉. 无不利.
Everything is auspicious.

No need to worry over gains and losses as your regrets and worries are vanishing. Everything is auspicious, so move forward as usual. Just remain happy and relaxed.

Topmost Nine (上九, Shang Jiu)
Advancement of one's own horns;　　　晉其角. 維用伐邑.
doing so to chastise the city.　　　厲吉. 无咎. 貞吝.
This is without fault.
Resoluteness brings fault.

If determined to travel, keep the forethought of it being dangerous, yet auspicious if no mistakes are made. In the end things do not go smoothly. Be resolute but show no expression of anger, then there will be no regret.

Alternate English Translations for the Hexagram of Jin, 晉

The Symbol of Forwardness [S]　　　*Advance* [C]
Progress [B] [L] [N] [WB]　　　*Proceeding Forward* [H]
Progress (Advance) [CS]　　　*Prospering* [K] [RS]
The Symbol of Progress [CC]

The Great Symbolism (大象, Da Xiang) says,

Brightness appears out from the Earth.	明出地.晉.
This is Jin. Superior persons, according with this, illuminate their own bright virtue.	君子以自照明德.

Sexagenary Placement

Heavenly Stem: Ding 丁 (4th Stem, Yin)—**Fire** (火, Huo)
Earthly Branch: Chou 丑 (2nd Branch, Yin)—**Ox** (牛, Niu)
Represents the *Year of the Fire Ox* (14th Year of the Sixty-Year Cycle)
Years: 1877 – 1937 – 1997 – 2057

Trigram Correlations

Upper Gua (Fire)

Li 離 **Represents:** Fire, Lightning, Sun, Middle Daughter
Actions: Clinging, Illuminating, Congregating
Influences: Fame, Reputation, Brightness, Elegance
Shape: Triangle   **Color:** Red
Body: Eyes   **Season:** Spring (Spring Equinox)
Moon Phase: Last Quarter
Animals: Earthly Rooster, Celestial Green Dragon
Directions: East (BH), South (AH)
Nine Palaces Numbers: Fu Xi: **8**
    Yu the Great: Ho River Map, **3**—Lo River Script, **9**
Internal Alchemy: Mercury, Qi
    Qi Center: Jiang Gong (Crimson Palace)
    Qi Meridian: Dai Mai (Belt Vessel)

#35 Advancement (Jin)

Lower Gua (Earth)

Kun 坤

Represents: Earth, Soil, Fields, Female, Mother, Empress
Actions: Receptive, Expanding, Yielding
Influences: Relationships, Love, Submission
Shape: Square   **Color:** Yellow
Body: Stomach   **Season:** Winter (Winter Solstice)
Moon Phase: New Moon
Animals: Earthly Ox, Celestial Black Tortoise
Directions: North (BH), Southwest (AH)
Nine Palaces Numbers: Fu Xi: **10**
   Yu the Great: Ho River Map, **1**—Lo River Script, **2**
Internal Alchemy: Tranquility, Void
   Qi Center: Hui Yin (Returning Yin)
   Qi Meridian: Ren Mai (Function Vessel)

Associated Developed Hexagrams of Jin

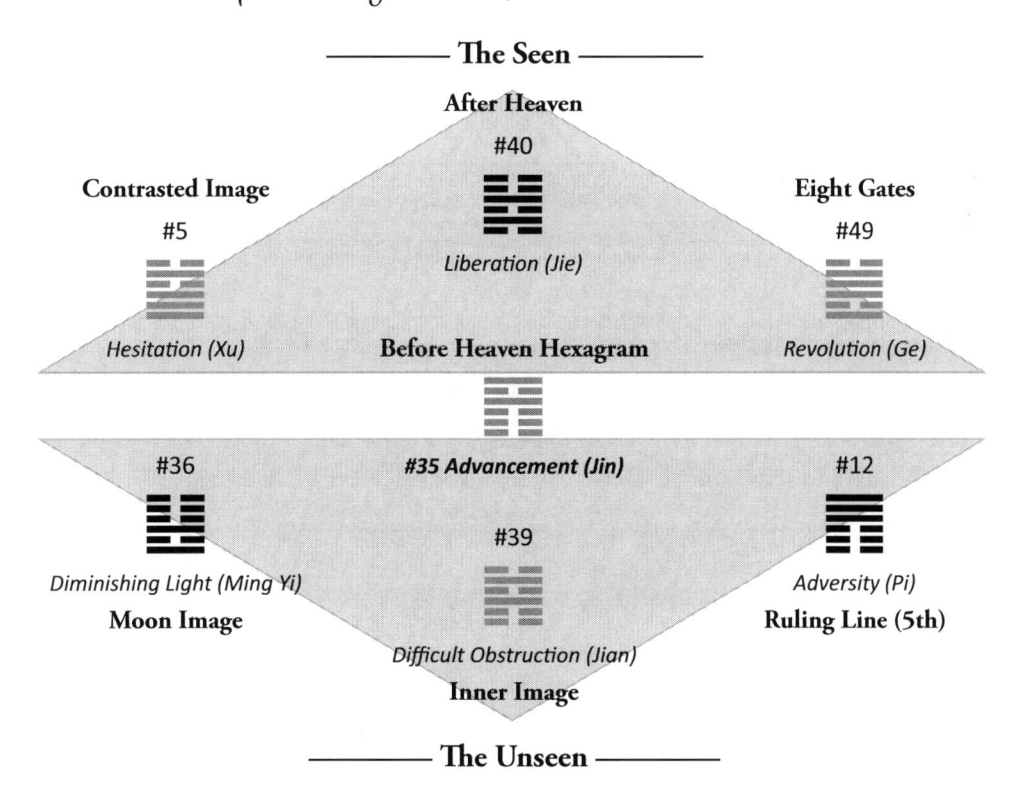

——— **The Seen** ———

After Heaven
#40
Liberation (Jie)

Contrasted Image
#5
Hesitation (Xu)

Eight Gates
#49
Revolution (Ge)

Before Heaven Hexagram

#35 Advancement (Jin)

#36
Diminishing Light (Ming Yi)
Moon Image

#39
Difficult Obstruction (Jian)
Inner Image

#12
Adversity (Pi)
Ruling Line (5th)

——— **The Unseen** ———

Ming Yi *Diminishing Light* 36

明夷

Kun (Earth) above
坤上
Kun Shang
Li (Fire) below
離下
Li Xia

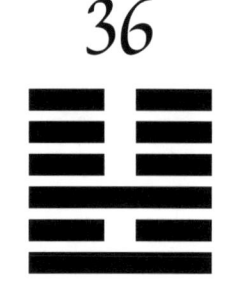

Moon/Yin Image

The Prediction (彖, Tuan)

Diminishing Light:
**Advantage is being resolute
through difficulties.**

明夷. 利艱貞.

This image warns that boasting of your accomplishments only arouses envy in others. A distant brightness descends upon the earth, indicating future plans should be made, especially in times of adverse circumstances. This is not a time to attempt to outwardly shine, better to rely on your internal light. Remain reserved and yielding while awaiting the passing of this darkness.

The Lines (爻, Yao)

First Nine (初 九, Chu Jiu)
**Diminishing Light in flying. The wings
drop. The wise person is moving. Three
days of fasting. Having somewhere to go.
The ruler has words.**

明夷于飛. 垂其翼.
君子于行. 三日不食.
有攸往. 主人有言.

A lone bird flies through the rays of the sun, but its left wing (due to the Yang line) is hanging down. A person of position is on a journey and has not eaten in three days, but must continue on as there is a message from a superior that must be received. These actions show persistence even though some find it suitable for ridicule.

Second Six (六 二, Liu Er)
**Diminishing Light. There is injury
in the left thigh. Saved by the strength
of a horse. Auspicious.**

明夷. 夷于左股.
用拯馬壯. 吉.

The left thigh has been injured, but the sun's rays are casting a shadow of the horse to the left, making it look more powerful. Even though wounded, help is being given. This is auspicious.

Third Nine (九三, Jiu San)
Diminishing Light goes south to hunt.	明夷于南狩.
Obtaining a Great Chief.	得其大首.
Do not be hasty, be resolute.	不可疾貞.

The hunting ground is shadowed by the setting sun. A great hunter arrives and shows where the big game is hiding in the South. Still, it is difficult to know what is going to happen, but one must act.

Fourth Six (六四, Liu Si)
Enters the left side of the stomach.	入于左腹.
Acquires Diminishing Light in the heart.	獲明夷之心.
Going and coming by the gate in the courtyard.	于出門庭.

The rays of the setting sun shine on the left side of the stomach and move up to shine on the heart. It would be wise to recognize the imminent danger at hand, but even though going in and out through the gate of the courtyard, the heart still feels illuminated.

Fifth Six (六五, Liu Wu)
Diminishing Light of Prince Ji.	箕子之明夷. 利貞.
Advantage in being resolute.	

After the Yin dynasty was overthrown, Prince Ji escaped and went into hiding. While underground, he found this was the right time to predict his future and so was able to persist in his own light.

Topmost Six (上六, Shang Jiu)
Not the light of night. First rising to Heaven.	不明晦. 初登于天.
Afterwards descending to Earth.	後入于地.

When the sun rises, it naturally moves across the sky and then falls below the horizon. This is the "naturally-just-so" of Heaven and Earth. Finally, the light has destroyed the darkness.

Alternate English Translations for the Hexagram of Ming Yi, 明夷

Darkening of the Light [CS] [WB]
Darkening of the Light, Injury [B]
*Darkening of the Light
    (The Darkened Light)* [L]
*Concealment of Illumination
    (Injury of Illumination)* [C]
The Symbol of Lack of Appreciation [CC]
Brilliance Injured [H]
The Time of Darkness [N]
Brightness Hidden [RS]
Brightness Hiding [K]
*The Symbol of the Appearance
    of Clear Intelligence Wounded* [S]

The Great Symbolism (大象, Da Xiang) says,

Brightness enters into the Earth.	明入地中. 明夷.
This is Ming Yi. The superior person,	君子以蒞眾.
according with this, oversees living beings	用晦而明.
by employing both darkness and brightness.	

Sexagenary Placement

Heavenly Stem: Gui 癸 (10th Stem, Yin)—**Water** (水, Shui)
Earthly Branch: Wei 未 (8th Branch, Yin)—**Goat** (羊, Yang)
Represents the *Year of the Water Goat* (20th Year of the Sixty-Year Cycle)
Years: 1883 – 1943 – 2003 – 2063

Trigram Correlations

Upper Gua (Earth)

Kun 坤   **Represents:** Earth, Soil, Fields, Female, Mother, Empress
Actions: Receptive, Expanding, Yielding
Influences: Relationships, Love, Submission
Shape: Square   **Color:** Yellow
Body: Stomach   **Season:** Winter (Winter Solstice)
Moon Phase: New Moon
Animals: Earthly Ox, Celestial Black Tortoise
Directions: North (BH), Southwest (AH)
Nine Palaces Numbers: Fu Xi: **10**
    Yu the Great: Ho River Map, **1**—Lo River Script, **2**
Internal Alchemy: Tranquility, Void

#36 Diminishing Light (Ming Yi)

Qi Center: Hui Yin (Returning Yin)
Qi Meridian: Ren Mai (Function Vessel)

Lower Gua (Fire)

☲ **Li** 離 **Represents:** Fire, Lightning, Sun, Middle Daughter
Actions: Clinging, Illuminating, Congregating
Influences: Fame, Reputation, Brightness, Elegance
Shape: Triangle **Color:** Red
Body: Eyes **Season:** Spring (Spring Equinox)
Moon Phase: Last Quarter
Animals: Earthly Rooster, Celestial Green Dragon
Directions: East (BH), South (AH)
Nine Palaces Numbers: Fu Xi: **8**
 Yu the Great: Ho River Map, **3**—Lo River Script, **9**
Internal Alchemy: Mercury, Qi
 Qi Center: Jiang Gong (Crimson Palace)
 Qi Meridian: Dai Mai (Belt Vessel)

Associated Developed Hexagrams of Ming Yi

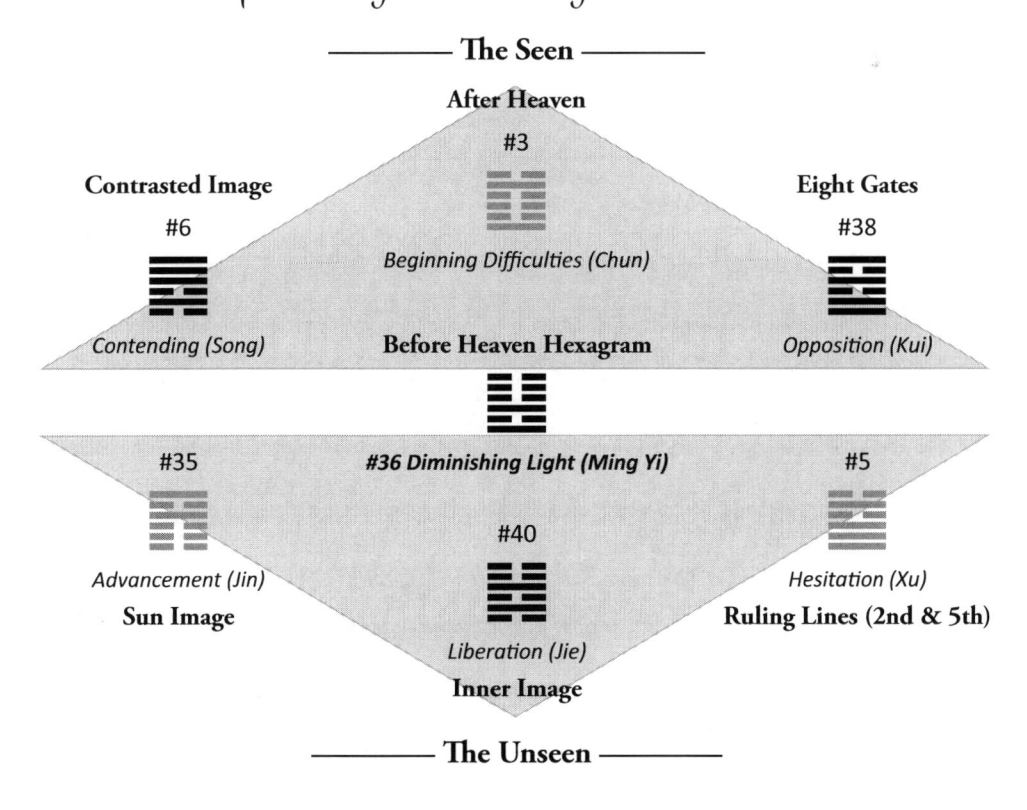

――― **The Seen** ―――

After Heaven
#3
Beginning Difficulties (Chun)

Contrasted Image
#6
Contending (Song)

Eight Gates
#38
Opposition (Kui)

Before Heaven Hexagram

#35
Advancement (Jin)
Sun Image

#36 Diminishing Light (Ming Yi)

#40
Liberation (Jie)
Inner Image

#5
Hesitation (Xu)
Ruling Lines (2nd & 5th)

――― **The Unseen** ―――

Jia Ren   *The Family*   37

家人

Xun (Wind) above
巽上
Xun Shang

Li (Fire) below
離下
Li Xia

Sun/Yang Image

The Prediction (彖, Tuan)

The Family:
There is advantage if the female is resolute.

家人. 利女貞.

Being filial to one's family and showing loyalty to friends is advantageous. So, it is proper and suitable for the female to be in charge of future plans for the home. The harmony of the individual should mirror the harmony of the family; the harmony of the family should mirror the harmony of society. The individual, then, needs to show loyalty through being responsible and sincere so one's family and society can be well organized. Rely on the female to make the family flourish.

The Lines (爻, Yao)

First Nine (初 九, **Chu Jiu**)
The Family has restrictions and regrets vanish.

閑有家悔亡.

If the home is spacious enough for the entire family there will be no regrets or worries.

Second Six (六 二, **Liu Er**)
Follows nothing in the preparation of food. Resoluteness is auspicious.

无攸遂在饋. 貞吉.

No employment or position is worth seeking at this time, so simply stay at home and prepare food. Do not indulge yourself excessively and persist gently in cooking for others. The future shows good fortune.

#37 The Family (Jia Ren)

Third Nine (九 三, Jiu San)
The Family is severely arguing.
Repentance and discipline are auspicious.
The wife and sons titter and laugh.
In the end there is regret.

家人嗃嗃.悔厲吉.
婦子嘻嘻.終吝.

If all the family members speak at once about what they want, this will bring misfortune and danger. If the talk can be disciplined and orderly, however, there will be good fortune. If the wife and children make too many jokes about each other this will invite trouble to the family's reputation and finances. Be tolerant of other people's flaws, yet resolute about your own discipline.

Fourth Six (六 四, Liu Si)
Enrichment of the home.
Great auspiciousness.

富家.大吉.

It is greatly auspicious to work hard and bring prosperity to the family.

Fifth Nine (九 五, Jiu Wu)
The king grants what is needed at home.
To be without worry is auspicious.

王假有家.勿恤吉.

The king wishes to be a guest in your home for a while. There is no need for concern or worry as this will bring great good fortune.

Topmost Nine (上 九, Shang Jiu)
Being both sincere and majestic to others.
In the end it is auspicious.

有孚威如.終吉.

Win the prestige of others and in the end this will be auspicious.

Alternate English Translations for the Hexagram of Jia Ren, 家人

The Symbol of the Family [CC] [S]
The Family (The Clan) [WB]
The Family [B] [L]
The Family (Proper Relations) [CS]
Dwelling People [K]

People in the Home [C]
Household [H]
Family [N]
Household People [RS]

The Great Symbolism (大象, Da Xiang) says,

From the Wind comes forth Fire. 風自火出. 家人.
This is Jia Ren. Superior persons, according 君子以言有物
with this, have substance to their words 而行有恒.
and show constancy in their actions.

Sexagenary Placement

Heavenly Stem: Geng 庚 (7th Stem, Yang)—**Metal** (金, Jin)
Earthly Branch: Wu 午 (7th Branch, Yang)—**Horse** (馬, Ma)
Represents the *Year of the Metal Horse* (7th Year of the Sixty-Year Cycle)
Years: 1870 – 1930 – 1990 – 2050

Trigram Correlations

Upper Gua (Wind)

Xun 巽
  Represents: Wind, Wood, Eldest Daughter
  Actions: Gentleness, Grounding, Penetrating, Spreading
  Influences: Prosperity, Abundance, Wealth
  Shape: Rectangle   **Color:** Purple
  Body: Waist and hips   **Season:** Beginning Summer
  Moon Phase: Waxing Gibbous
  Animals: Earthly Fowl, Celestial Golden Rooster
  Directions: Southwest (BH), Southeast (AH)
  Nine Palaces Numbers: Fu Xi: **9**
      Yu the Great: Ho River Map, **2**—Lo River Script, **4**
  Internal Alchemy: Breath and Mobilizing Qi
      Qi Center: Yu Zhen (Jade Pillow)
      Qi Meridian: Yin Wei Mai (Yin Preserving Vessel)

Lower Gua (Fire)

☲ **Li** 離
Represents: Fire, Lightning, Sun, Middle Daughter
Actions: Clinging, Illuminating, Congregating
Influences: Fame, Reputation, Brightness, Elegance
Shape: Triangle   **Color:** Red
Body: Eyes   **Season:** Spring (Spring Equinox)
Moon Phase: Last Quarter
Animals: Earthly Rooster, Celestial Green Dragon
Directions: East (BH), South (AH)
Nine Palaces Numbers: Fu Xi: **8**
　Yu the Great: Ho River Map, **3**—Lo River Script, **9**
Internal Alchemy: Mercury, Qi
　Qi Center: Jiang Gong (Crimson Palace)
　Qi Meridian: Dai Mai (Belt Vessel)

Associated Developed Hexagrams of Jia Ren

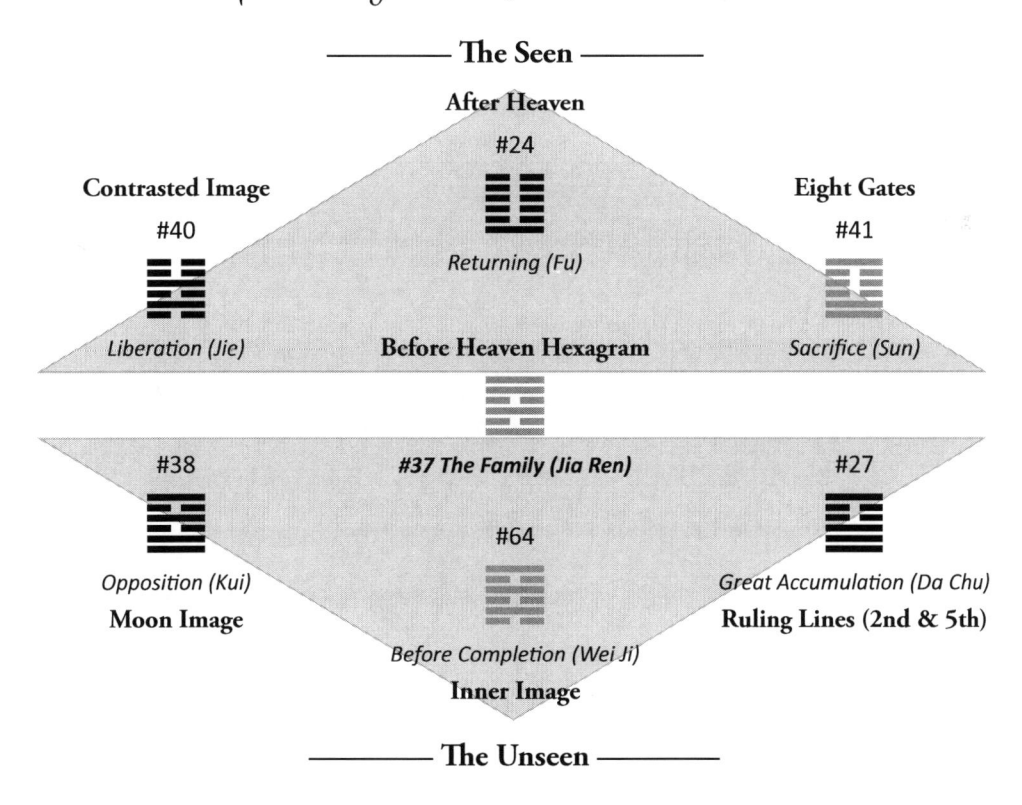

——— **The Seen** ———

After Heaven
#24
☷☳ *Returning (Fu)*

Contrasted Image
#40
Liberation (Jie)

Eight Gates
#41
Sacrifice (Sun)

Before Heaven Hexagram

#37 The Family (Jia Ren)

#38
Opposition (Kui)
Moon Image

#64
Before Completion (Wei Ji)
Inner Image

#27
Great Accumulation (Da Chu)
Ruling Lines (2nd & 5th)

——— **The Unseen** ———

Kui

Opposition

38

睼

Li (Fire) above
離上
Li Shang

Dui (Valley) below
兌下
Dui Xia

Moon/Yin Image

The Prediction (彖, Tuan)

Opposition:
Small affairs. Auspicious. 睽.小事吉.

Always show kindness to those less fortunate. Even though fire burns upward and water flows downward, and each opposes the other, they both maintain a like intention of natural order. So even in small matters, if opposites operate like this it will be auspicious. Take small steps so not to offend others and then the obstacle can be overcome. Understand that your opposition is just one end or side of the entire situation.

The Lines (爻, Yao)

First Nine (初 九, Chu Jiu)
Regret vanishes. Losing the horses,   悔亡.喪馬勿逐.
but no need to search for them.   自復.見惡人.无咎.
They will return of themselves.
Bad people are seen. Without fault.

All worries and regrets are gone as the missing horses have been returned without having to search for them. Even if bad-intentioned people appear there will be no trouble. Reconciliation can never be accomplished through force, and is pointless to try.

Second Nine (九 二, Jiu Er)
Meeting the master in a side passage.   遇主于巷.无咎.
Without fault.

You meet your master in the back streets while conducting your daily business and he advises you to compromise. Nothing unfavorable occurs from this meeting or advice.

Third Six (六三, Liu San)

Seeing their carriage pulled back and the oxen stopped. The head is shaved and the nose is cut off. No good beginning, but having a good end.

見輿曳其牛掣.
其人天且劓.
无初有終.

You happen upon a cart carrying goods, and the ox pulling the cart raises his horns at you. The driver is a man whose head is shaved and tattooed and his nose has been cut off as punishment for a past crime. This shows a terrible start of things, but the end is not all that bad.

Fourth Nine (九四, Jiu Si)

Solitary Opposition. Meeting with the Great Sage. There is sincere communication. Without fault.

睽孤. 遇元夫.
交孚. 厲无咎.

Leaving home and walking alone you come across a man whose feet are bound. At first it appears strange and dangerous, but it turns out there is nothing unusual or dangerous at all. A knowing person appears and explains the situation.

Fifth Six (六五, Liu Wu)

Regret vanishes. Chewing skin for their ancestors. What fault is there in going?

悔亡. 厥宗噬膚.
往何咎.

All regrets and worries are gone. People of the same family are eating meat at a feast in honor of their ancestors. You question yourself about joining them and sharing in the feast. There is no error in meeting with kindred spirits.

Topmost Nine (上九, Shang Jiu)

Solitary Opposition. Seeing pigs enduring the mud. The cart is full of ghosts. First drawing the bow, then later he unbends it. Not a robber, but takes a marriageable maiden. In moving, one meets a gentle rain. Auspicious.

睽孤. 見豕負塗.
載鬼. 一車.
先張之弧.
後說之弧.
匪寇婚媾.
往遇雨. 則吉.

Leaving home alone you see some pigs whose backs are smeared in mud and a cart full of people who look ghostly. This first alarms you and you pull up your bow to shoot, but they immediately greet you cheerfully. You offer them wine when you discover they are not ghosts or robbers, rather suitors returning women who were captured from the village back home. When you turn to look at the women, it begins to rain. The pigs and cart are then all cleaned, and this is an omen of auspiciousness.

Alternate English Translations for the Hexagram of Kui, 睽

The Symbol of Strangeness and Disunion [S]
Opposition [L] [WB]
The Estranged, Opposites [B]
Opposition (Estrangement) [CS]
Diverging [K]

Diversity [H]
Opposition—Disharmony [N]
Polarizing [RS]
Disharmony [C]
The Symbol of Opposition [CC]

The Great Symbolism (大象, Da Xiang) says,

Fire above and below a Marsh. This is Kui.
In showing deference, the superior person,
according with this, maintains fellowship.

上火下澤. 睽.
君子以同而異.

Sexagenary Placement

Heavenly Stem: Jia 甲 (1st Stem, Yang)—**Wood** (木, Mu)
Earthly Branch: Yin 寅 (3rd Branch, Yang)—**Tiger** (虎, Hu)
Represents the *Year of the Wood Tiger* (51st Year of the Sixty-Year Cycle)
Years: 1854 – 1914 – 1974 – 2034

Trigram Correlations

Upper Gua (Fire)

Li 離

Represents: Fire, Lightning, Sun, Middle Daughter
Actions: Clinging, Illuminating, Congregating
Influences: Fame, Reputation, Brightness, Elegance
Shape: Triangle **Color:** Red
Body: Eyes **Season:** Spring (Spring Equinox)
Moon Phase: Last Quarter
Animals: Earthly Rooster, Celestial Green Dragon
Directions: East (BH), South (AH)
Nine Palaces Numbers: Fu Xi: **8**
  Yu the Great: Ho River Map, **3**—Lo River Script, **9**
Internal Alchemy: Mercury, Qi
  Qi Center: Jiang Gong (Crimson Palace)
  Qi Meridian: Dai Mai (Belt Vessel)

Lower Gua (Valley)

☱ **Dui** 兑 **Represents:** Valley, River, Lake/Marsh, Youngest Daughter
Actions: Joyous, Opening, Stimulating
Influences: Family, Future, Collecting, Pleasure, Absorbing, Complacency.
Shape: Introverted Triangle   **Color:** Brown
Body: Mouth   **Season:** Beginning Spring
Moon Phase: Waning Gibbous
Animals: Earthly Goat, Celestial Great Roc
Directions: Southeast (BH), West (AH)
Nine Palaces Numbers: Fu Xi: 5
  Yu the Great: Ho River Map, 4—Lo River Script, 7
Internal Alchemy: Po (Earthly) Spirit
  Qi Center: Xuan Guan (Mysterious Pass)
  Qi Meridian: Yang Wei Mai (Yang Preserving Vessel)

Associated Developed Hexagrams of Kui

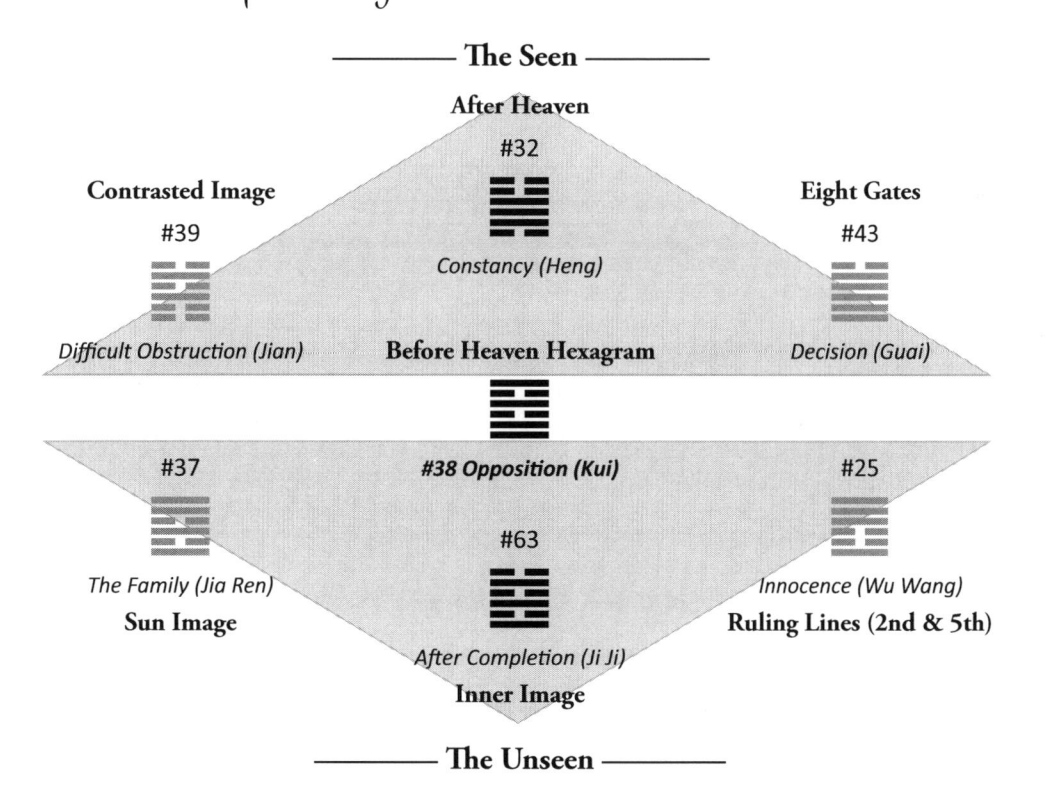

───── **The Seen** ─────

After Heaven
#32
Constancy (Heng)

Contrasted Image
#39
Difficult Obstruction (Jian)

Eight Gates
#43
Decision (Guai)

Before Heaven Hexagram

#38 Opposition (Kui)

#37
The Family (Jia Ren)
Sun Image

#63
After Completion (Ji Ji)
Inner Image

#25
Innocence (Wu Wang)
Ruling Lines (2nd & 5th)

───── **The Unseen** ─────

Jian

蹇

Difficult Obstruction

39

Kan (Water) above
坎 上
Kan Shang
Gen (Mountain) below
艮 下
Gen Xia

Sun/Yang Image

The Prediction (彖, Tuan)

Difficult Obstruction:
There is advantage in the Southwest.
No advantage in the Northeast.
Advantage in seeing an elder.
Being resolute is auspicious.

蹇. 利西南. 不利東北.
利見大人. 貞吉.

This image advises to look first and apply caution before making any great leap. Surrounded by hardships and difficulties, take pause, reflect, and seek out solutions. Associations with the Southwest (Xun, Wind) are most favorable, but those from the Northeast (Zhen, Thunder) are unfavorable. Seek advice from a person of wisdom and then plan for the future.

The Lines (爻, Yao)

First Six (初 六, Chu Liu)
Going leads to Difficult Obstruction.
Arriving meets praise.

往蹇. 來譽.

There will be hardships in going to a destination, but honors will be bestowed when returning. When going do not be hasty; when returning be still.

Second Six (六 二, Liu Er)
The king's minister meets Difficult
Obstruction upon Difficult Obstruction.
Not your own cause.

王臣蹇蹇. 匪躬之故.

Those in power and influence over the situation are experiencing many obstructions, but this is not caused by you.

#39 Difficult Obrstruction (Jian)

Third Nine (九 三, Jiu San)
Moving is Difficult Obstruction, 　　　　往 蹇 來 反.
both in arriving and returning.

There are too many obstructions and difficulties in going forward, or in returning. Trying to force a solution will only bring more danger.

Fourth Six (六 四, Liu Si)
Moving is Difficult Obstruction, 　　　　往 蹇 來 連
but arriving is union.

Too many obstructions and difficulties in going forward all alone, but if you return and wait, someone will support and join you in your struggle.

Fifth Nine (九 五, Jiu Wu)
Meeting great Difficult Obstruction, 　　　大 蹇 朋 來.
but friends arrive.

When hardships and difficulties are met, you show great personal courage, attracting friends to come to your aid.

Topmost Six (上 六, Shang Liu)
Moving is Difficult Obstruction, 　　　　往 蹇 來 碩. 吉.
but coming back meets with greatness. 　　利 見 大 人.
Auspicious. Advantage in seeing an elder.

Many difficulties and obstructions have been met, but great wealth and honors are brought back. The situation is very auspicious, but it is still important to acquire the counsel of a wise person.

Alternate English Translations for the Hexagram of Jian, 蹇

The Symbol of Difficulty [S]　　　　　　*Halting (Trouble)* [C]
Obstruction [L] [N] [WB]　　　　　　　*Hardship* [H]
Trouble [B]　　　　　　　　　　　　　*Limping* [RS]
Impediments [CS]　　　　　　　　　　*Difficult/Limping* [K]
The Symbol of Difficulty [CC]

The Great Symbolism (大象, Da Xiang) says,

Above the Mountain there is Water. 　　山上有水. 蹇.
This is Jian. Superior persons, 　　君子以反身修德.
according with this, turn themselves
around to cultivate their virtue.

Sexagenary Placement

Heavenly Stem: Jia 甲 (1st Stem, Yang)—**Wood** (木, Mu)
Earthly Branch: Shen 申 (9th Branch, Yang)—**Monkey** (猴, Hou)
Represents the *Year of the Wood Monkey* (21st Year of the Sixty-Year Cycle)
Years: 1884 – 1944 – 2004 – 2064

Trigram Correlations

Upper Gua (Water)

Kan 坎 　　**Represents:** Water, Moon, Springs/Streams, Middle Son
Actions: Peril, Danger, and Difficulty.
Influences: Abysmal Life Path and Vocation
Shape: Wave　　　　　　**Color:** Black
Body: Ears　　　　　　　**Season:** Autumn (Autumn Equinox)
Moon Phase: First Quarter
Animals: Earthly Pig, Celestial White Tiger
Directions: West (BH), North (AH)
Nine Palaces Numbers: Fu Xi: 4
　　Yu the Great: Ho River Map, 7—Lo River Script, 1
Internal Alchemy: Essence, Jing, Lead
　　Qi Center: Shuang Guan (Double Pass)
　　Qi Meridian: Chong Mai (Penetrating Vessel)

#39 Difficult Obstruction (Jian)

Lower Gua (Mountain)

☶ **Gen** 艮
- **Represents:** Mountain, Towers, Youngest Son
- **Actions:** Stillness, Binding, Stopping
- **Influences:** Knowledge, Wisdom, Skill, Determination
- **Shape:** Vertical Column   **Color:** Blue
- **Body:** Hands and arms   **Season:** Beginning Autumn
- **Moon Phase:** Waxing Crescent
- **Animals:** Earthly Dog, Celestial Vermilion Snake
- **Directions:** Northwest (BH), Northeast (AH)
- **Nine Palaces Numbers:** Fu Xi: 7
  Yu the Great: Ho River Map, **6**— Lo River Script, **8**
- **Internal Alchemy:** Hun (Heavenly) Spirit
  Qi Center: Jing Men (Essence Gate)
  Qi Meridian: Yang Qiao Mai (Yang Heel Vessel)

Associated Developed Hexagrams of Jian

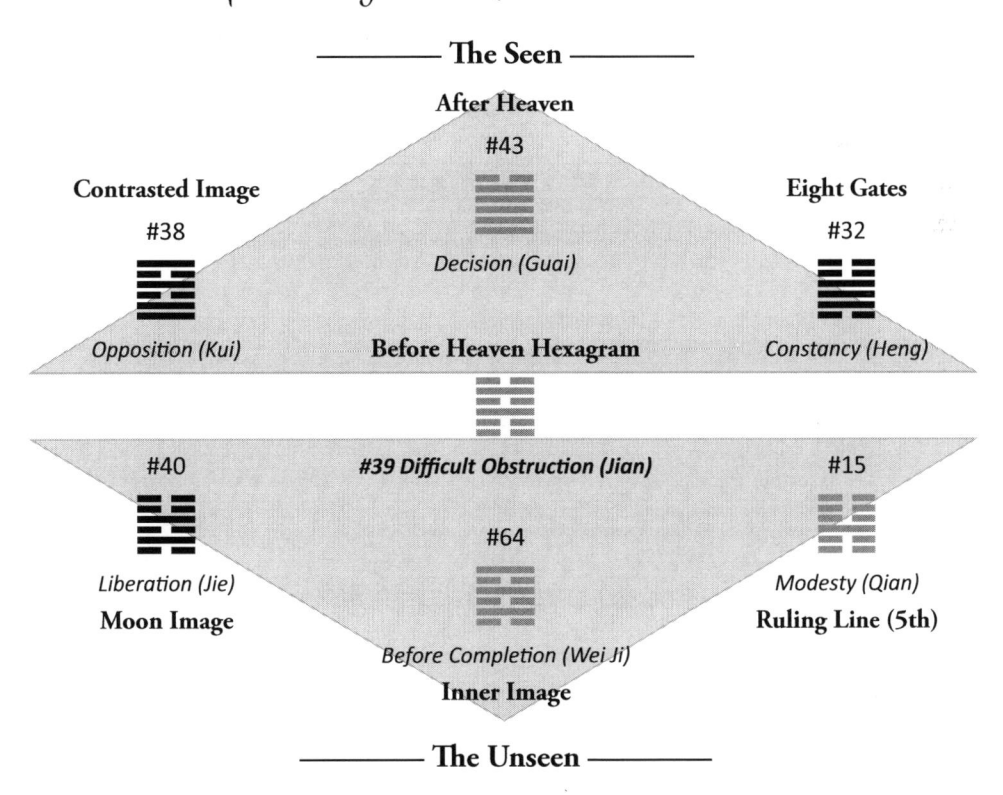

───── **The Seen** ─────

After Heaven
#43
Decision (Guai)

Contrasted Image
#38
Opposition (Kui)

Before Heaven Hexagram

Eight Gates
#32
Constancy (Heng)

#39 Difficult Obstruction (Jian)

#40
Liberation (Jie)
Moon Image

#64
Before Completion (Wei Ji)
Inner Image

#15
Modesty (Qian)
Ruling Line (5th)

───── **The Unseen** ─────

Jie

解

Liberation

40

Zhen (Thunder) above
震上
Zhen Shang
Kan (Water) below
坎下
Kan Xia

Moon/Yin Image

The Prediction (彖, Tuan)

Liberation:
There is advantage in the Southwest. 解.利西南.
Going nowhere. One's own returning 无所往.其來復吉.
is auspicious. Have somewhere to go. 有攸往.夙吉.
Early morning is auspicious.

This image shows that one must forgive him or herself for past errors and forget about them. Liberation is about taking on the tasks of problem solving. Things associated with the Southwest (Xun, Wind) are favorable, so avoid going in other directions. Problems are beginning to ease, but this is no time to celebrate. It's best if you return to a simple and normal life, and take care of all the loose ends in your life. In going, understand you must return from where you started. This is auspicious. If deciding to leave again, it is most auspicious if you begin the journey early in the morning.

The Lines (爻, Yao)

First Six (初 六, Chu Liu)
Without fault. 无咎.

No errors or mistakes are being made. All troubles are past and you should express gratitude.

Second Nine (九 二, Jiu Er)
Hunting three foxes in the field. 田獲三狐.
Receives yellow arrows. Being resolute 得黄失.貞吉.
is auspicious.

Three foxes are caught in the hunting fields. Gold-plated bronze arrowheads are found in their bodies—a very auspicious omen. Now is the time to keep to the Middle Way.

#40 Liberation (Jie)

Third Six (六三, Liu San)
Burdened, yet riding. The carriage is attacked by robbers. Being resolute brings regret.

負且乘. 致寇至. 貞吝.

You have filled your cart with goods and set off to move them. This, however, has attracted the attention of robbers who then ambush you on the road. So, do not be determined in transporting the goods, otherwise great trouble results. Best to remain humble and protect your good fortune.

Fourth Nine (九四, Jiu Si)
Liberation in the great toe. Friends arrive and then there is sincerity.

解而拇. 朋至斯孚.

Your big toes were bound but are now untied, but it is still too late as the robbers have already taken your goods. Friends come to help, but you must get rid of bad friends as their bad habits only bind you. Keep close with good friends as they are liberating.

Fifth Six (六五, Liu Wu)
The wise person was entangled, but receives Liberation. Auspicious. There is sincerity in the inferior person.

君子維有解. 吉.
有孚于小人.

The wise person was bound by the robbers and then freed by friends. This is auspicious because the wise person then captures the robbers.

Topmost Six (上六, Shang Liu)
The duke shoots at a hawk on top of a high wall, hits it, and everything is of advantage.

公用射隼于高墉之上.
獲之无不利.

The leader draws a bow and shoots at a hawk sitting high upon the city wall and the arrow hits the hawk. This is auspicious. It shows a leader removing inferior influences through force.

Alternate English Translations for the Hexagram of Jie, 解

The Symbol of Loosening [S]
Deliverance [WB]
Release [B]
Deliverance (Release, Clarification) [CS]
Liberation (Solution) [C]
The Symbol of Deliverance [CC]

Relief [H]
Dissolution of the Problem [N]
Unraveling [RS]
Liberation [L]
Loosening/Deliverance [K]

The Great Symbolism (大象, Da Xiang) says,

The workings of Thunder and Rain. This is Jie.	雷雨作.解.
The superior person, according with this, pardons transgressions and is lenient in dealing with crimes.	君子以赦 過宥罪.

Sexagenary Placement

Heavenly Stem: Geng 庚 (7th Stem, Yang)—**Metal** (金, Jin)
Earthly Branch: Zi 子 (1st Branch, Yang)—**Rat** (鼠, Shu)
Represents the *Year of the Metal Rat* (37th Year of the Sixty-Year Cycle)
Years: 1900 – 1960 – 2020 – 2080

Trigram Correlations

Upper Gua (Thunder)

Zhen 震   **Represents:** Thunder, Earthquake, Eldest Son
Actions: Arousing, Shaking, Initiating
Influences: Foundations, Past Actions, Excitement.
Shape: Vertical Column   **Color:** Green
Body: Feet and legs   **Season:** Beginning Winter
Moon Phase: Waning Crescent
Animals: Earthly Dragons, Celestial Dragon-Horse
Directions: Northeast (BH), East (AH)
Nine Palaces Numbers: Fu Xi: **3**
    Yu the Great: *Ho River Map,* **8**—*Lo River Script,* **3**
Internal Alchemy: Mind-Intention
    Qi Center: Dan Tian (Elixir Field)
    Qi Meridian: Yin Qiao Mai (Yin Heel Vessel)

#40 Liberation (Jie)

Lower Gua (Water)

☵ **Kan** 坎
Represents: Water, Moon, Springs/Streams, Middle Son
Actions: Peril, Danger, and Difficulty.
Influences: Abysmal Life Path and Vocation
Shape: Wave   **Color:** Black
Body: Ears   **Season:** Autumn (Autumn Equinox)
Moon Phase: First Quarter
Animals: Earthly Pig, Celestial White Tiger
Directions: West (BH), North (AH)
Nine Palaces Numbers: Fu Xi: 4
   Yu the Great: Ho River Map, 7—Lo River Script, 1
Internal Alchemy: Essence, Jing, Lead
   Qi Center: Shuang Guan (Double Pass)
   Qi Meridian: Chong Mai (Penetrating Vessel)

Associated Developed Hexagrams of Jie

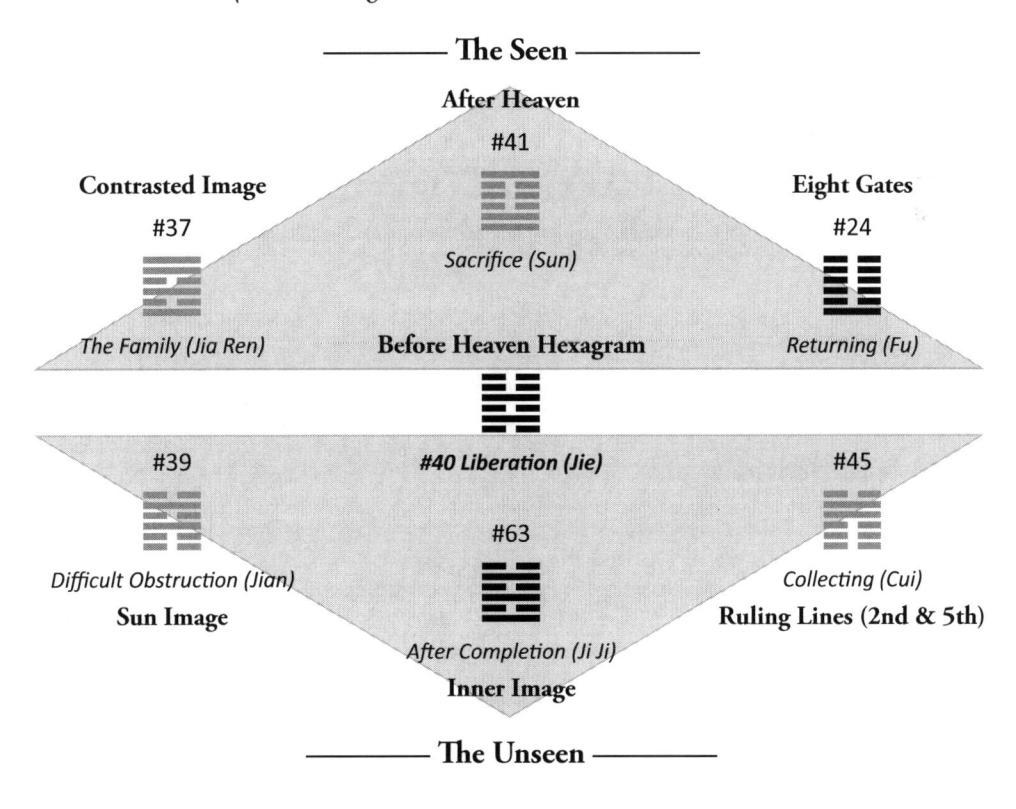

——— **The Seen** ———

After Heaven
#41
Sacrifice (Sun)

Contrasted Image
#37
The Family (Jia Ren)

Eight Gates
#24
Returning (Fu)

Before Heaven Hexagram
#40 Liberation (Jie)

#39
Difficult Obstruction (Jian)
Sun Image

#63
After Completion (Ji Ji)
Inner Image

#45
Collecting (Cui)
Ruling Lines (2nd & 5th)

——— **The Unseen** ———

Sun 損

Sacrifice

41

Gen (Mountain) above
艮上
Gen Shang
Dui (Valley) below
兌下
Dui Xia

Sun/Yang Image

The Prediction (彖, Tuan)

Sacrifice:
Having sincerity. Great auspiciousness.
Without fault if able to be resolute.
Advantage in having somewhere to go.
How is it to be employed? Use of two
bamboo baskets filled with grain
for the sacrifice.

損.有孚.元吉.无咎可貞.
利有攸往.曷之用.
二簋可用享.

The greatest sacrifice and charity begins within the home. Those who are against you have been restrained and everything is auspicious with no mistakes made from the very beginning. This situation demands restraint, discipline, and simplicity. Refrain from any expression of anger to strengthen your inner fortitude. This is a good time to plan for the future and move forward. When making a sacrifice to the spirits, offer two containers of food.

The Lines (爻, Yao)

First Nine (初九, Chu Jiu)
Private affairs are hurried. Without fault.
Sacrifice is deliberate.

已事遄往.无咎.酌損之.

Be reverent and solemn when offering sacrifices within the ceremony, yet do not delay making the sacrifices. No errors have been made, but be frugal in conduct. Help is offered, but none of this is beyond your own strengths.

#41 Sacrifice (Sun)

Second Nine (九二, Jiu Er)
Advantage in being resolute.
Action is unfortunate.
Increasing is not Sacrifice.

利貞.征凶.弗損益之.

Travel is dangerous. Make offerings of expenditures intended for travels, then funds can be further increased.

Third Six (六三, Liu San)
Three people walking. Sacrifice
by one person. The lone person
will find a companion.

三人行.則損一人.
一人行.則得其友.

Three people head out on a journey, but one will leave the group during the journey. The person who leaves will find a companion.

Fourth Six (六四, Liu Si)
Sacrifice of one's own illness. To cause
a hastening has joy. Without fault.

損其疾.使遄有喜.无咎.

If finding a good treatment when falling ill, the recovery will be quick. No errors are made.

Fifth Six (六五, Liu Wu)
Given an increase. Ten pairs
of tortoise shells. Incapable of refusing.
Great auspiciousness.

或益之.十朋之龜.
弗克違.元吉.

Someone has given you ten pairs of tortoise shells for divining your future. Worth ten strings of cash, this gift cannot be refused because it creates an opening for further good fortune.

Topmost Nine (上九, Shang Jiu)
Increasing without Sacrifice. Without fault.
Being resolute is auspicious. There is
advantage in having somewhere to go.
Acquire a minister who is without a clan.

弗損益之.无咎.貞吉.
利有攸往.得臣无家.

Nothing bad is in this situation as it portends good fortune, especially if savings are augmented. Develop your prospects by moving forward, and seek out a hardworking and honest person to handle your affairs.

Alternate English Translations for the Hexagram of Sun, 損

The Symbol of Lessening [S]
Decrease [L] [WB]
Loss, Reduction [B]
Decrease (Loss) [CS]
The Symbol of Diminution [CC]

Reduction [C]
Decreasing [H]
Sacrifice—Decrease [N]
Diminishing [K] [RS]

The Great Symbolism (大象, Da Xiang) says,

Below the Mountain there is a Marsh. 　　山下有澤. 損.
This is Sun. The superior person, according 　君子以懲忿窒欲.
with this, controls anger and restrains desires.

Sexagenary Placement

Heavenly Stem: Xin 辛 (8th Stem, Yin)—**Metal** (金, Jin)
Earthly Branch: Mao 卯 (4th Branch, Yin)—**Rabbit** (兔, Tu)
Represents the *Year of the Metal Rabbit* (28th Year of the Sixty-Year Cycle)
Years: 1891 – 1951 – 2011 – 2071

Trigram Correlations

Upper Gua (Mountain)

Gen 艮　　**Represents:** Mountain, Towers, Youngest Son
Actions: Stillness, Binding, Stopping
Influences: Knowledge, Wisdom, Skill, Determination
Shape: Vertical Column　　**Color:** Blue
Body: Hands and arms　　**Season:** Beginning Autumn
Moon Phase: Waxing Crescent
Animals: Earthly Dog, Celestial Vermilion Snake
Directions: Northwest (BH), Northeast (AH)
Nine Palaces Numbers: Fu Xi: 7
　　Yu the Great: Ho River Map, **6**— Lo River Script, **8**
Internal Alchemy: Hun (Heavenly) Spirit
　　Qi Center: Jing Men (Essence Gate)
　　Qi Meridian: Yang Qiao Mai (Yang Heel Vessel)

#41 Sacrifice (Sun)

Lower Gua (Valley)

Dui 兌

Represents: Valley, River, Lake/Marsh, Youngest Daughter
Actions: Joyous, Opening, Stimulating
Influences: Family, Future, Collecting, Pleasure, Absorbing, Complacency.
Shape: Introverted Triangle   **Color:** Brown
Body: Mouth   **Season:** Beginning Spring
Moon Phase: Waning Gibbous
Animals: Earthly Goat, Celestial Great Roc
Directions: Southeast (BH), West (AH)
Nine Palaces Numbers: Fu Xi: 5
    Yu the Great: Ho River Map, 4—Lo River Script, 7
Internal Alchemy: Po (Earthly) Spirit
    Qi Center: Xuan Guan (Mysterious Pass)
    Qi Meridian: Yang Wei Mai (Yang Preserving Vessel)

Associated Developed Hexagrams of Sun

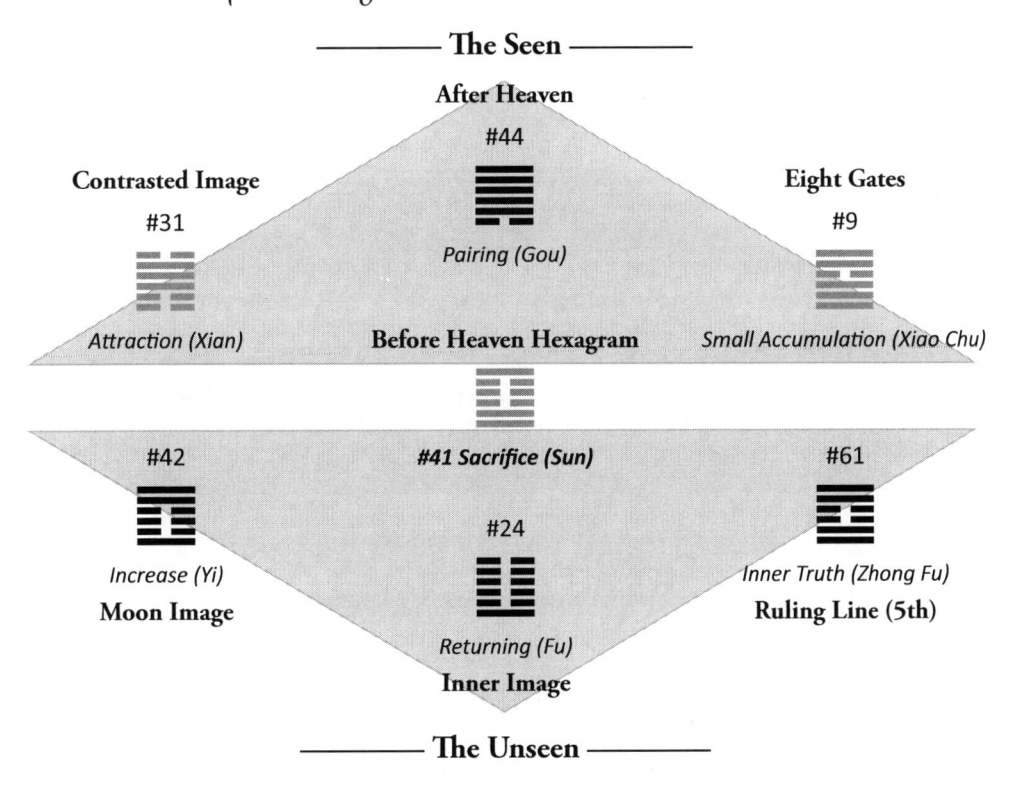

The Seen

After Heaven
#44
Pairing (Gou)

Contrasted Image
#31
Attraction (Xian)

Eight Gates
#9
Small Accumulation (Xiao Chu)

Before Heaven Hexagram

#42
Increase (Yi)
Moon Image

#41 Sacrifice (Sun)

#24
Returning (Fu)
Inner Image

#61
Inner Truth (Zhong Fu)
Ruling Line (5th)

The Unseen

Yi

益

Increase

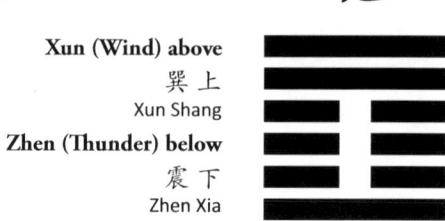

42

Xun (Wind) above
巽上
Xun Shang
Zhen (Thunder) below
震下
Zhen Xia

Moon/Yin Image

The Prediction (彖, Tuan)

Increase:
Advantage in having somewhere to go.
Advantage in fording the great stream.

益. 利有攸往. 利涉大川.

This image is revealing that fate has taken your side, and there's an increase in your life and wealth. The image of Thunder properly moves to influence Wind, so it is a time of progress and development. Do not waste this opportune time while it lasts. Equally consider the needs of others and help where and when you can. There is benefit in having somewhere to travel, particularly in crossing over a great waterway.

The Lines (爻, Yao)

First Nine (初 九, Chu Jiu)
Advantage in undertaking a great doing.
Great auspiciousness. Without fault.

利用為大作. 元吉. 无咎.

This is a very opportune time to display and make use of your skills and talents. Just do not give way to selfishness. No errors are made, everything is auspicious from the beginning.

Second Six (六 二, Liu Er)
Perhaps given an increase of ten pairs
of tortoise shells. Incapable of refusing.
Perpetual resoluteness is auspicious.
The king makes offerings to the
supreme ruler. Auspicious.

或益之十朋之龜.
弗克違. 永貞吉.
王用亨于帝. 吉.

You receive ten pairs of tortoise shells for divining your future. This gift creates an opening for long-term good fortune. A leader making an offering or sacrifice to the highest ruler is very auspicious.

Third Six (六 三, Liu San)
Using the affairs of misfortune for Increase.   益之用凶事.无咎.
Without fault. Acting on sincerity from   有孚中行.告公用圭.
within. Announces publicly those
to be employed to officiate the records.

There is no error in using the increase of wealth to take care of situations of misfortune. Those scheming against you have been restrained. Keep to the Middle Way and offer reports to the leader while holding a jade tablet (a symbol of respect and authority) in front of your chest.

Fourth Six (六 四, Liu Si)
Acting from within. Advises the duke to comply.   中行.告公從.
There is advantage in using trust when the   利用為依遷國.
movement is to re-establish the capital.

Keep to the Middle Way and report to the leader through the closest subordinates. You can only hope the leader will listen to your suggestions and find you trustworthy. This is a good time to move to the capital of the kingdom (move to a new home or change your place of business).

Fifth Nine (九 五, Jiu Wu)
Possessing sincerity and kindness of the   有孚惠心.勿問元吉.
heart. Without question, great auspiciousness.   有孚惠我德.
Possessing sincerity and kindness is my virtue.

To those who scheme against you, offer comfort. Do not punish them for their transgressions, because later they will repay you through acts of kindness and goodwill.

Topmost Nine (上 九, Shang Jiu)
No Increase. Others attack.   莫益之.或擊之.
Not constant in the regulation   立心勿恆.凶.
of the heart. Misfortune.

You have received no income and have suffered even further misfortunes. This is because you did not share your increase in wealth. None of your ambitions can be pursued and the entire situation is ominous.

Alternate English Translations for the Hexagram of Yi, 益

The Symbol of Addition [S]   *Increasing* [H]
Increase [C] [L] [WB]   *Benefit—Increase* [N]
Gain [B]   *Augmenting* [K] [RS]
Increase (Gain) [CS]   *The Symbol of Addition* [CC]

The Great Symbolism (大象, Da Xiang) says,

Wind and Thunder. This is Yi. 　風雷.益.
The superior person, according with 　君子以見善則遷.
this, seeing the good, moves toward it, 　有過則改.
and if having faults, reforms.

☷ Sexagenary Placement

Heavenly Stem: Gui 癸 (10th Stem, Yin)—**Water** (水, Shui)
Earthly Branch: Si 巳 (6th Branch, Yin)—**Snake** (蛇, She)
Represents the *Year of the Water Snake* (30th Year of the Sixty-Year Cycle)
Years: 1893 – 1953 – 2013 – 2073

Trigram Correlations

Upper Gua (Wind)

☴ **Xun** 巽   **Represents:** Wind, Wood, Eldest Daughter
Actions: Gentleness, Grounding, Penetrating, Spreading
Influences: Prosperity, Abundance, Wealth
Shape: Rectangle   **Color:** Purple
Body: Waist and hips   **Season:** Beginning Summer
Moon Phase: Waxing Gibbous
Animals: Earthly Fowl, Celestial Golden Rooster
Directions: Southwest (BH), Southeast (AH)
Nine Palaces Numbers: Fu Xi: **9**
　　Yu the Great: Ho River Map, **2**—Lo River Script, **4**
Internal Alchemy: Breath and Mobilizing Qi
　　Qi Center: Yu Zhen (Jade Pillow)
　　Qi Meridian: Yin Wei Mai (Yin Preserving Vessel)

#42 Increase (Yi)

Lower Gua (Thunder)

Zhen 震

Represents: Thunder, Earthquake, Eldest Son
Actions: Arousing, Shaking, Initiating
Influences: Foundations, Past Actions, Excitement.
Shape: Vertical Column **Color:** Green
Body: Feet and legs **Season:** Beginning Winter
Moon Phase: Waning Crescent
Animals: Earthly Dragons, Celestial Dragon-Horse
Directions: Northeast (BH), East (AH)
Nine Palaces Numbers: Fu Xi: 3
 Yu the Great: Ho River Map, 8—Lo River Script, 3
Internal Alchemy: Mind-Intention
 Qi Center: Dan Tian (Elixir Field)
 Qi Meridian: Yin Qiao Mai (Yin Heel Vessel)

Associated Developed Hexagrams of Yi

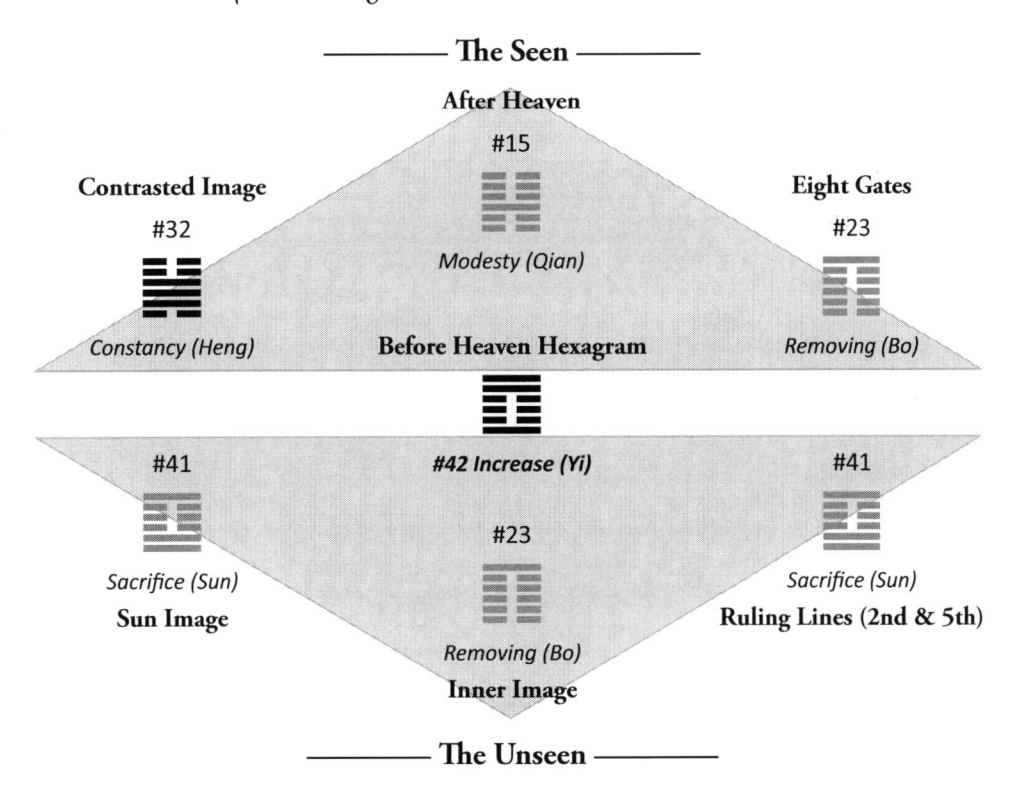

——— **The Seen** ———

After Heaven
#15
Modesty (Qian)

Contrasted Image
#32
Constancy (Heng)

Eight Gates
#23
Removing (Bo)

Before Heaven Hexagram

#42 Increase (Yi)

#23
Removing (Bo)
Inner Image

#41
Sacrifice (Sun)
Sun Image

#41
Sacrifice (Sun)
Ruling Lines (2nd & 5th)

——— **The Unseen** ———

Guai

夬

Decision

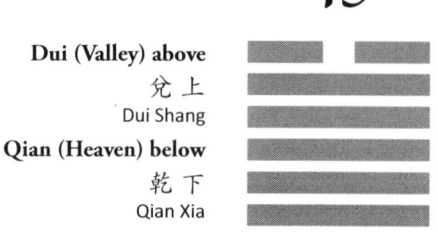

43

Dui (Valley) above
兌 上
Dui Shang

Qian (Heaven) below
乾 下
Qian Xia

Sun/Yang Image

The Prediction (彖, Tuan)

Decision:
Praising the king at the royal court. Acting sincere has danger. It is announced to the city. No advantage in going to arms. Advantage in having somewhere to go.

夬．揚于王庭．孚號有厲．
告自邑．不利即戎．
利有攸往．

This image advises to avoid indulging in petty desires and self interests. Just be open and honest. A decision has been made in the royal court and the present danger has been announced by warning all the people. There is no good end in applying force to this situation, so it's better to use diplomacy and peaceful measures.

The Lines (爻, Yao)

First Nine (初 九, Chu Jiu)
Strength in advancing the toes.
Moving forward, but not superior,
and a cause for fault.

壯于前趾．往不勝為咎．

You were too confident about your footing when moving forward and so you were not successful because of your mistakes. This shows you took on a project that was beyond your capabilities.

Second Nine (九 二, Jiu Er)
Showing alarm. In the darkness of the night people go to arms. There will be no pity.

惕號．莫夜有戎．勿恤．

You are showing alarm and shout out to everyone, "A fight will happen tonight," but the attackers show no pity or remorse for their cruel actions. This shows you must anticipate the danger of this situation and be cautious in your reactions.

Third Nine (九 三, Jiu San)

Strength in the face, there is misfortune.	壯于頄.有凶.君子夬夬.
The wise person chooses to depart. In solitary action there is a meeting with a gentle rain. Getting wet and becoming indignant. Without fault.	獨行遇雨.苦濡有慍.无咎.

The face has been injured and this is a bad omen. It seems everyone has misunderstood you and so you feel hurt. You determine to leave and go it alone, but then get caught in the rain. Your clothes are soaked and you get angry. Yet, no real mistakes are being made.

Fourth Nine (九 四, Jiu Si)

The buttock is without flesh, so your walking is hesitant. The sheep are led about, regrets vanish. Hearing these words, they will not be believed.	臀无膚.其行次且. 牽羊悔亡.聞言不信.

The buttocks has been badly injured and so movement is difficult. There is regret about having led the sheep, but soon the regrets vanish. When others hear your story, they do not believe you because they witnessed your obstinate behavior and so their ears are deafened to your explanation.

Fifth Nine (九 五, Jiu Wu).

Edible greens in dry soil need to be uprooted. Acting in the middle is without fault.	莧陸夬夬.中行无咎.

The plants are not weeds but edible greens and so should be used before they wither. There is no error in following the Middle Way.

Topmost Six (上 六, Shang Liu)

No more making appeals. There is misfortune.	无號.終有凶.

The shouting and screaming has finally ended, but there is still misfortune. With victory there always follows a defeat.

Alternate English Translations for the Hexagram of Guai, 夬

The Symbol of Decision [S]
Break-through (Resolution) [WB]
Resolution [B] [N]
Resoluteness (Removal) [CS]
The Symbol of Resoluteness [CC]

Parting [C] [RS]
Eliminating [H]
Determination [L]
Deciding/Parting [K]

The Great Symbolism (大象, Da Xiang) says,

A Marsh above in Heaven. This is Guai. Superior persons, according with this, bestow prosperity and extend it to all those below them, and avoid dwelling on their own virtue.

澤上於天. 夬.
君子以施祿及下.
居德則忌.

Sexagenary Placement

Heavenly Stem: Ren 壬 (9th Stem, Yang)—**Water** (水, Shui)
Earthly Branch: Xu 戌 (11th Branch, Yang)—**Dog** (狗, Gou)
Represents the *Year of the Water Dog* (59th Year of the Sixty-Year Cycle)
Years: 1862 – 1922 – 1982 – 2042

Trigram Correlations

Upper Gua (Valley)

Dui 兑 **Represents:** Valley, River, Lake/Marsh, Youngest Daughter
Actions: Joyous, Opening, Stimulating
Influences: Family, Future, Collecting, Pleasure, Absorbing, Complacency.
Shape: Introverted Triangle   **Color:** Brown
Body: Mouth   **Season:** Beginning Spring
Moon Phase: Waning Gibbous
Animals: Earthly Goat, Celestial Great Roc
Directions: Southeast (BH), West (AH)
Nine Palaces Numbers: Fu Xi: 5
    Yu the Great: Ho River Map, 4—Lo River Script, 7
Internal Alchemy: Po (Earthly) Spirit

Qi Center: Xuan Guan (Mysterious Pass)
Qi Meridian: Yang Wei Mai (Yang Preserving Vessel)

Lower Gua (Heaven)

Qian 乾 **Represents:** Heaven, Sky, Male, Father, Emperor
Actions: Creative Principle, Persisting, Forceful
Influences: Blessings, Good Fortune, Strength, Spiritual Power
Shape: Circle **Color:** White
Body: Head **Season:** Summer (Summer Solstice)
Moon Phase: Full Moon
Animals: Earthly Horse, Celestial Red Phoenix
Directions: South (BH), Northwest (AH)
Nine Palaces Numbers: Fu Xi: 2
 Yu the Great: Ho River Map, 9—Lo River Script, 6
Internal Alchemy: Clarity, Illumination
 Qi Center: Ni Wan (Mud Pellet)
 Qi Meridian: Du Mai (Control Vessel)

Associated Developed Hexagrams of Guai

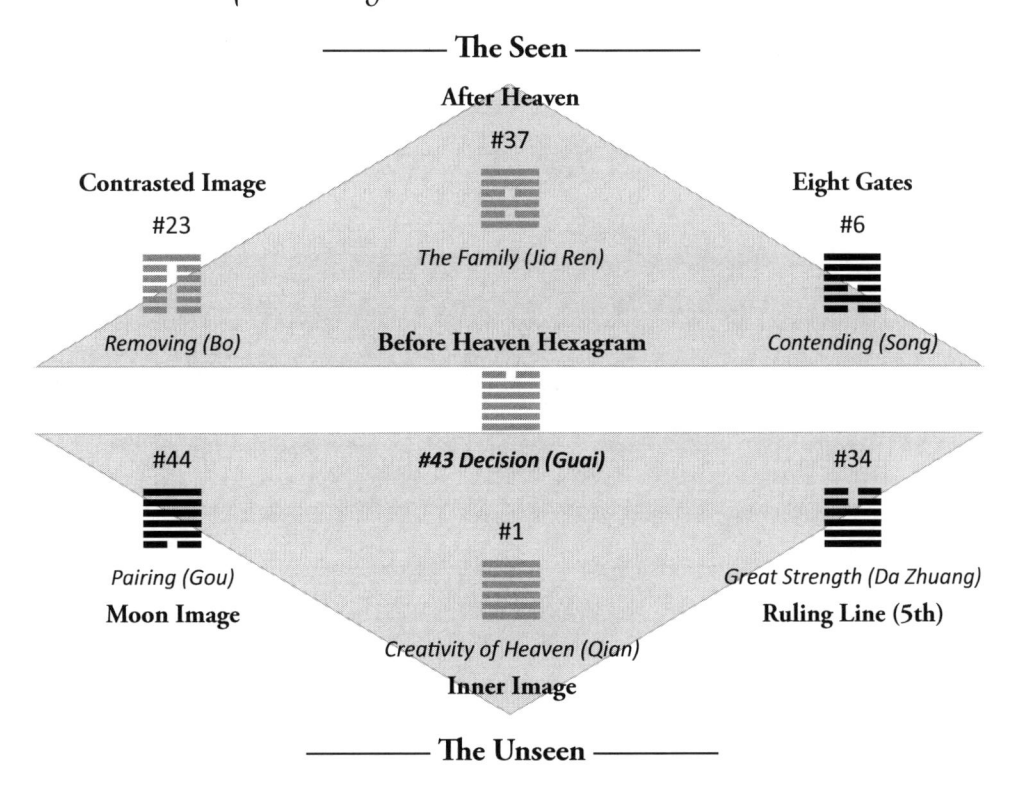

——— **The Seen** ———

After Heaven
#37

Contrasted Image **Eight Gates**
#23 #6

The Family (Jia Ren)

Removing (Bo) **Before Heaven Hexagram** *Contending (Song)*

#44 *#43 Decision (Guai)* #34

#1

Pairing (Gou) *Great Strength (Da Zhuang)*
Moon Image **Ruling Line (5th)**

Creativity of Heaven (Qian)
Inner Image

——— **The Unseen** ———

Gou 姤

Pairing   44

Qian (Heaven) above
乾上
Qian Shang
Xun (Wind) below
巽下
Xun Xia

Moon/Yin Image

The Prediction (彖, Tuan)

Pairing:
The female is strong, so there is no use in choosing the female.

姤. 女 壯. 勿 用 取 女.

This image indicates to apply reason and caution to the situation. Everything looks good on the surface, but underneath looms misfortune The female is stronger than you and very controlling, so do not choose her for marriage. Things that are yielding, like water, can likewise be very strong and unyielding.

The Lines (爻, Yao)

First Six (初 六, Chu Liu)
Fastened onto a metal drag. To be resolute is auspicious. Having somewhere to go, yet unfortunate signs will appear. A lean pig truly falters and wriggles.

繫于金. 貞吉. 有攸往.
見凶. 贏豕孚蹢躅.

To put on the brakes and halt your actions brings good fortune. If continuing to move on, an ominous omen appears, a wild pig running about erratically and squealing loudly. This shows that you should avoid and reject those who exhibit bad habits and behaviors.

Second Nine (九 二, Jiu Er)
Possessing a bundle of fish is without fault. No advantage for guests.

包有魚. 无咎. 不利賓.

There is no error in having fish in the kitchen, but the fish are not the kind suitable for serving to guests.

Third Nine (九三, Jiu San)
The buttock is without flesh, so walking is hesitant. Danger. No great fault.

臀无膚.其行次且.厲无大咎.

The buttocks has been injured and so movement is difficult and dangerous. Do not try to force things at this time, but nothing more will occur that could lead to misfortune.

Fourth Nine (九四, Jiu Si)
A bundle, but no fish. Misfortunes arise.

包无魚.起凶.

The basket is empty and so there are no fish in the kitchen. Misfortune will appear, as there is no means of support.

Fifth Nine (九五, Jiu Wu)
Melons beneath the willow tree. Restraint of qualities; benefit falls from Heaven.

以杞包瓜.含章.有隕自天.

The sprigs of a willow tree are covering ripe melons. Restrain from greed as these melons were placed there by Heaven. This shows you should regulate yourself and not interfere with the natural working of things.

Topmost Nine (上九, Shang Jiu)
Encountering their horns. Regret, but without fault.

姤其角.吝.无咎.

The horns become struck and this encounter brings regret. Being aloof has caused the conflict (encountering their horns) because others want to be recognized by you. But this is still no great disaster.

Alternate English Translations for the Hexagram of Gou, 姤

The Symbol of Meeting [S]
Coming to Meet [WB]
Contact (Relationships) [CS]
Contact (Sexual Intercourse, Meeting, Etc.) [B]
The Symbol of Coming to Meet [CC]

Encountering [H] [L]
Encounter—Meeting Together [N]
Coupling [K] [RS]
Meeting [C]

The Great Symbolism (大象, Da Xiang) says,

Beneath Heaven there is Wind. This is Gou. 　　天下有風. 姤. 后
The ruler, according with this, grants decrees 　以施命誥四方.
and proclaims them to the four directions.

䷍ Sexagenary Placement

Heavenly Stem: Geng 庚 (7th Stem, Yang)—**Metal** (金, Jin)
Earthly Branch: Xu 戌 (11th Branch, Yang)—**Dog** (狗, Gou)
Represents the *Year of the Metal Dog* (47th Year of the Sixty-Year Cycle)
Years: 1850 – 1910 – 1970 – 2030

Trigram Correlations

Upper Gua (Heaven)

☰ **Qian** 乾　　**Represents:** Heaven, Sky, Male, Father, Emperor
　　　　　　　Actions: Creative Principle, Persisting, Forceful
　　　　　　　Influences: Blessings, Good Fortune, Strength, Spiritual Power
　　　　　　　Shape: Circle　　　　　**Color:** White
　　　　　　　Body: Head　　　　　　**Season:** Summer (Summer Solstice)
　　　　　　　Moon Phase: Full Moon
　　　　　　　Animals: Earthly Horse, Celestial Red Phoenix
　　　　　　　Directions: South (BH), Northwest (AH)
　　　　　　　Nine Palaces Numbers: Fu Xi: **2**
　　　　　　　　　Yu the Great: Ho River Map, **9**—Lo River Script, **6**
　　　　　　　Internal Alchemy: Clarity, Illumination
　　　　　　　　　Qi Center: Ni Wan (Mud Pellet)
　　　　　　　　　Qi Meridian: Du Mai (Control Vessel)

Lower Gua (Wind)

☴ Xun 巽

Represents: Wind, Wood, Eldest Daughter
Actions: Gentleness, Grounding, Penetrating, Spreading
Influences: Prosperity, Abundance, Wealth
Shape: Rectangle   **Color:** Purple
Body: Waist and hips   **Season:** Beginning Summer
Moon Phase: Waxing Gibbous
Animals: Earthly Fowl, Celestial Golden Rooster
Directions: Southwest (BH), Southeast (AH)
Nine Palaces Numbers: Fu Xi: **9**
  Yu the Great: Ho River Map, **2**—Lo River Script, **4**
Internal Alchemy: Breath and Mobilizing Qi
  Qi Center: Yu Zhen (Jade Pillow)
  Qi Meridian: Yin Wei Mai (Yin Preserving Vessel)

Associated Developed Hexagrams of Gou

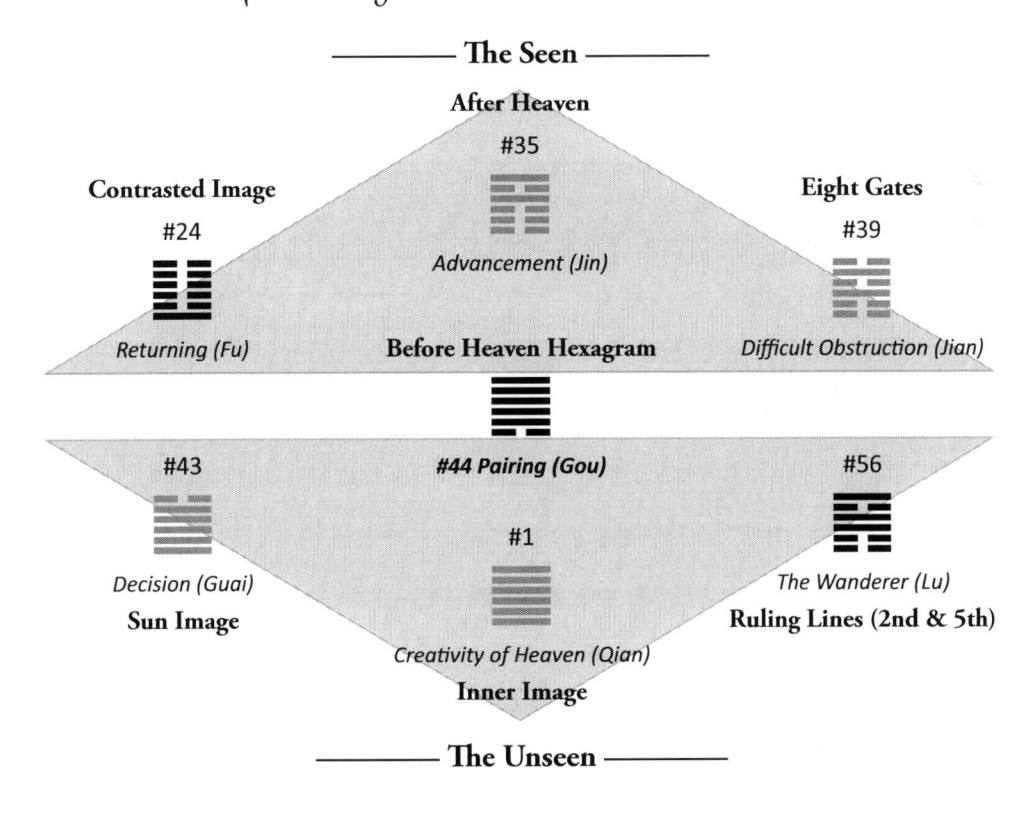

The Seen

After Heaven
#35
Advancement (Jin)

Contrasted Image
#24
Returning (Fu)

Eight Gates
#39
Difficult Obstruction (Jian)

Before Heaven Hexagram
#44 Pairing (Gou)

#43
Decision (Guai)
Sun Image

#1
Creativity of Heaven (Qian)
Inner Image

#56
The Wanderer (Lu)
Ruling Lines (2nd & 5th)

The Unseen

Cui

萃

Collecting

45

Dui (Valley) above
兑上
Dui Shang
Kun (Earth) below
坤下
Kun Xia

Sun/Yang Image

The Prediction (象, Tuan)

Collecting:

Perseverance. The king draws near to the ancestral temple. Advantage in seeing an elder. Perseverance. Advantage in being resolute. Employing a great sacrifice is auspicious. Advantage in having somewhere to go.

萃.亨.王假有廟.
利見大人.亨.
利貞.用大牲吉.
利有攸往.

Seek to acquire harmonious relationships, as gathering with friends and associates brings good fortune. With the king sitting in court, this is the correct time for capable and learned people to appear, giving aid to future plans and carrying them out for success. It is most auspicious if a great offering is made for future success. However, be cautious. Whenever groups are formed for a collective purpose there is the potential for something to go wrong. Just be prudent in your actions. Be well prepared and capable of quickly responding to any unexpected problems.

The Lines (爻, Yao)

First Six (初 六, Chu Liu)
Initially there is sincerity, but not in the end. Perhaps disorder. All at once grasping and then laughing. Moving forward there is no pity. Without fault.

有孚不終.乃亂乃萃.
若號.一握為笑.
勿恤往.无咎.

No good accommodations were made for those in your service and so initially they were in disorder. First they were shouting and complaining, but when proper accommodations were acquired, they felt gleeful and satisfied. They were told initially not to worry as this was really no problem. Bringing clarity to the situation by recognition of the confusion is of utmost importance.

#45 Collecting (Cui)

Second Six (六二, Liu Er)
Guiding is auspicious. Without fault. 引吉.无咎.孚乃利用禴.
Be sincere in employing the sacrificial
offerings, advantageous.

Good fortune has been increased because of sound errorless guidance. Your intuition of the situation is of great value. Those in service to you can be employed in the sacrificial ceremonies.

Third Six (六三, Liu San)
Collecting and then sighing. Nowhere 萃如嗟如.无攸利.
is there advantage. Leaving is without fault. 往无咎.小吝.
Minor regrets.

The gathering of people proves unfavorable and everyone is sighing. Even though it is not wrong to move forward there will still be some trouble. It seems everyone is confused, so it is important to trust in your intuition and clarity.

Fourth Nine (九四, Jiu Si)
Great auspiciousness. Without fault. 大吉.无咎.

The situation is extremely fortunate and no mistakes are being made. The entire group is acting unselfishly so there is no problem in continuing.

Fifth Nine (九五, Jiu Wu)
Collecting to have position. Without fault. 萃有位.无咎.匪孚.
There is no sincerity. Greatness is long-lasting 元永贞.悔亡.
when resolute. Regrets vanish.

Each person in the gathering takes his or her proper seat, so there's no mistake in organizing this meeting. Those who oppose you are restrained and cause no trouble. Some superficial people are within the group, but just remain resolute. A prediction was made for a long-term plan, and everything will go well from the beginning. All concerns will vanish.

Topmost Six (上六, Shang Liu)
Harboring sighs and tears. Without fault. 齎咨涕洟.无咎.

Unwarranted crying and sighing, tears streaming down their faces, but even so, nothing bad has really happened. Issues have been completely misunderstood, so sadness prevails. You should not worry, however, as there's no blame in any of this.

Alternate English Translations for the Hexagram of Cui, 萃

The Symbol of Gathering Into One [S]
Gathering Together (Massing) [WB]
Gathering Together, Assembling [B] [CS]
Gathering [C] [L]
Bringing Together [H]
Congregation—Gathering the Essence [N]
Clustering [K] [RS]
The Symbol of Collection [CC]

The Great Symbolism (大象, Da Xiang) says,

A Marsh on the Earth. This is Cui.
The superior person, according with this, does away with weapons of war, yet guards against unseen incidents.

澤上於地. 萃.
君子以除戎器.
戒不虞.

Sexagenary Placement

Heavenly Stem: Ren 壬 (9th Stem, Yang)—**Water** (水, Shui)
Earthly Branch: Yin 寅 (3rd Branch, Yang)—**Tiger** (虎, Hu)
Represents the *Year of the Water Tiger* (39th Year of the Sixty-Year Cycle)
Years: 1842 – 1902 – 1962 – 2022

Trigram Correlations

Upper Gua (Valley)

Dui 兑
- **Represents:** Valley, River, Lake/Marsh, Youngest Daughter
- **Actions:** Joyous, Opening, Stimulating
- **Influences:** Family, Future, Collecting, Pleasure, Absorbing, Complacency.
- **Shape:** Introverted Triangle   **Color:** Brown
- **Body:** Mouth   **Season:** Beginning Spring
- **Moon Phase:** Waning Gibbous
- **Animals:** Earthly Goat, Celestial Great Roc
- **Directions:** Southeast (BH), West (AH)
- **Nine Palaces Numbers:** Fu Xi: 5
    Yu the Great: Ho River Map, 4—Lo River Script, 7
- **Internal Alchemy:** Po (Earthly) Spirit
    Qi Center: Xuan Guan (Mysterious Pass)
    Qi Meridian: Yang Wei Mai (Yang Preserving Vessel)

#45 Collecting (Cui)

Lower Gua (Earth)

Kun 坤   **Represents:** Earth, Soil, Fields, Female, Mother, Empress
Actions: Receptive, Expanding, Yielding
Influences: Relationships, Love, Submission
Shape: Square   **Color:** Yellow
Body: Stomach   **Season:** Winter (Winter Solstice)
Moon Phase: New Moon
Animals: Earthly Ox, Celestial Black Tortoise
Directions: North (BH), Southwest (AH)
Nine Palaces Numbers: Fu Xi: **10**
    Yu the Great: Ho River Map, **1**—Lo River Script, **2**
Internal Alchemy: Tranquility, Void
    Qi Center: Hui Yin (Returning Yin)
    Qi Meridian: Ren Mai (Function Vessel)

Associated Developed Hexagrams of Cui

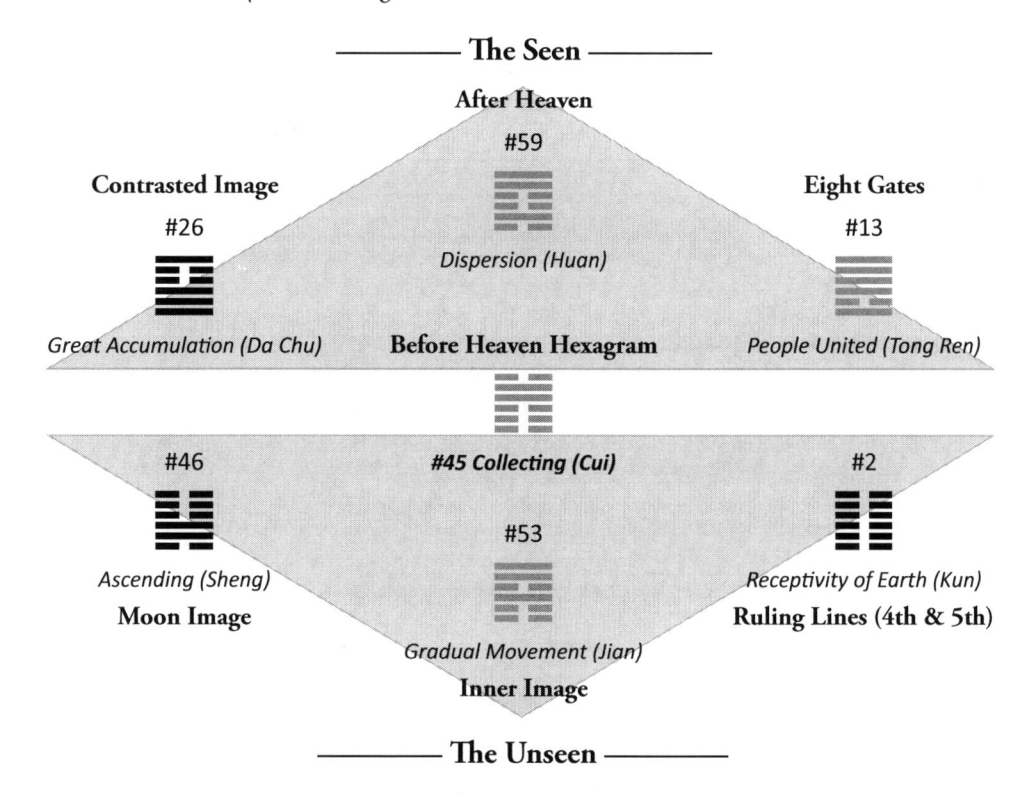

——— **The Seen** ———

After Heaven
#59
Dispersion (Huan)

Contrasted Image
#26
Great Accumulation (Da Chu)

Eight Gates
#13
People United (Tong Ren)

Before Heaven Hexagram

#45 Collecting (Cui)

#46
Ascending (Sheng)
Moon Image

#53
Gradual Movement (Jian)
Inner Image

#2
Receptivity of Earth (Kun)
Ruling Lines (4th & 5th)

——— **The Unseen** ———

Sheng
升

Ascending

46

Kun (Earth) above
坤上
Kun Shang
Xun (Wind) below
巽下
Xun Xia

Moon/Yin Image

The Prediction (彖, Tuan)

Ascending:
Great perseverance. Useful to see an elder.　　升.元亨.用見大人.
Without pity. Advancing to the South　　　　勿恤.南征吉.
is auspicious.

This images indicates there's nothing to fear and that one should be advancing to the southerly direction (the position of Qian, Heaven). This is a time of great change as an ascension is occurring. Take small steps forward and rely on your will power. With Ascending, there is good fortune from the very beginning, and a great person will appear and help show how to take advantage of the present opportunities. Traveling to the South is very auspicious.

The Lines (爻, Yao)

First Six (初六, Chu Liu)
Sincere Ascending. Great auspiciousness.　　允升.大吉.

There is a true belief of the Ascending and this brings good fortune. To be sincere in your ascension, rely on your humility and be sensitive to others and the situation.

Second Nine (九二, Jiu Er)
Sincerity will make the sacrificial　　　　　孚乃利用禴.无咎.
offering advantageous. Without fault.

There is no error in using those subordinate to you in helping with the summer sacrificial ceremonies. The ascension is unconventional but there is no error in this.

#46 Ascending (Sheng)

Third Nine (九 三, **Jiu San**)
Ascending to an empty city.　　　升 虛 邑.

Ascending a hill to a city on top of it, but it turns out the city is empty. Beware when the ascension seems easy, as this is an illusion.

Fourth Six (六 四, **Jiu Si**)
Employed by the king to make　　王 用 亨 岐 山. 吉. 无 咎.
offerings on Mount Qi. Auspicious.
Without fault.

The king employed you to make offerings on top of Mount Qi. This is very auspicious and there are no errors in doing this. Push yourself to reach the top, then the goal can be obtained.

Fifth Six (六 五, **Liu Wu**)
Being resolute is auspicious.　　　貞 吉. 升 階.
Ascending the stairs of rank.

Examining the possible prospects is auspicious and will create a promotion in rank. Going up the stairs means to take things step by step and to remain calm.

Topmost Six (上 六, **Shang Liu**)
Obscure Ascending. Advantage　　冥 升. 利 于 不 息 之 貞.
in being unceasingly resolute.

As if climbing a mountain in the dark, you must be constantly mindful of making plans for the future. Be constantly resolute, not giving way to blind ambitions.

Alternate English Translations for the Hexagram of Sheng, 升

The Symbol of Rising and Advancing [S]　　　*Rising* [C] [N]
Pushing Upward [WB]　　　　　　　　　　*Growing Upward* [H]
Ascending, Promotion [B]　　　　　　　　 *Ascending* [K] [L] [RS]
Rising (Ascending) [CS]　　　　　　　　　*The Symbol of Pushing Upwards* [CC]

185

The Great Symbolism (大象, Da Xiang) says,

Within the Earth, Wood is produced.	地中生木. 升.
This is Sheng. Superior persons, according	君子以順德.
with this, are docile about their virtue	積小以高大.
but store up the small until they	
are lofty and great.	

䷭ Sexagenary Placement

Heavenly Stem: Bing 丙 (3rd Stem, Yang)—**Fire** (火, Huo)
Earthly Branch: Wu 午 (7th Branch, Yang)—**Horse** (馬, Ma)
Represents the *Year of the Fire Horse* (43rd Year of the Sixty-Year Cycle)
Years: 1846 – 1906 – 1966 – 2026

Trigram Correlations

Upper Gua (Earth)

☷ **Kun** 坤
- **Represents:** Earth, Soil, Fields, Female, Mother, Empress
- **Actions:** Receptive, Expanding, Yielding
- **Influences:** Relationships, Love, Submission
- **Shape:** Square   **Color:** Yellow
- **Body:** Stomach   **Season:** Winter (Winter Solstice)
- **Moon Phase:** New Moon
- **Animals:** Earthly Ox, Celestial Black Tortoise
- **Directions:** North (BH), Southwest (AH)
- **Nine Palaces Numbers:** Fu Xi: **10**
    Yu the Great: Ho River Map, **1**—Lo River Script, **2**
- **Internal Alchemy:** Tranquility, Void
    Qi Center: Hui Yin (Returning Yin)
    Qi Meridian: Ren Mai (Function Vessel)

Lower Gua (Wind)

Xun 巽
Represents: Wind, Wood, Eldest Daughter
Actions: Gentleness, Grounding, Penetrating, Spreading
Influences: Prosperity, Abundance, Wealth
Shape: Rectangle **Color:** Purple
Body: Waist and hips **Season:** Beginning Summer
Moon Phase: Waxing Gibbous
Animals: Earthly Fowl, Celestial Golden Rooster
Directions: Southwest (BH), Southeast (AH)
Nine Palaces Numbers: Fu Xi: 9
  Yu the Great: Ho River Map, 2—Lo River Script, 4
Internal Alchemy: Breath and Mobilizing Qi
  Qi Center: Yu Zhen (Jade Pillow)
  Qi Meridian: Yin Wei Mai (Yin Preserving Vessel)

Associated Developed Hexagrams of Sheng

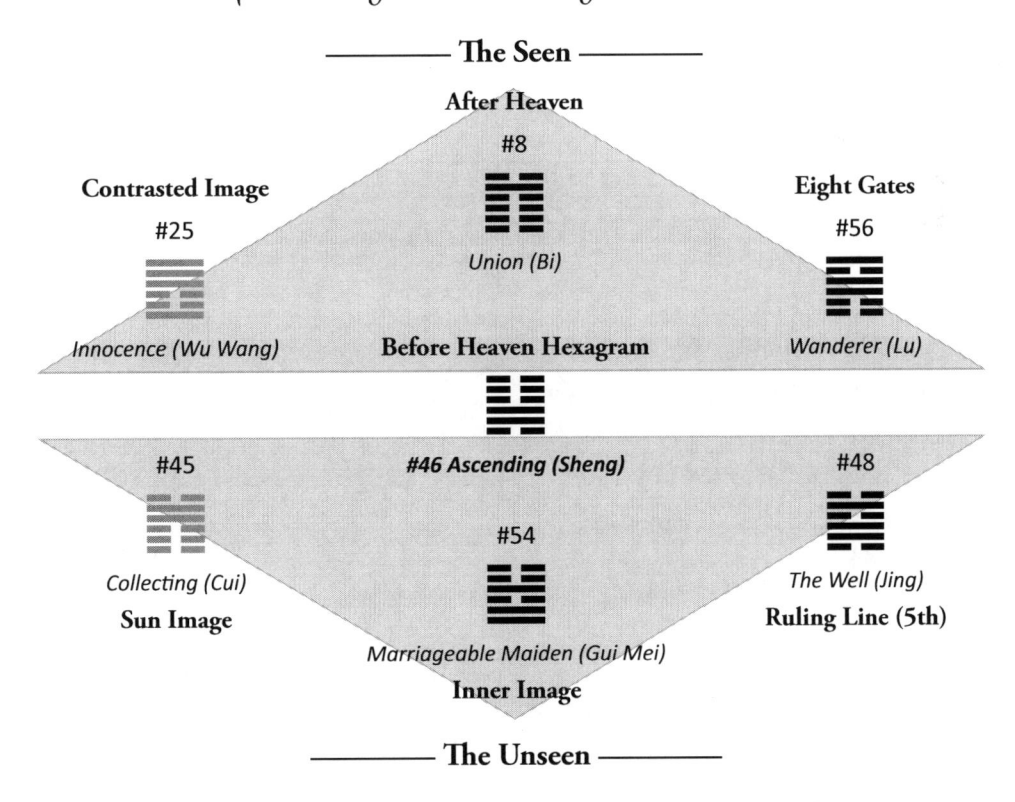

——— **The Seen** ———

After Heaven
#8
Union (Bi)

Contrasted Image
#25
Innocence (Wu Wang)

Eight Gates
#56
Wanderer (Lu)

Before Heaven Hexagram
#46 Ascending (Sheng)

#45
Collecting (Cui)
Sun Image

#54
Marriageable Maiden (Gui Mei)
Inner Image

#48
The Well (Jing)
Ruling Line (5th)

——— **The Unseen** ———

Kun

困

Oppression

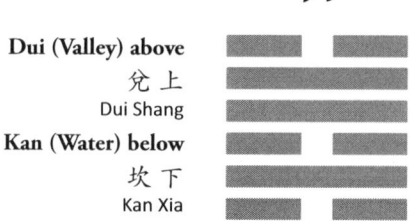

47

Dui (Valley) above
兑 上
Dui Shang
Kan (Water) below
坎 下
Kan Xia

Sun/Yang Image

The Prediction (象, Tuan)

Oppression:
Perseverance and resoluteness.
The elder is auspicious. Without fault.
Having words, but not believed.

困.亨貞.大人吉.无咎.
有言不信.

This image indicates that people should cultivate themselves by reforming their behavior. It is an auspicious time to consult with a learned and wise person. Although there's nothing wrong in consulting with an elder, others will find difficulty in believing your words. This is a very trying and difficult time for you, but remain cheerful and grateful for all you have, and above all do not let the situation break your spirit. Within misfortune, good fortune will always sprout forth, like a dried seed regenerating itself.

The Lines (爻, Yao)

First Six (初 六, Chu Liu)
The buttocks is in Oppression from
the trunk of a tree. Entering a dark valley.
Three years no one is seen.

臀困于株木.入于幽谷.
三歲不覿.

Sit within a dark valley beneath a large tree and remain in seclusion for three years. Do not let the gloom overshadow your hopes and dreams.

Second Nine (九 二, Jiu Er)
Oppression with wine and food. A man
with the red ceremonial sash is coming.
Advantage in using perseverance at the
sacrificial rites. Advance brings misfortune.
Without fault.

困于酒食.朱紱方來.
利用亨祀.征凶.无咎.

There's an addiction to wine and food. A person comes and gives you a ceremonial red sash that should be worn for engaging in a sacrificial offering ceremony. Danger if going on travels at this time. Fortunately, the crisis of addiction is survived. The external appears fine, but the internal needs your attention. The root of all addiction lies within yourself.

Third Six (六 三, Liu San)

Oppression on a rock. Leaning on thorny brambles. Entering into one's own palace. Doesn't see one's own wife. Misfortune.	困于石．據于蒺藜． 入于其宮．不見其妻．凶．

Within a rocky enclave you are left stranded, but you manage to escape by crawling over thorns and bushes. When you return home your wife is gone. You have been irrational about things and so have exhausted yourself. This situation is very ominous and misfortune follows.

Fourth Nine (九 四, Jiu Si)

The arrival is slow and composed. Oppression in a golden carriage. There is regret in the end.	來徐徐．困于金車．吝有終．

Things arrive and happen slowly. You were stranded on a heavy golden carriage and the journey did not go smoothly. You reach your destination, but there are regrets. Misguided, you were given bad advice, and because of this you harbor regret.

Fifth Nine (九 五, Jiu Wu)

The nose has been cut off. Oppression comes from those in red sashes. Pleasures come slowly. Advantageous to make use of sacrifices.	劓刖．困于赤紱． 乃徐有說．利用祭祀．

The nose is injured while stranded among people wearing red sashes, but the opportunity to escape them will occur. No one is supporting you, so you must remain composed. It is wise and correct to ask Heaven for help. Offer sacrifices out of gratitude to Heaven for future good fortune.

Topmost Six (上 六, Shang Liu)

Oppression comes from creeping and climbing plants in a high and tottering position. Telling one's self, "To move is to repent." Having repented, advancing is then auspicious.	困于葛藟．于臲卼． 曰動悔．有悔征吉．

Stranded on a high tree covered with creeping and climbing vegetation, it is very precarious. You tell yourself, "If I move, I will regret it." If you repent and reform, however, advancing will be auspicious. These difficulties are of no great importance. Moving forward is important.

Alternate English Translations for the Hexagram of Kun, 困

The Symbol of Repression and Confinement [S]
Oppression (Exhaustion) [WB]
Adversity, Weariness [B]
Adversity (Exhaustion) [CS]
Exhaustion [C]
The Symbol of Repression [CC]

Exhausting [H]
Besieged—Entrapped—Exhausted [N]
Confinement [RS]
Oppression [L]
Confining [K]

The Great Symbolism (大象, Da Xiang) says,

A Marsh without Water. This is Kun. Superior persons, according with this, stake their lives to complete their will.

澤无水. 困. 君子以.
致命遂志.

Sexagenary Placement

Heavenly Stem: Jia 甲 (1st Stem, Yang)—**Wood** (木, Mu)
Earthly Branch: Zi 子 (1st Branch, Yang)—**Rat** (鼠, Shu)
Represents the *Year of the Wood Rat* (1st Year of the Sixty-Year Cycle)
Years: 1864 – 1924 – 1984 – 2044

Trigram Correlations

Upper Gua (Valley)

Dui 兌
 Represents: Valley, River, Lake/Marsh, Youngest Daughter
 Actions: Joyous, Opening, Stimulating
 Influences: Family, Future, Collecting, Pleasure, Absorbing, Complacency.
 Shape: Introverted Triangle   **Color:** Brown
 Body: Mouth   **Season:** Beginning Spring
 Moon Phase: Waning Gibbous
 Animals: Earthly Goat, Celestial Great Roc
 Directions: Southeast (BH), West (AH)
 Nine Palaces Numbers: Fu Xi: 5
  Yu the Great: Ho River Map, 4—Lo River Script, 7
 Internal Alchemy: Po (Earthly) Spirit
  Qi Center: Xuan Guan (Mysterious Pass)
  Qi Meridian: Yang Wei Mai (Yang Preserving Vessel)

#47 Oppression (Kun)

Lower Gua (Water)

Kan 坎
- **Represents:** Water, Moon, Springs/Streams, Middle Son
- **Actions:** Peril, Danger, and Difficulty.
- **Influences:** Abysmal Life Path and Vocation
- **Shape:** Wave   **Color:** Black
- **Body:** Ears   **Season:** Autumn (Autumn Equinox)
- **Moon Phase:** First Quarter
- **Animals:** Earthly Pig, Celestial White Tiger
- **Directions:** West (BH), North (AH)
- **Nine Palaces Numbers:** Fu Xi: 4
  - Yu the Great: Ho River Map, 7—Lo River Script, 1
- **Internal Alchemy:** Essence, Jing, Lead
  - Qi Center: Shuang Guan (Double Pass)
  - Qi Meridian: Chong Mai (Penetrating Vessel)

Associated Developed Hexagrams of Kun

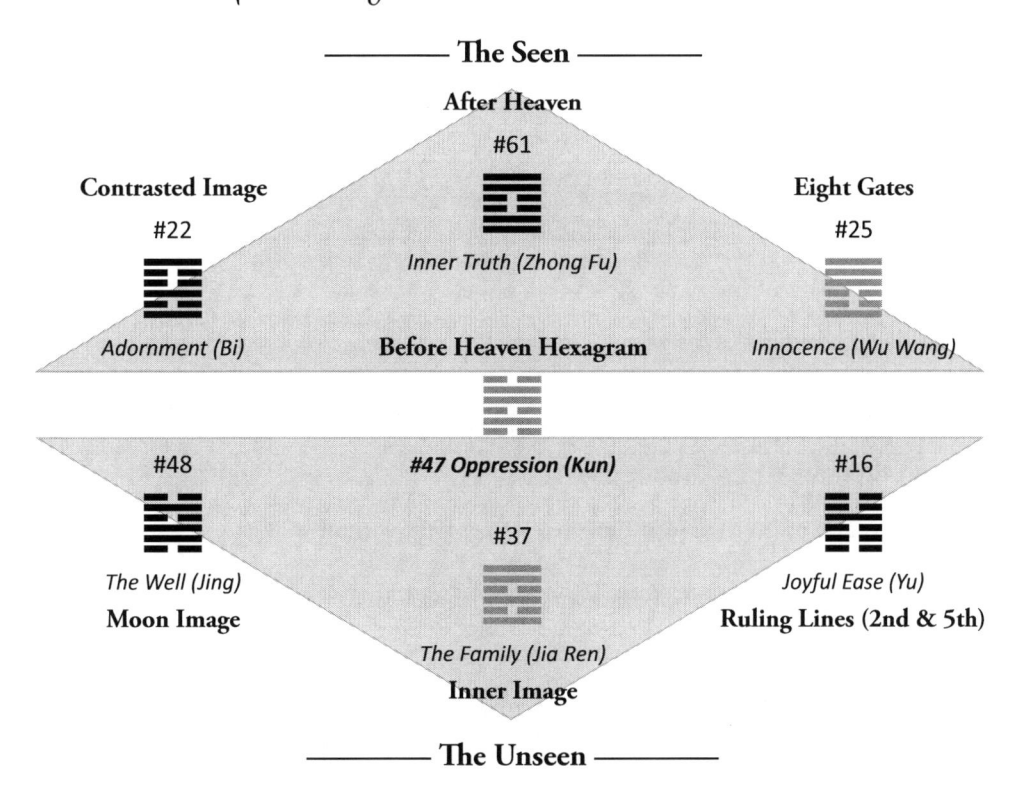

——— **The Seen** ———

After Heaven
#61
Inner Truth (Zhong Fu)

Contrasted Image
#22
Adornment (Bi)

Eight Gates
#25
Innocence (Wu Wang)

Before Heaven Hexagram

#47 Oppression (Kun)

#48
The Well (Jing)
Moon Image

#37
The Family (Jia Ren)
Inner Image

#16
Joyful Ease (Yu)
Ruling Lines (2nd & 5th)

——— **The Unseen** ———

Jing
井

The Well　　48

Kan (Water) above
坎 上
Kan Shang
Xun (Wind) below
巽 下
Xun Xia

Moon/Yin Image

The Prediction (彖, Tuan)

The Well:
Changing the city, but not changing　　井.改邑不改井.
The Well. Not losing and not gaining.　　无喪无得.
They come and go from well to well.　　往來井井.
The rope nearly reaches, but not quite.　　汔至亦未繘井.
The jug breaks. Misfortune.　　羸其瓶.凶.

This image shows to use your courage of convictions and to hold onto your principles. The entire village has been changed, but not The Well. There is no gain or loss to the well, but more people come to get water. The well is used up and you can see mud at the bottom. The rope does not reach far enough and the jug for retrieving water breaks. No one comes to repair the well, which is a really bad omen.

The Lines (爻, Yao)

First Six (初 六, Chu Liu)
The Well is muddy and no one drinks　　井泥不食.舊井无禽.
from it. Not even the birds and animals.

The well is too muddied and unclean to use. It is in such dire need of repair, not even birds or animals come to it. This shows there is no clarity or spiritual awareness of the situation. Everything looks cloudy and murky.

Second Nine (九 二, Jiu Er)
The Well is like a valley and fish shoot out.　　井谷射鮒.甕敝漏.
The jug is ruined and the water leaks out.

Like a stream running through the valley, small fish are jumping in the well. A spear jabbing at the fish hits the water jug and breaks it. This shows you are not using your best qualities and skills.

Third Nine (九 三, Jiu San)
The Well is cleared, but not to be drunk from.　　井渫不食. 為我心惻.
My heart acts with sorrow. The water might　　可用汲. 王明. 並受其福.
be drawn and used. The king is wise,
and together we receive good fortune.

There is concern and worry that the water in the well is too dirty to drink. Through the wisdom of the ruler, the water was made drinkable, and so everyone is relieved and happy. This shows that your qualities and skills are going unrecognized.

Fourth Six (六 四, Liu Si)
The Well is repaired. Without fault.　　井甃. 无咎.

A strong lining has been added to the well so that it will not deteriorate again. This shows that you need to take the time and put in the effort to restore yourself.

Fifth Nine (九 五, Jiu Wu)
The Well is clear.　　井冽. 寒泉食.
The cool spring water is drinkable.

The water in the well is clear. Cool spring water makes the water a joy to drink. This shows that your potential is really great but is not used or recognized by others. You cleared the well but receive no credit for it.

Topmost Six (上 六, Shang Liu)
The Well is restored, but not covered.　　井收勿幕. 有孚元吉.
Having sincerity brings great auspiciousness.

People are constantly drawing water from the well and so it is left uncovered. This new well has brought a new beginning of auspiciousness and renewal. This shows your efforts have benefitted everyone and this brings you great good fortune.

Alternate English Translations for the Hexagram of Jing, 井

The Symbol of the Well [S]　　　　*Replenishing* [H]
The Well [C] [CS] [K] [L] [RS] [WB]　　*Well* [N]
A Well [B]　　　　*The Symbol of the Source* [CC]

The Great Symbolism (大象, Da Xiang) says,

Above Wood there is Water. This is Jing.　　木上有水. 井.
The superior person, according with this,　　君子以勞民勸相.
encourages and stimulates the people
to be mutually helpful.

Sexagenary Placement

Heavenly Stem: Ren 壬 (9th Stem, Yang)—**Water** (水, Shui)
Earthly Branch: Wu 午 (7th Branch, Yang)—**Horse** (馬, Ma)
Represents the *Year of the Water Horse* (19th Year of the Sixty-Year Cycle)
Years: 1882 – 1942 – 2002 – 2062

Trigram Correlations

Upper Gua (Water)

Kan 坎　　**Represents:** Water, Moon, Springs/Streams, Middle Son
　　　　Actions: Peril, Danger, and Difficulty.
　　　　Influences: Abysmal Life Path and Vocation
　　　　Shape: Wave　　　　**Color:** Black
　　　　Body: Ears　　　　**Season:** Autumn (Autumn Equinox)
　　　　Moon Phase: First Quarter
　　　　Animals: Earthly Pig, Celestial White Tiger
　　　　Directions: West (BH), North (AH)
　　　　Nine Palaces Numbers: Fu Xi: 4
　　　　　　Yu the Great: Ho River Map, 7—Lo River Script, 1
　　　　Internal Alchemy: Essence, Jing, Lead
　　　　　　Qi Center: Shuang Guan (Double Pass)
　　　　　　Qi Meridian: Chong Mai (Penetrating Vessel)

Lower Gua (Wind)

☴ Xun 巽
- **Represents:** Wind, Wood, Eldest Daughter
- **Actions:** Gentleness, Grounding, Penetrating, Spreading
- **Influences:** Prosperity, Abundance, Wealth
- **Shape:** Rectangle   **Color:** Purple
- **Body:** Waist and hips   **Season:** Beginning Summer
- **Moon Phase:** Waxing Gibbous
- **Animals:** Earthly Fowl, Celestial Golden Rooster
- **Directions:** Southwest (BH), Southeast (AH)
- **Nine Palaces Numbers:** Fu Xi: 9
   Yu the Great: Ho River Map, 2—Lo River Script, 4
- **Internal Alchemy:** Breath and Mobilizing Qi
   Qi Center: Yu Zhen (Jade Pillow)
   Qi Meridian: Yin Wei Mai (Yin Preserving Vessel)

Associated Developed Hexagrams of Jing

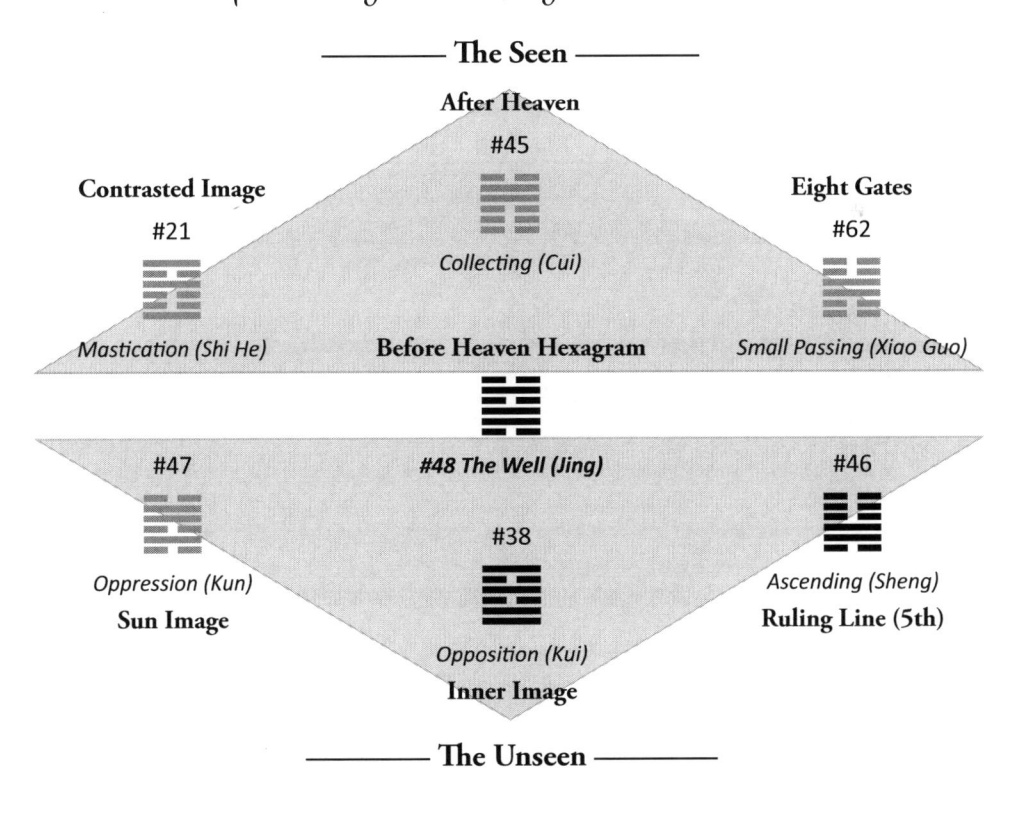

— The Seen —

After Heaven
#45
Collecting (Cui)

Contrasted Image
#21
Mastication (Shi He)

Eight Gates
#62
Small Passing (Xiao Guo)

Before Heaven Hexagram
#48 The Well (Jing)

#47
Oppression (Kun)
Sun Image

#38
Opposition (Kui)
Inner Image

#46
Ascending (Sheng)
Ruling Line (5th)

— The Unseen —

Ge

革

Revolution

49

Dui (Valley) above
兑 上
Dui Shang
Li (Fire) below
離 下
Li Xia

Sun/Yang Image

The Prediction (彖, Tuan)

Revolution:
On the proper day they will trust him.
Great perseverance. Advantage in being resolute. Regret vanishes.

革. 已日乃孚. 元亨.
利貞. 悔亡.

This image shows to look at traditions and make these your guidelines. From the time of Zi (11:00 p.m. to 1:00 a.m.) will come Wu (11:00 a.m. to 1:00 p.m.), and the sun will shine brightly over you. Change is inevitable, so look at the direction things are going and simply follow without struggle. Through this you can gain clarity and eliminate the chaos. It will be as if everywhere shines good weather. Planning for the future will eliminate all worries.

The Lines (爻, Yao)

First Nine (初 九, Chu Jiu)
Bound with the skin of a yellow ox.

鞏用黃牛之革.

Seeking to make something strong and hold fast, use the hide of an ox. This shows the time for change is not quite right, so be patient and wait.

Second Six (六 二, Liu Er)
On the proper day there will be Revolution.
Advancing is auspicious. Without fault.

已日乃革之. 征吉. 无咎.

The sun moves to the hour of Wu. It moves to the center of the sky and so things are seen very clearly and reforms can be set in place. This shows that before change there should be proper preparation. This is a very auspicious time for traveling. No mistakes are made.

Third Nine (九三, Jiu San)
To advance brings misfortune. Even though resolute discipline is needed. Three times the words of Revolution are given. There is sincerity.

征凶.貞厲.革言三就.有孚.

Traveling is ominous and even though the prediction shows danger, discipline and sincerity produce a good result. Not the time to act in haste, nor to be ruthless, it is best to engage in discussions. Three times there was talk about revolt, and by overseeing and guiding those in opposition, the discussion became sincere about planning the revolution.

Fourth Nine (九四, Jiu Si)
Regret vanishes. Having sincerity. Changing destiny is auspicious.

悔亡.有孚.改命吉.

All regrets and anxieties vanish, and sincere intent is focused. All this is a result of the destiny of revolution being auspicious. It's as if change itself is in charge.

Fifth Nine (九五, Jiu Wu)
The elder is as changeable as a tiger. Before divining there must be sincerity.

大人虎變.未占有孚.

Just as the fur of a tiger changes according to the needs of the season, a good leader changes according to both the will of Heaven and the needs of the people. The leader is bold, and Heaven favors the bold. All those in opposition are quelled and no divination need be done.

Topmost Six (上六, Shang Jiu)
The wise person is as changeable as a leopard. Only the face of an inferior person changes in Revolution. Advancing brings misfortune. Abiding in resoluteness is auspicious.

君子豹變.小人革面.
征凶.居貞吉.

Just as a leopard changes its spots, the wise person should only engage in Revolution according to the will of Heaven or the needs of the people. The noise of the radical factions are quiet and they make small steps. The common person can only change superficially, not fundamentally. Travel at this time is ominous, so dwelling near the home is auspicious.

Alternate English Translations for the Hexagram of Ge, 革

The Symbol of Change [S]
Revolution (Molting) [WB]
Revolution, Leather, Skin [B]
Change (Revolution) [CS]
Skinning/Revolution [K]

Revolution [C] [L]
Abolishing the Old [H]
Revolution—Reform [N]
Skinning [RS]
The Symbol of Change [CC]

The Great Symbolism (大象, Da Xiang) says,

Within the Marsh there is Fire. This is Ge. 　　澤中有火.革.
The superior person, according with this, 　　君子以治曆明時.
puts the calendar in order, making clear
the times of the seasons.

Sexagenary Placement

Heavenly Stem: Ji 己 (6th Stem, Yin)—**Earth** (土, Tu)
Earthly Branch: You 酉 (10th Branch, Yin)—**Rooster** (雞, Ji)
Represents the *Year of the Earth Rooster* (46th Year of the Sixty-Year Cycle)
Years: 1849 – 1909 – 1969 – 2029

Trigram Correlations

Upper Gua (Valley)

Dui 兌　**Represents:** Valley, River, Lake/Marsh, Youngest Daughter
Actions: Joyous, Opening, Stimulating
Influences: Family, Future, Collecting, Pleasure, Absorbing, Complacency.
Shape: Introverted Triangle　**Color:** Brown
Body: Mouth　　　　　　　**Season:** Beginning Spring
Moon Phase: Waning Gibbous
Animals: Earthly Goat, Celestial Great Roc
Directions: Southeast (BH), West (AH)
Nine Palaces Numbers: Fu Xi: 5
　　　Yu the Great: Ho River Map, 4—Lo River Script, 7
Internal Alchemy: Po (Earthly) Spirit
　　　Qi Center: Xuan Guan (Mysterious Pass)
　　　Qi Meridian: Yang Wei Mai (Yang Preserving Vessel)

Lower Gua (Fire)

☲ **Li** 離

Represents: Fire, Lightning, Sun, Middle Daughter
Actions: Clinging, Illuminating, Congregating
Influences: Fame, Reputation, Brightness, Elegance
Shape: Triangle **Color:** Red
Body: Eyes **Season:** Spring (Spring Equinox)
Moon Phase: Last Quarter
Animals: Earthly Rooster, Celestial Green Dragon
Directions: East (BH), South (AH)
Nine Palaces Numbers: Fu Xi: **8**
    Yu the Great: Ho River Map, **3**—Lo River Script, **9**
Internal Alchemy: Mercury, Qi
    Qi Center: Jiang Gong (Crimson Palace)
    Qi Meridian: Dai Mai (Belt Vessel)

Associated Developed Hexagrams of Ge

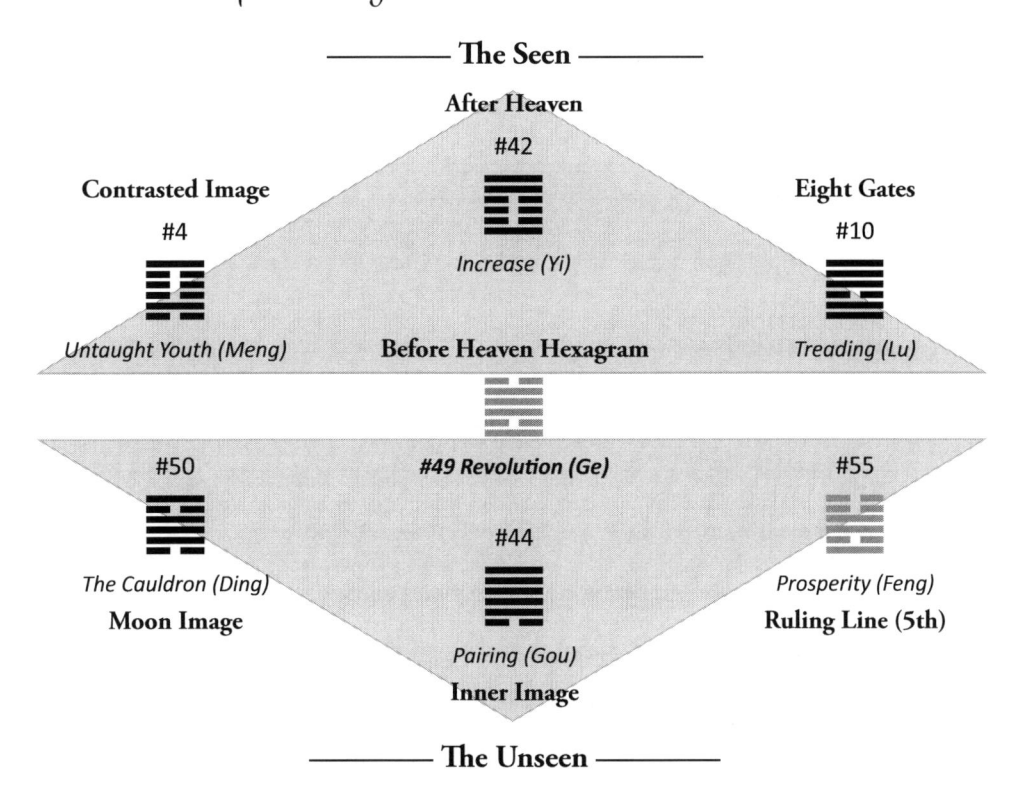

——— **The Seen** ———

After Heaven
#42
Increase (Yi)

Contrasted Image
#4
Untaught Youth (Meng)

Eight Gates
#10
Treading (Lu)

Before Heaven Hexagram

#50
The Cauldron (Ding)
Moon Image

#49 Revolution (Ge)
#44
Pairing (Gou)
Inner Image

#55
Prosperity (Feng)
Ruling Line (5th)

——— **The Unseen** ———

Ding 鼎 — The Cauldron — 50

Li (Fire) above
離上
Li Shang
Xun (Wind) below
巽下
Xun Xia

Moon/Yin Image

The Prediction (象, Tuan)

The Cauldron:
Great auspiciousness. Perseverance.   鼎. 元吉. 亨.

This image shows there is a possibility of danger in the immediate sense, but it will not last long and soon pass. The cauldron is an image of a vessel for cooking and for making sacrifices. Both cooking and making sacrifices are very auspicious and from the start success is being formed. Just as Wind nourishes the flame (Fire), the discipline of making sacrifices nourishes spiritual growth. Seek to nourish your qi and there will be spiritual progress and good fortune from Heaven.

The Lines (爻, Yao)

First Six (初六, Chu Liu)
The Cauldron has toppled off its legs.   鼎顛趾. 利出否.
Advantage in dispersing the wrong.   得妾以其子. 无咎.
Acquiring a concubine to have a son.
Without fault.

The legs of the cauldron are pointing upward, so the situation is upside down. This makes it right to take in a concubine and her child (or to have a child with her) because the wife is estranged. There is no error here because this shows goodwill within being humble.

Second Nine (九二, Jiu Er)
In The Cauldron there is food.   鼎有實. 我仇有疾.
My wife has an illness and cannot   不我能即. 吉.
approach me. Auspicious.

There is cooked food in the cauldron, but the wife is ill and cannot eat with her husband. She will achieve spiritual strength from this and he will be properly nourished, so it is auspicious.

Third Nine (九三, Jiu San)

The ears of The Cauldron have been changed. His actions are thus stopped. The fat of the pheasant is not eaten. When the rain arrives, regret wanes. The end is auspicious.

鼎耳革．其行塞．雉膏不食．
方雨虧悔．終吉．

An ear was broken off the cauldron. Leaving the home will not go well because no one will recognize him nor give him recognition. Avoid eating the fat of the pheasant as it can create an illness. When the dark clouds disperse, the rain is gentle and so there is no more fear. This proves to bring forth a fortunate surprise. Everything is auspicious in the end.

Fourth Nine (九四, Jiu Si)

The legs of The Cauldron are damaged. The duke's food in The Cauldron has spilled out. He blushes shamefully. Misfortune.

鼎折足．覆公餗．其形渥．凶．

The cauldron is tipped over and the legs have been broken. The food in the cauldron was for an honored guest but it has spilt onto the floor and is now dirty. This shows there was a lack of caution, care, and devotion to the cauldron, bringing misfortune.

Fifth Six (六五, Liu Wu)

The Cauldron has yellow ears. The carrying rings are gold. Advantage in being resolute.

鼎黃耳．金鉉．利貞．

The golden ears of the cauldron sparkle and shine brilliantly. This is a very auspicious time to plan for the future and move forward. The persistence of remaining cautious, providing care, and showing sincere devotion to the cauldron reaps great rewards.

Topmost Nine (上九, Shang Jiu)

The Cauldron has carrying rings made of jade. Great auspiciousness. Everything is beneficial.

鼎玉鉉．大吉．无不利．

The carrying rings on the cauldron are made of precious jade and so tinkle when heated. This signals extremely good fortune and causes everything to be advantageous. Heated jade cures all illnesses and brings restoration to things in need of repair. The sage bestowed a blessing upon you, a blessing of jade.

Alternate English Translations for the Hexagram of Ding, 鼎

The Symbol of the Cauldron [S]
The Cauldron [C] [L] [WB]
A Sacrificial Vessel [B]
Cauldron—Harmonization & Stability [N]

Establishing the New [H]
The Cauldron (Sacrificial Vessel) [CS]
The Vessel [K] [RS]
The Symbol of Nourishment [CC]

The Great Symbolism (大象, Da Xiang) says,

Above Wood there is Fire. This is Ding. 木上有火. 鼎.
Superior persons, according with this, 君子以正位凝命.
establish their position by bringing
their destiny to pass.

Sexagenary Placement

Heavenly Stem: Ji 己 (6th Stem, Yin)—**Earth** (土, Tu)
Earthly Branch: Hai 亥 (12th Branch, Yin)—**Pig** (猪, Zhu)
Represents the *Year of the Earth Pig* (36th Year of the Sixty-Year Cycle)
Years: 1839 – 1899 – 1959 – 2019

Trigram Correlations

Upper Gua (Fire)

Li 離

Represents: Fire, Lightning, Sun, Middle Daughter
Actions: Clinging, Illuminating, Congregating
Influences: Fame, Reputation, Brightness, Elegance
Shape: Triangle   **Color:** Red
Body: Eyes   **Season:** Spring (Spring Equinox)
Moon Phase: Last Quarter
Animals: Earthly Rooster, Celestial Green Dragon
Directions: East (BH), South (AH)
Nine Palaces Numbers: Fu Xi: 8
    Yu the Great: Ho River Map, **3**—Lo River Script, **9**
Internal Alchemy: Mercury, Qi
    Qi Center: Jiang Gong (Crimson Palace)
    Qi Meridian: Dai Mai (Belt Vessel)

#50 The Cauldron (Ding)

Lower Gua (Wind)

☴ **Xun** 巽
Represents: Wind, Wood, Eldest Daughter
Actions: Gentleness, Grounding, Penetrating, Spreading
Influences: Prosperity, Abundance, Wealth
Shape: Rectangle   **Color:** Purple
Body: Waist and hips   **Season:** Beginning Summer
Moon Phase: Waxing Gibbous
Animals: Earthly Fowl, Celestial Golden Rooster
Directions: Southwest (BH), Southeast (AH)
Nine Palaces Numbers: Fu Xi: **9**
   Yu the Great: Ho River Map, **2**—Lo River Script, **4**
Internal Alchemy: Breath and Mobilizing Qi
   Qi Center: Yu Zhen (Jade Pillow)
   Qi Meridian: Yin Wei Mai (Yin Preserving Vessel)

Associated Developed Hexagrams of Ding

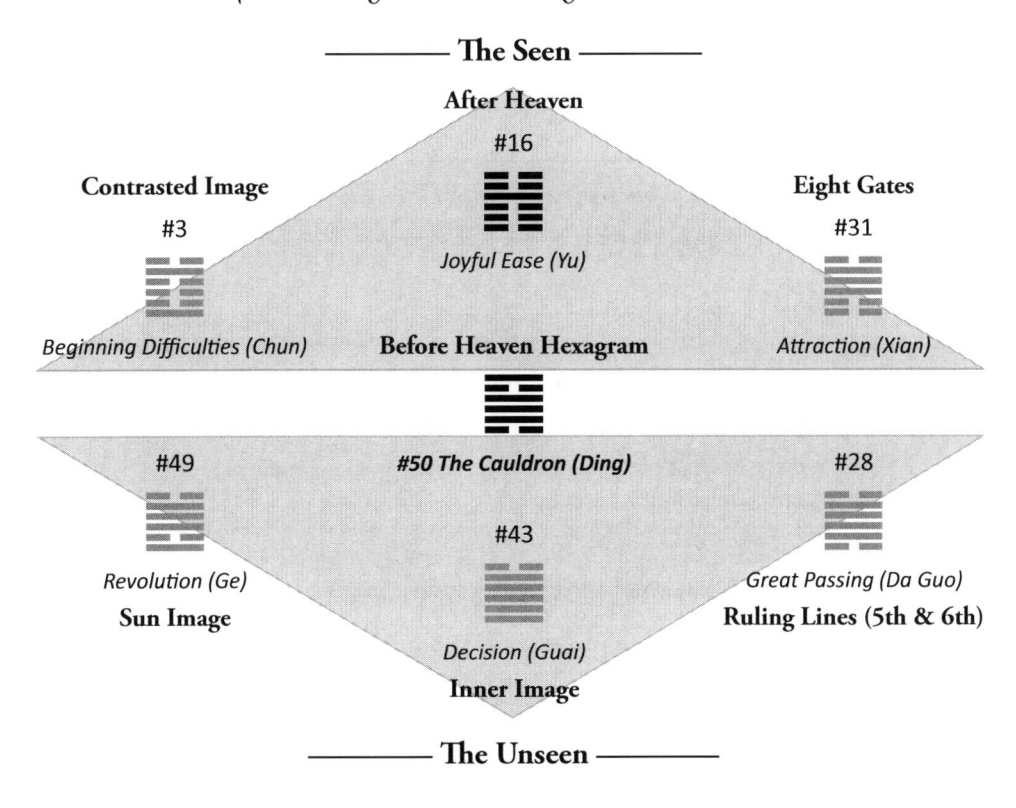

——— **The Seen** ———

After Heaven
#16
Joyful Ease (Yu)

Contrasted Image
#3
Beginning Difficulties (Chun)

Eight Gates
#31
Attraction (Xian)

Before Heaven Hexagram

#50 The Cauldron (Ding)

#49
Revolution (Ge)
Sun Image

#43
Decision (Guai)
Inner Image

#28
Great Passing (Da Guo)
Ruling Lines (5th & 6th)

——— **The Unseen** ———

Zhen

震

Arousing Movement

51

Zhen (Thunder) above
震上
Zhen Shang

Zhen (Thunder) below
震下
Zhen Xia

Sun/Yang Image

The Prediction (象, Tuan)

Arousing Movement, Thunder:
Perseverance. Terrified by the arrival of the sounds of Arousing Movement. Smiling while talking and laughing cheerfully. For a hundred miles there is fright of the Arousing Movement. No spilling of the sacrificial spirits from the ladle.

震.亨.震來虩虩.笑言啞啞.
震驚百里.不喪匕鬯.

This image shows that great changes are expected and needed. But within Arousing Movement, everything does go well. Even though the sound of the thunder frightens people, they are still carrying on with jovial talk and laughing. The thunder was strong, heard a hundred miles away, yet no one spilled a drop of wine from their wine ladles. This shows that catastrophes and great fear can be experienced and managed if one remains spiritually resolute.

The Lines (爻, Yao)

First Nine (初 九, Chu Jiu)
Terrified by the coming sounds of Arousing Movement. Afterwards talking cheerfully and laughing. Auspicious.

震來虩虩.恐致福也.
笑言啞啞.吉.

Even though the thunder was frightening, afterwards people continued having good cheer and felt relief. This is a very auspicious omen of things to come.

Second Six (六 二, Liu Er)
With Arousing Movement comes peril. Losing a large treasure after traveling to nine tombs. No pursuing. In seven days it will again be obtained.

震來厲.億喪貝.躋于九陵.
勿逐.七日得.

The thunder was loud and strong, shaking everything. A large treasure was lost when traveling to nine ancestral graves, but there's no need to try to recover it because it will be returned within seven days. Even though the loss was great, in the end it really didn't matter, so it's best to always stay unattached.

Third Six (六 三, Liu San)
Arousing Movement causes fear and uneasiness. The action of Arousing Movement is without error.

震蘇蘇. 震行无眚.

The sound and shaking of the thunder frightens and numbs you, but as you walk through it no injury or disasters occur.

Fourth Nine (九 四, Jiu Si)
Arousing Movement is pursued into the mire.

震逐泥.

The lightning struck down into muddy waters and that is all that occurred. You were just dazed and confused, so take the time to wait and regain clarity.

Fifth Six (六 五, Liu Wu)
Arousing Movement comes and goes, causing peril. Nothing large is lost in having affairs.

震往來厲. 億无喪有事.

The thunder and lightning are intermittent, causing fear each time. Nothing of value is lost, but there is work to do. One shock after another has put you off balance, but just keep centered and upright.

Topmost Six (上 六, Shang Liu)
Arousing Movement startles and shakes. Looking about scared and terrified. Advancing brings misfortune. Arousing Movement does not strike him, but his neighbor. Without fault. There is talk of a marriageable maiden.

震索索. 視矍矍.
征凶. 震不于其躬.
于其鄰. 无咎.
婚媾有言.

The thunder startled and scared everyone. Do not go out into the storm for it is dangerous. The lightning strikes a close neighbor, but you are safe. It's as if everyone is in a panic while you are sitting still, but, in sitting still, everyone begins gossiping about how you need to marry.

Alternate English Translations for the Hexagram of Zhen, 震

The Symbol of Startling Movement [S]
The Arousing (Shock, Thunder) [WB]
Thunder [B] [C]
Thunder (Arousing) [CS]
Shake [K]

Taking Action [H]
The Arousing—Force of Thunder [N]
The Shake [RS]
Thunder (Shock) [L]
The Symbol of Exciting Power [CC]

The Great Symbolism (大象, Da Xiang) says,

Continuous Lightning. This is Zhen. 洊雷．震．君子以
The superior person, according with this, 恐懼修省．
is cautious, apprehensive, and alert
when cultivating.

Sexagenary Placement

Heavenly Stem: Yi 乙 (2nd Stem, Yin)—**Wood** (木, Mu)
Earthly Branch: Chou 丑 (2nd Branch, Yin)—**Ox** (牛, Niu)
Represents the *Year of the Wood Ox* (2nd Year of the Sixty-Year Cycle)
Years: 1865 – 1925 – 1985 – 2045

Trigram Correlations

Upper Gua (Thunder)

Zhen 震   **Represents:** Thunder, Earthquake, Eldest Son
Actions: Arousing, Shaking, Initiating
Influences: Foundations, Past Actions, Excitement.
Shape: Vertical Column   **Color:** Green
Body: Feet and legs   **Season:** Beginning Winter
Moon Phase: Waning Crescent
Animals: Earthly Dragons, Celestial Dragon-Horse
Directions: Northeast (BH), East (AH)
Nine Palaces Numbers: Fu Xi: 3
  Yu the Great: Ho River Map, **8**—Lo River Script, **3**
Internal Alchemy: Mind-Intention
  Qi Center: Dan Tian (Elixir Field)
  Qi Meridian: Yin Qiao Mai (Yin Heel Vessel)

#51 Arousing Movement (Zhen)

Lower Gua (Thunder)

Zhen 震

Represents: Thunder, Earthquake, Eldest Son
Actions: Arousing, Shaking, Initiating
Influences: Foundations, Past Actions, Excitement.
Shape: Vertical Column   **Color:** Green
Body: Feet and legs   **Season:** Beginning Winter
Moon Phase: Waning Crescent
Animals: Earthly Dragons, Celestial Dragon-Horse
Directions: Northeast (BH), East (AH)
Nine Palaces Numbers: Fu Xi: 3
  Yu the Great: Ho River Map, 8—Lo River Script, 3
Internal Alchemy: Mind-Intention
  Qi Center: Dan Tian (Elixir Field)
  Qi Meridian: Yin Qiao Mai (Yin Heel Vessel)

Associated Developed Hexagrams of Zhen

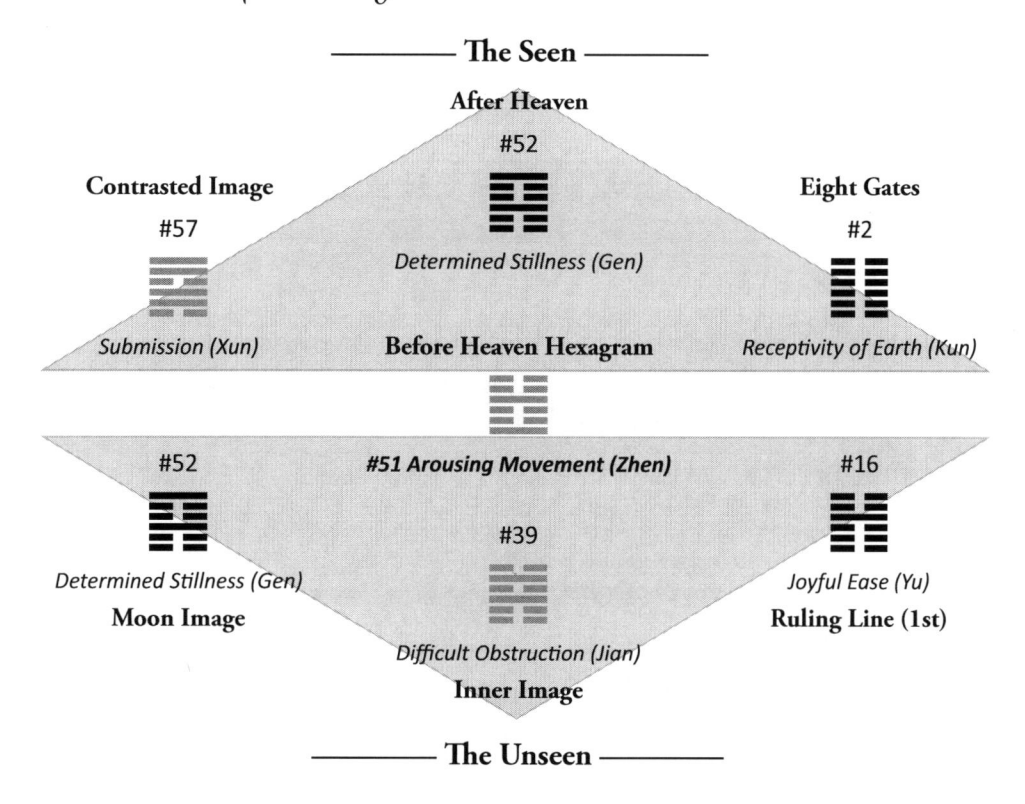

— **The Seen** —

After Heaven
#52
Determined Stillness (Gen)

Contrasted Image
#57
Submission (Xun)

Eight Gates
#2
Receptivity of Earth (Kun)

Before Heaven Hexagram
#51 Arousing Movement (Zhen)

#52
Determined Stillness (Gen)
Moon Image

#39
Difficult Obstruction (Jian)
Inner Image

#16
Joyful Ease (Yu)
Ruling Line (1st)

— **The Unseen** —

Gen

艮

Determined Stillness

52

Gen (Mountain) above
艮上
Gen Shang

Gen (Mountain) below
艮下
Gen Xia

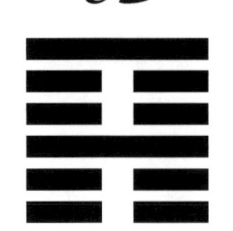

Moon/Yin Image

The Prediction (彖, Tuan)

Stillness of a Mountain:
Determined Stillness is to one's own back.
No longer aware of one's own body.
Activity in one's own courtyard. Does not
see one's own people. Without fault.

艮其背. 不獲其身. 行其庭.
不見其人. 无咎.

This image indicates that those who use wisdom are granted good fortune and favors. You stopped to look behind you and forgot about your own body. You went into your courtyard looking for others, but no one was there. Your tranquility has gathered great power. There is a time for stillness, and a time for movement. Through your tranquility, you have created a distance from the everyday worries of life. Nothing is wrong with this.

The Lines (爻, Yao)

First Six (初 六, Chu Liu)
Determined Stillness in the toes.
Without fault. Resolute continuance
is beneficial.

艮其趾. 无咎. 利永貞.

You stopped to check your feet and everything was all right. It is good to continue your plan of action, but it is best to remain tranquil and not drift off course.

Second Six (六 二, Liu Er)
Determined Stillness in the calves of the legs.
There is no help from one's own following.
One's mind is not keen.

艮其腓. 不拯其隨.
其心不快.

You stopped to check your calf, but it is weak. You cannot continue because you have no help from anyone. Your mind is sorrowful about the situation because you followed the wrong master and you need to let him go.

Third Nine (九 三, Jiu San)
Determined Stillness in one's own loins. The girdle is aligned. Discipline sets the heart aglow.

艮其限. 列其夤. 厲薰心.

You stopped to check your waist and loins and discover a pulled or torn muscle, which worries you. However, with determination you can continue. It is best to seek true peace, but not through repressive ideas of discipline.

Fourth Six (六 四, Liu Si)
Determined Stillness in one's own body. Without fault.

艮其身. 无咎.

You stopped to check your whole body and nothing is wrong. This shows there is unrest and doubt, but pay no attention and continue being still.

Fifth Six (六 五, Liu Wu)
Determined Stillness in one's own jawbones. Having words that are orderly. Regret vanishes.

艮其輔. 言有序. 悔亡.

You stopped to check your cheeks and jawbones. Speak carefully, guard your speech, and use few words, making sure what you say is orderly. In this way you will have no regrets.

Topmost Nine (上 九, Shang Jiu)
Determined Stillness is sincere. Auspicious.

敦艮. 吉.

To be sincere means you are concerned about what you want to become. This shows that your spiritual achievement is noble, and the situation is auspicious.

Alternate English Translations for the Hexagram of Gen, 艮

The Symbol of Checking and Stopping [S]
Keeping Still, Mountain [CS] [WB]
Desisting, Stilling [B]
Mountain [C]
Bound [K]

Keeping Still [H]
Keeping Still—Impediment [N]
The Bound [RS]
Stillness [L]
The Symbol of Stability [CC]

The Great Symbolism (大象, Da Xiang) says,

Mountains united. This is Gen. Superior persons, according with this, do not take their thoughts beyond their position.

兼山.艮.君子以思不出其位.

Sexagenary Placement

Heavenly Stem: Xin 辛 (8th Stem, Yin)—**Metal** (金, Jin)
Earthly Branch: Wei 未 (8th Branch, Yin)—**Goat** (羊, Yang)
Represents the *Year of the Metal Goat* (8th Year of the Sixty-Year Cycle)
Years: 1871 – 1931 – 1991 – 2051

Trigram Correlations

Upper Gua (Mountain)

Gen 艮   **Represents:** Mountain, Towers, Youngest Son
Actions: Stillness, Binding, Stopping
Influences: Knowledge, Wisdom, Skill, Determination
Shape: Vertical Column   **Color:** Blue
Body: Hands and arms   **Season:** Beginning Autumn
Moon Phase: Waxing Crescent
Animals: Earthly Dog, Celestial Vermilion Snake
Directions: Northwest (BH), Northeast (AH)
Nine Palaces Numbers: Fu Xi: 7
   Yu the Great: Ho River Map, **6**— Lo River Script, **8**
Internal Alchemy: Hun (Heavenly) Spirit
   Qi Center: Jing Men (Essence Gate)
   Qi Meridian: Yang Qiao Mai (Yang Heel Vessel)

Lower Gua (Mountain)

Gen 艮

Represents: Mountain, Towers, Youngest Son
Actions: Stillness, Binding, Stopping
Influences: Knowledge, Wisdom, Skill, Determination
Shape: Vertical Column   **Color:** Blue
Body: Hands and arms   **Season:** Beginning Autumn
Moon Phase: Waxing Crescent
Animals: Earthly Dog, Celestial Vermilion Snake
Directions: Northwest (BH), Northeast (AH)
Nine Palaces Numbers: Fu Xi: 7
   Yu the Great: Ho River Map, **6**— Lo River Script, **8**
Internal Alchemy: Hun (Heavenly) Spirit
   Qi Center: Jing Men (Essence Gate)
   Qi Meridian: Yang Qiao Mai (Yang Heel Vessel)

Associated Developed Hexagrams of Gen

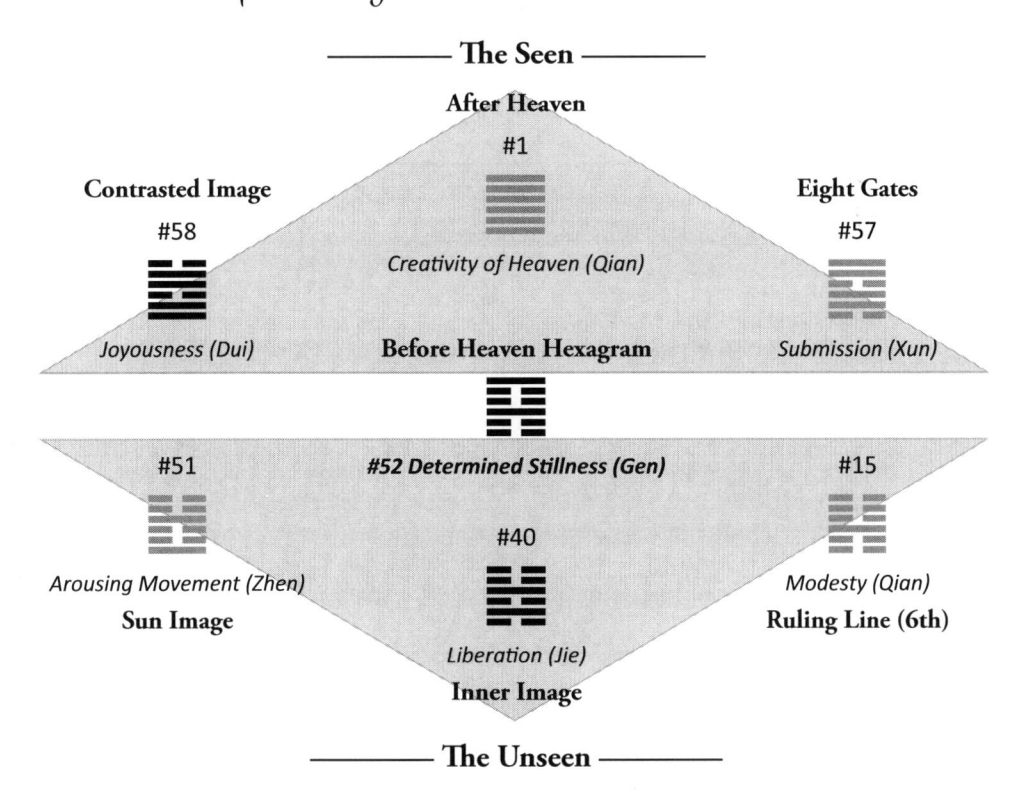

——— **The Seen** ———

After Heaven
#1
Creativity of Heaven (Qian)

Contrasted Image
#58
Joyousness (Dui)

Eight Gates
#57
Submission (Xun)

Before Heaven Hexagram

#52 Determined Stillness (Gen)

#51
Arousing Movement (Zhen)
Sun Image

#40
Liberation (Jie)
Inner Image

#15
Modesty (Qian)
Ruling Line (6th)

——— **The Unseen** ———

Jian

漸

Gradual Movement

53

Xun (Wind) above
巽 上
Xun Shang
Gen (Mountain) below
艮 下
Gen Xia

Sun/Yang Image

The Prediction (彖, Tuan)

Gradual Movement:
The marriage of a young female.
Auspicious. Advantage in being resolute.

漸. 女 歸 吉. 利 貞.

This image advises to pay great attention to the facts. There is a gradual movement toward the marriage of a young woman. She is auspicious, so there is advantage in pursuing her. This is a time to avoid the futile efforts of trying to get things to move quicker. Let things develop and come to fruition gradually, step by step. You will need great patience to sustain yourself in this situation. Above all do not underestimate your own worth and charisma.

The Lines (爻, Yao)

First Six (初 六, Chu Liu)
Gradual Movement of the wild geese on the shore. Someone young is in danger and spoken against. Without fault.

鴻 漸 于 于. 小 子 厲 有 言. 无 咎.

Many geese keep coming in and landing on the shore. There is a young person who is in immediate danger and others are talking badly about this person, yet there really will be no big trouble. You make some initial errors, so just slow down the pace.

Second Six (六 二, Liu Er)
Gradual Movement of wild geese onto large rocks. Eating and drinking in joyful ease. Auspicious.

鴻 漸 于 磐. 飲 食 衎 衎. 吉.

The geese have landed onto large rocks where there is plentiful food and drink, so they are joyous and comfortable. This is a very good omen. Enjoy your rest and the safety of this time. Likewise, engage in sharing with others.

Third Nine (九 三, Jiu San)

Gradual Movement of wild geese onto dry land. The man goes but does not return. The wife is pregnant but does not offer birth. Misfortune. Advantage is resisting bandits.

鴻漸于陸. 夫征不復.
婦孕不育. 凶. 利禦寇.

The geese were forced to land upon dry ground. The husband left to travel but has not returned. The wife is pregnant and at home alone. Although this is not auspicious, it, at least, prevents thieves from coming. It is good not to provoke conflicts or arguments, then all can go well.

Fourth Six (六 四, Liu Si)

Gradual Movement of wild geese into trees. Perhaps landing on flat branches. Without fault.

鴻漸于木. 或得其桷. 无咎.

The geese try to land in the trees but they can only find balance on the flat branches (because of their webbed feet). This causes no danger. It shows that you should be grateful for every humble dwelling you encounter.

Fifth Nine (九 五, Jiu Wu)

Gradual Movement of wild geese onto dry land. For three years the wife does not become pregnant. In the end no obstruction. Auspicious.

鴻漸于陸. 婦三歲不孕.
終莫之勝. 吉.

The geese fly away but find dry ground on which to land. The wife is unable to become pregnant for three years, and so was without child. Her life is auspicious, though, and without any other obstacles. This shows the progress was too hasty, which only invited you to be isolated.

Topmost Nine (上 九, Shang Jiu)

Gradual Movement of wild geese unto dry land. The feathers can be used in ceremonies. Auspicious.

鴻漸于陸. 其羽可用為儀. 吉.

All the geese have landed upon dry land. Their fallen feathers are then used as decoration for ceremonies. This is a good omen. It means your work has been completed and good fortune will follow.

Alternate English Translations for the Hexagram of Jian, 漸

The Symbol of Progressive Advance [S]
Development (Gradual Progress) [WB]
Gradual Development (Progress) [CS]
Gradual Progress [B] [C]
Gradual Advance [K]
Developing Gradually [H]
Gradualness [N]
Infiltrating [RS]
Gradual Development [L]
The Symbol of Gradual Progress [CC]

The Great Symbolism (大象, Da Xiang) says,

A Mountain and above it is Wood. This is Jian. Superior persons, according with this, maintain their worthy virtue for the good of the common people.

山上有木. 漸.
君子以居賢德善俗.

Sexagenary Placement

Heavenly Stem: Bing 丙 (3rd Stem, Yang)—**Fire** (火, Huo)
Earthly Branch: Shen 申 (9th Branch, Yang)—猴 **Monkey** (Hou)
Represents the *Year of the Fire Monkey* (33rd Year of the Sixty-Year Cycle)
Years: 1836 – 1896 – 1956 – 2016

Trigram Correlations

Upper Gua (Wind)

Xun 巽   **Represents:** Wind, Wood, Eldest Daughter
Actions: Gentleness, Grounding, Penetrating, Spreading
Influences: Prosperity, Abundance, Wealth
Shape: Rectangle   **Color:** Purple
Body: Waist and hips   **Season:** Beginning Summer
Moon Phase: Waxing Gibbous
Animals: Earthly Fowl, Celestial Golden Rooster
Directions: Southwest (BH), Southeast (AH)
Nine Palaces Numbers: Fu Xi: **9**
    Yu the Great: Ho River Map, **2**—Lo River Script, **4**
Internal Alchemy: Breath and Mobilizing Qi
    Qi Center: Yu Zhen (Jade Pillow)
    Qi Meridian: Yin Wei Mai (Yin Preserving Vessel)

#53 Gradual Movement (Jian)

Lower Gua (Mountain)

Gen 艮

Represents: Mountain, Towers, Youngest Son
Actions: Stillness, Binding, Stopping
Influences: Knowledge, Wisdom, Skill, Determination
Shape: Vertical Column   **Color:** Blue
Body: Hands and arms   **Season:** Beginning Autumn
Moon Phase: Waxing Crescent
Animals: Earthly Dog, Celestial Vermilion Snake
Directions: Northwest (BH), Northeast (AH)
Nine Palaces Numbers: Fu Xi: 7
  Yu the Great: Ho River Map, 6— Lo River Script, 8
Internal Alchemy: Hun (Heavenly) Spirit
  Qi Center: Jing Men (Essence Gate)
  Qi Meridian: Yang Qiao Mai (Yang Heel Vessel)

Associated Developed Hexagrams of Jian

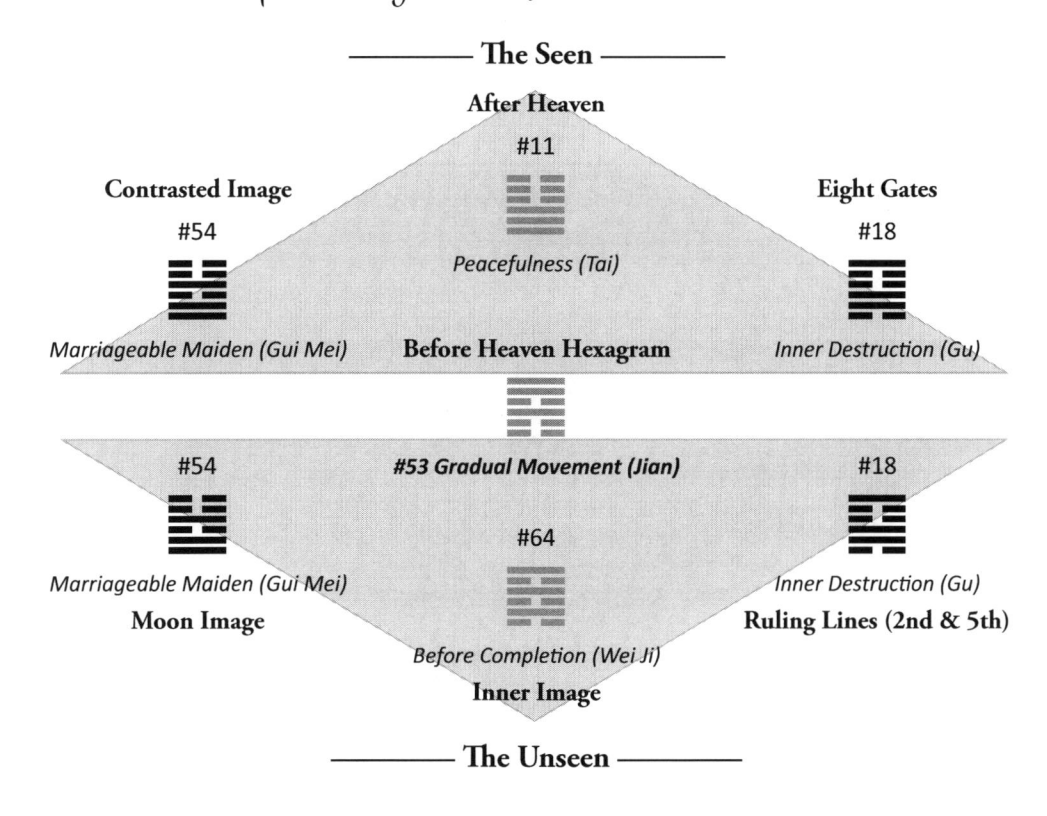

——— **The Seen** ———

After Heaven
#11
Peacefulness (Tai)

Contrasted Image
#54
Marriageable Maiden (Gui Mei)

Eight Gates
#18
Inner Destruction (Gu)

Before Heaven Hexagram

#53 Gradual Movement (Jian)

#54
Marriageable Maiden (Gui Mei)
Moon Image

#64
Before Completion (Wei Ji)
Inner Image

#18
Inner Destruction (Gu)
Ruling Lines (2nd & 5th)

——— **The Unseen** ———

Gui Mei *Marriageable Maiden* 54

Zhen (Thunder) above
震 上
Zhen Shang

Dui (Valley) below
兌 下
Dui Xia

Moon/Yin Image

The Prediction (彖, Tuan)

Marriageable Maiden:
**Advancing brings misfortune.
Nothing is of benefit.**

歸妹. 征凶. 无有利.

This image shows that people should make good use of their talents. The woman is engaged, so to advance further with talk of marriage will only cause her to retreat and bring you misfortune. Nothing will go as planned or smoothly. It is best to exercise great tact and show great respect towards her. Make compromises and avoid conflicts. Keep your mind fixed on the end goal and this will flourish into a close relationship.

The Lines (爻, Yao)

First Nine (初 九, **Chu Jiu**)
The Marriageable Maiden is to be a concubine. Lamed, yet able to walk. Advancing is auspicious.

歸妹以娣. 跛能履. 征吉.

The woman getting married brings along her younger sister. Even though she has a limp, she can move well. Advancing this situation brings good fortune. This shows you can move forward despite being in an inferior position.

Second Nine (九 二, **Jiu Er**)
A one-eyed man is able to see. There is advantage for the recluse to be resolute.

眇能視. 利幽人之貞.

When the left eye is closed it is a sign of enlightenment. The recluse should resolutely continue cultivating. This shows to maintain loyalty even if being in isolation and feeling lonely.

#54 Marriageable Maiden (Gui Mei)

Third Six (六 三, Liu San)
The Marriageable Maiden's wedding
is postponed. Marriage will be late,
but the time will come.

歸妹以須. 反歸以娣.

The woman's marriage is postponed because the elder sister will marry the man. After some time it is decided the younger sister will also marry him. This shows the first opportunity is actually a lowly position.

Fourth Nine (九 四, Jiu Si)
The Marriageable Maiden is to be
a maidservant. Instead she
marries as a concubine.

歸妹愆期. 遲歸有時.

The woman postpones her marriage to wait for a better opportunity. She decides on another man and to be a concubine instead. The intention is sincere and little can be lost in advancing.

Fifth Six (六 五, Liu Wu)
The emperor gives an embroidered
robe to the Marriageable Maiden,
but it is not as splendid as the one
for the younger sister. The moon
is nearly full. Auspicious.

帝乙歸妹. 其君之袂.
不如其娣之袂良.
月幾望. 吉.

The emperor is going to marry off his daughters. The elder's robes are not of the same high beauty as the one given to her younger sister, who is to marry the same man. If the wedding occurs on the day of the full moon it will be very auspicious. This shows to accept the situation without bitterness, then good fortune will come under the fullness of the moon.

Topmost Six (上 六, Shang Liu)
The female has a basket. It is empty.
The man stabs the goat. There is no blood.
Nothing is of advantage.

女承筐. 无實. 士刲羊.
无血. 无攸利.

The woman carries a basket, but it is empty. The man cuts the goat, but no blood comes forth. Neither of these two are in a favorable situation. This shows there really is no sincerity, and without it all is meaningless.

Alternate English Translations for the Hexagram of Gui Mei, 歸妹

The Marrying Maiden [CS] [WB]
The Marriageable Maiden [B]
Making a Young Girl Marry [C]
The Symbol of the Marriage
    of the Younger Sister [S]
The Symbol of Marriage [CC]

Marriage [N]
Converting Maidenhood [RS]
The Marrying Girl [L]
Marrying Maiden [H]
Marrying the Maiden [K]

The Great Symbolism (大象, Da Xiang) says,

A Marsh and above it there is Thunder. This is Gui Mei. The superior person, according with this, regards the far-distant end to know the errors in the beginning.

澤上有雷.歸妹.
君子以永終知敝.

Sexagenary Placement

Heavenly Stem: Bing 丙 (3rd Stem, Yang)—**Fire** (火, Huo)
Earthly Branch: Yin 寅 (3rd Branch, Yang)—**Tiger** (虎, Hu)
Represents the *Year of the Fire Tiger* (3rd Year of the Sixty-Year Cycle)
Years: 1866 – 1926 – 1986 – 2046

Trigram Correlations

Upper Gua (Thunder)

Zhen 震

- **Represents:** Thunder, Earthquake, Eldest Son
- **Actions:** Arousing, Shaking, Initiating
- **Influences:** Foundations, Past Actions, Excitement.
- **Shape:** Vertical Column   **Color:** Green
- **Body:** Feet and legs   **Season:** Beginning Winter
- **Moon Phase:** Waning Crescent
- **Animals:** Earthly Dragons, Celestial Dragon-Horse
- **Directions:** Northeast (BH), East (AH)
- **Nine Palaces Numbers:** Fu Xi: **3**
    - Yu the Great: Ho River Map, **8**—Lo River Script, **3**
- **Internal Alchemy:** Mind-Intention
    - Qi Center: Dan Tian (Elixir Field)
    - Qi Meridian: Yin Qiao Mai (Yin Heel Vessel)

#54 Marriageable Maiden (Gui Mei)

Lower Gua (Valley)

☱ Dui 兑

Represents: Valley, River, Lake/Marsh, Youngest Daughter
Actions: Joyous, Opening, Stimulating
Influences: Family, Future, Collecting, Pleasure, Absorbing, Complacency.
Shape: Introverted Triangle   **Color:** Brown
Body: Mouth   **Season:** Beginning Spring
Moon Phase: Waning Gibbous
Animals: Earthly Goat, Celestial Great Roc
Directions: Southeast (BH), West (AH)
Nine Palaces Numbers: Fu Xi: 5
    Yu the Great: Ho River Map, 4—Lo River Script, 7
Internal Alchemy: Po (Earthly) Spirit
    Qi Center: Xuan Guan (Mysterious Pass)
    Qi Meridian: Yang Wei Mai (Yang Preserving Vessel)

Associated Developed Hexagrams of Gui Mei

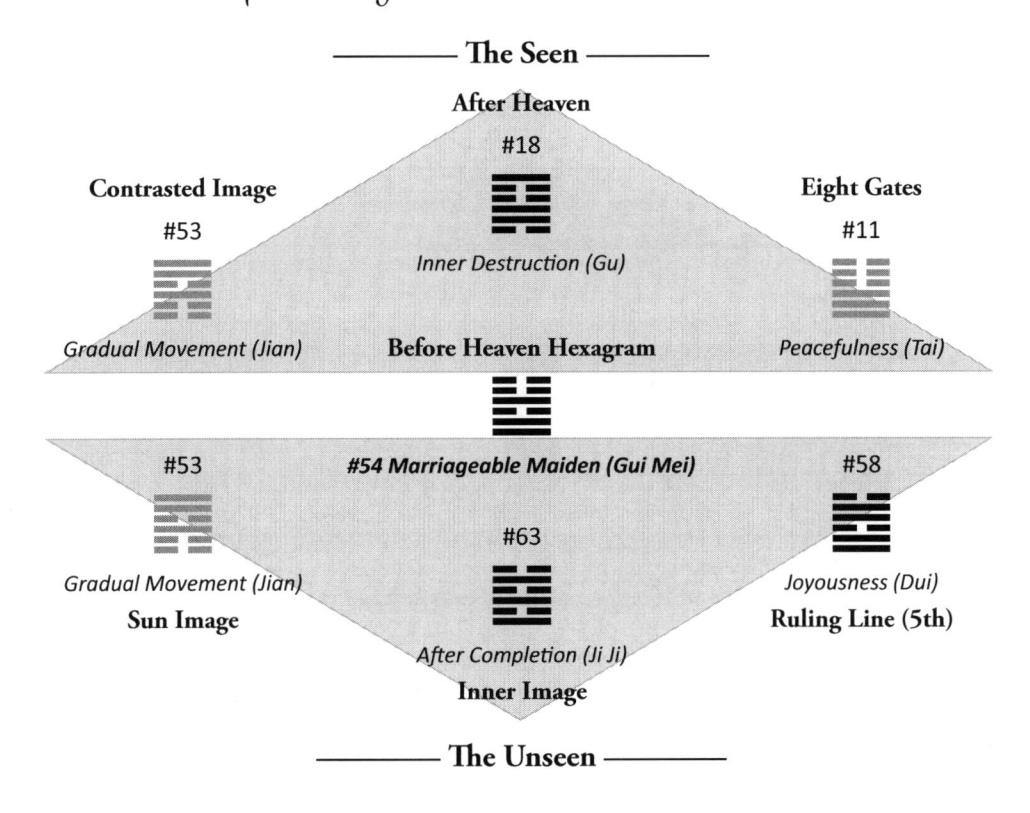

——— **The Seen** ———

After Heaven
#18
Inner Destruction (Gu)

Contrasted Image
#53
Gradual Movement (Jian)

Eight Gates
#11
Peacefulness (Tai)

Before Heaven Hexagram
#54 Marriageable Maiden (Gui Mei)

#53
Gradual Movement (Jian)
Sun Image

#63
After Completion (Ji Ji)
Inner Image

#58
Joyousness (Dui)
Ruling Line (5th)

——— **The Unseen** ———

Feng 豐

Prosperity — 55

Zhen (Thunder) above
震上
Zhen Shang
Li (Fire) below
離下
Li Xia

Sun/Yang Image

The Prediction (彖, Tuan)

Prosperity:
Perseverance. The king reaches to greatness. Without any sorrow. He should be as the midday sun.

豐. 亨. 王假之. 勿憂宜日中.

This image indicates that when a person shares a problem, it becomes half of the solution. This image is of prosperity because the king himself arrives to preside over a ceremony, so there will be no need to worry. The ceremony will be most favorable if conducted at noon. Prosperity should be enjoyed while it lasts because fortunes inevitably diminish. So sharing your prosperity with others and accepting its disappearance lessens the sorrow and anger afterwards.

The Lines (爻, Yao)

First Nine (初 九, Chu Jiu)
Meeting both his mate and master. Though it has been ten days, this is without fault. To advance has honor.

遇其配主. 雖旬无咎.
往有尚.

You have come together with a wealthy family and so find both a mate and master. Within ten days there will be no more troubles. To advance in this situation brings honor and rewards. This shows a very beneficial association is possible.

Second Six (六 二, Liu Er)
Prosperity of his shields. At the midday sun the Dipper constellation is seen. Going, he will acquire suspicion and anger. Truth brings approval. Auspicious.

豐其蔀. 日中見斗.
往得疑疾. 有孚發若. 吉.

Even though the brightness of the sun was hidden and the sky grew dark, the Big Dipper could be seen clearly at midday. Walking on, you feel a sense of suspicion and anger, but once you realize this was an eclipse you see it as an auspicious omen.

Third Nine (九 三, Jiu San)

Prosperity flows to him. At the midday sun the star Mei is seen. He breaks his right arm. Without fault.	豐其沛.日中見沫. 折其右肱.无咎.

Even though rewards have flowed to him, the morning star is seen in the midday sun (because of the eclipse). He breaks his right arm, so the arm must be bound, but this is not too serious and all will be well.

Fourth Nine (九 四, Jiu Si)

Prosperity of his shields. At the midday sun the Dipper constellation can be seen. Meeting his noble master Yi. Auspicious.	豐其蔀.日中見斗. 遇其夷主.吉.

The daytime light was cut off by the eclipse, and the Big Dipper is seen at midday, but this is auspicious because one meets with the leader of the Yi clan. Though considered as barbarians, the Yi clan bring good fortune.

Fifth Six (六 五, Liu Wu)

Honor comes. Having Prosperity and praise. Auspicious.	來章.有慶譽.吉.

The light of the sun has returned and everyone is celebrating. An extremely auspicious time, this shows the master gave very wise counsel and advised to be modest in one's prosperity.

Topmost Six (上 六), Shang Liu)

Prosperity in his household. Shielding one's own family. Spying through one's own door. But when examining it, no one is there. For three years there is no audience. Unfortunate.	豐其屋.蔀其家.闚其戶. 闃其无人.三歲不覿.凶.

The house is big and well protected. He wants to spy on others in the house, but no one is there. For three years there will be no visitors. This is a very ill-omened situation, which shows that the prosperity was excessive and so he becomes isolated and left alone.

Alternate English Translations for the Hexagram of Feng, 豐

The Symbol of Prosperity [CC] [S]
Abundance (Fullness) [WB]
Abundance [B] [CS] [H]
Richness [C]
Over—Capacity [N]
Abounding [K] [RS]
Greatness [L]

The Great Symbolism (大象, Da Xiang) says,

Thunder and Lightning arrive together. This is Feng. The superior person, according with this, deliberates the litigation, and then considers the punishments.

雷電皆至.豐.
君子以折折致刑.

Sexagenary Placement

Heavenly Stem: Bing 丙 (3rd Stem, Yang)—**Fire** (火, Huo)
Earthly Branch: Xu 戌 (11th Branch, Yang)—**Dog** (狗, Gou)
Represents the *Year of the Fire Dog* (23rd Year of the Sixty-Year Cycle)
Years: 1886 – 1946 – 2006 – 2066

Trigram Correlations

Upper Gua (Thunder)

Zhen 震　　**Represents:** Thunder, Earthquake, Eldest Son
Actions: Arousing, Shaking, Initiating
Influences: Foundations, Past Actions, Excitement.
Shape: Vertical Column　　**Color:** Green
Body: Feet and legs　　**Season:** Beginning Winter
Moon Phase: Waning Crescent
Animals: Earthly Dragons, Celestial Dragon-Horse
Directions: Northeast (BH), East (AH)
Nine Palaces Numbers: Fu Xi: **3**
　　Yu the Great: Ho River Map, **8**—Lo River Script, **3**
Internal Alchemy: Mind-Intention
　　Qi Center: Dan Tian (Elixir Field)
　　Qi Meridian: Yin Qiao Mai (Yin Heel Vessel)

#55 Prosperity (Feng)

Lower Gua (Fire)

☲ **Li** 離
Represents: Fire, Lightning, Sun, Middle Daughter
Actions: Clinging, Illuminating, Congregating
Influences: Fame, Reputation, Brightness, Elegance
Shape: Triangle   **Color:** Red
Body: Eyes   **Season:** Spring (Spring Equinox)
Moon Phase: Last Quarter
Animals: Earthly Rooster, Celestial Green Dragon
Directions: East (BH), South (AH)
Nine Palaces Numbers: Fu Xi: **8**
   Yu the Great: Ho River Map, **3**—Lo River Script, **9**
Internal Alchemy: Mercury, Qi
   Qi Center: Jiang Gong (Crimson Palace)
   Qi Meridian: Dai Mai (Belt Vessel)

Associated Developed Hexagrams of Feng

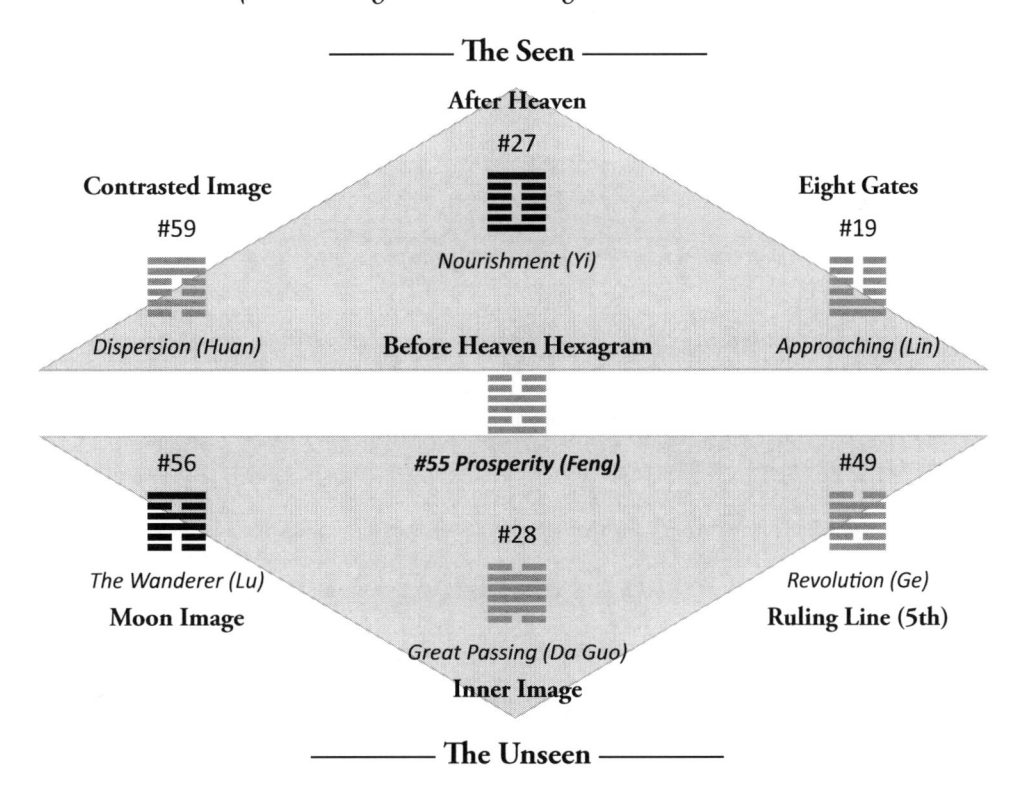

———— **The Seen** ————

After Heaven
#27
Nourishment (Yi)

Contrasted Image
#59
Dispersion (Huan)

Eight Gates
#19
Approaching (Lin)

Before Heaven Hexagram

#55 Prosperity (Feng)

#56
The Wanderer (Lu)
Moon Image

#28
Great Passing (Da Guo)
Inner Image

#49
Revolution (Ge)
Ruling Line (5th)

———— **The Unseen** ————

Lu

旅

The Wanderer

56

Li (Fire) above
離 上
Li Shang

Gen (Mountain) below
艮 下
Gen Xia

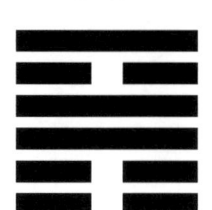

Moon/Yin Image

The Prediction (彖, Tuan)

The Wanderer:
A little perseverance. The Wanderer
is resolute and auspicious.

旅. 小 亨. 旅 貞 吉.

This image shows that if the tongue is restrained, wisdom can flow to the head. The wandering has went well and the journey was fruitful. It is auspicious to plan your future while wandering. It is good to see yourself as a wanderer upon the face of the Earth and you will be seen as nothing more than that to others. Whether you wander internally or externally, your influence will not be long lasting. As a wanderer, you must adopt the attitudes of patience and yielding in the face of what you encounter.

The Lines (爻, Yao)

First Six (初 六, Chu Liu)
The Wanderer is petty and contemptible;
thus, he creates calamities.

旅 瑣 瑣. 斯 其 所 取 災.

The wanderer pays too much attention to the trivial, and this brings about trouble. Like a person playing with a rabbit, he does not see the tiger about to pounce. This shows that your dignity has been compromised for small favors, and this brings misfortune.

Second Six (六 二, Liu Er)
The Wanderer is now in the lodging house.
Carrying his wealth, he acquires a good
servant of virtue.

旅 即 次. 懷 其 資. 得 童 僕 貞.

The wanderer decides to stay at an inn, using his money to hire a servant who serves him well. This shows there is a good companionship bringing good fortune.

Third Nine (九 三, Jiu San)
The Wanderer's lodging house is set on fire and he loses his good servant. Resoluteness brings danger.

旅焚其次. 喪其童僕. 貞厲.

A fire starts at the inn and a good servant is lost. This is a bad omen. This shows that the wanderer has burned some bridges and has put himself in danger.

Fourth Nine (九 四, Jiu Si)
The Wanderer is resting. Having his wealth and axe. But his heart is not cheerful.

旅于處. 得其資斧. 我心不快.

The wanderer stops to rest and finds money and an axe, but neither of these make him feel happy. This shows the wanderer has found shelter but not a home, for he knows he must leave in a short while.

Fifth Six (六 五, Liu Wu)
He shoots a pheasant. One arrow is lost. In the end he receives praise and a decree.

射雉. 一矢亡. 終以譽命.

Spotting a pheasant, he shoots his arrow at it. He misses and so loses an arrow, but in the end he is honored with a decree. The wanderer has found acceptance amongst strangers and so is praised for his talents.

Topmost Nine (上 九, Shang Jiu)
The bird's nest catches on fire in the tree. The stranger first laughs. Afterwards, he wails and weeps. He loses the ox by being lax. Misfortune.

鳥焚其巢. 旅人先笑後號咷.
喪牛于易. 凶.

Seeing a nest burning in a tree is an ominous omen. When engaged in trading with a stranger, the stranger laughs at first, then cries later. From not paying attention, his ox has wandered off. Extremely misfortunate, this shows a loss from being careless. There is great regret and remorse.

Alternate English Translations for the Hexagram of Lu, 旅

The Symbol of Traveller [S]
The Wanderer [WB]
The Traveller [B] [CS]
Travel [C]
The Symbol of Wandering [CC]

Travelling [H] [N]
Sojourning [RS]
The Exile [L]
Sojourning/Quest [K]

The Great Symbolism (大象, Da Xiang) says,

Above the Mountain there is Fire. This is Lu.　　山上有火. 旅.
The superior person, according with this,　　　君子以明愼用刑.
uses both wisdom and caution in punishments,　而不留獄.
and does not detain litigation.

Sexagenary Placement

Heavenly Stem: Jia 甲 (1st Stem, Yang)—**Wood** (木, Mu)
Earthly Branch: Xu 戌 (11th Branch, Yang)—**Dog** (狗, Gou)
Represents the *Year of the Wood Dog* (11th Year of the Sixty-Year Cycle)
Years: 1874 – 1934 – 1994 – 2054

Trigram Correlations

Upper Gua (Fire)

Li 離

Represents: Fire, Lightning, Sun, Middle Daughter
Actions: Clinging, Illuminating, Congregating
Influences: Fame, Reputation, Brightness, Elegance
Shape: Triangle　　　**Color:** Red
Body: Eyes　　　　　**Season:** Spring (Spring Equinox)
Moon Phase: Last Quarter
Animals: Earthly Rooster, Celestial Green Dragon
Directions: East (BH), South (AH)
Nine Palaces Numbers: Fu Xi: **8**
　　Yu the Great: Ho River Map, **3**—Lo River Script, **9**
Internal Alchemy: Mercury, Qi
　　Qi Center: Jiang Gong (Crimson Palace)
　　Qi Meridian: Dai Mai (Belt Vessel)

#56 The Wanderer (Lu)

Lower Gua (Mountain)

☶ Gen 艮

Represents: Mountain, Towers, Youngest Son
Actions: Stillness, Binding, Stopping
Influences: Knowledge, Wisdom, Skill, Determination
Shape: Vertical Column   **Color:** Blue
Body: Hands and arms   **Season:** Beginning Autumn
Moon Phase: Waxing Crescent
Animals: Earthly Dog, Celestial Vermilion Snake
Directions: Northwest (BH), Northeast (AH)
Nine Palaces Numbers: Fu Xi: 7
   Yu the Great: Ho River Map, 6— Lo River Script, 8
Internal Alchemy: Hun (Heavenly) Spirit
   Qi Center: Jing Men (Essence Gate)
   Qi Meridian: Yang Qiao Mai (Yang Heel Vessel)

Associated Developed Hexagrams of Lu

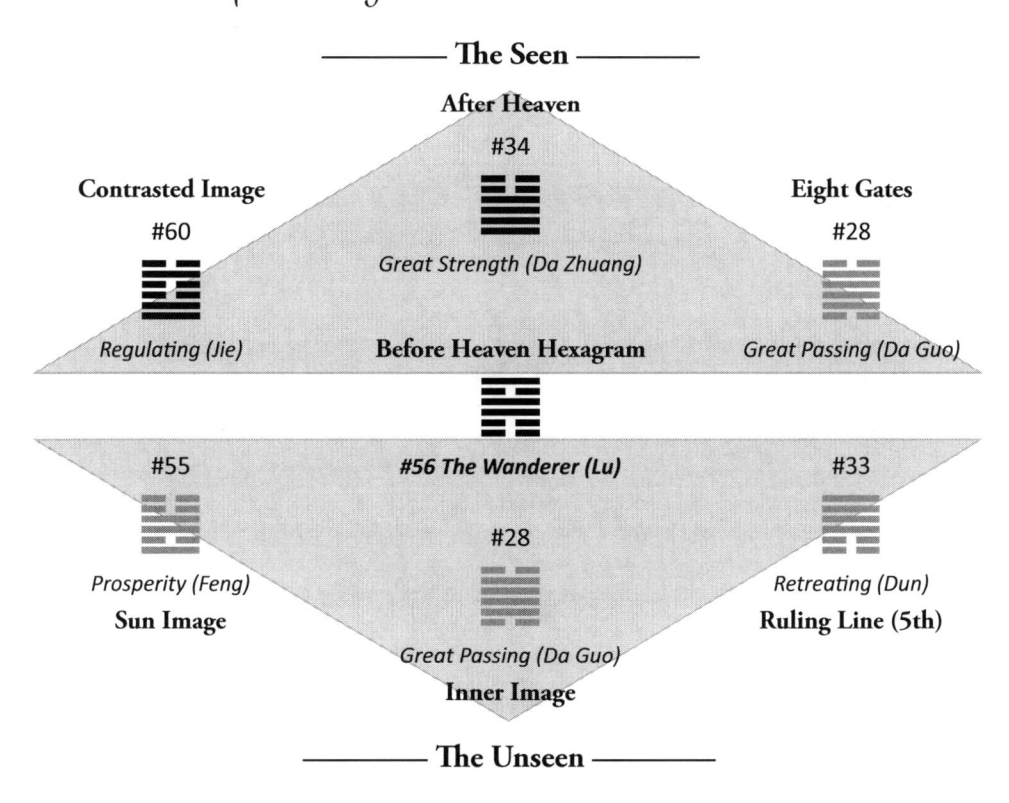

——— **The Seen** ———

After Heaven
#34
Great Strength (Da Zhuang)

Contrasted Image
#60
Regulating (Jie)

Eight Gates
#28
Great Passing (Da Guo)

Before Heaven Hexagram

#56 The Wanderer (Lu)

#55
Prosperity (Feng)
Sun Image

#28
Great Passing (Da Guo)
Inner Image

#33
Retreating (Dun)
Ruling Line (5th)

——— **The Unseen** ———

Xun

巽

Submission

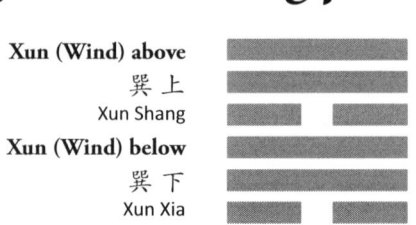

57

Xun (Wind) above
巽 上
Xun Shang
Xun (Wind) below
巽 下
Xun Xia

Sun/Yang Image

The Prediction (象, Tuan)

Submission:

A little perseverance. Advantage in having somewhere to go. Advantage in seeing an elder.

巽. 小 亨. 利 有 攸 往. 利 見 大 人.

This image shows to move step by step with no hurried or rash actions. This is the right time to go somewhere to meet with a great person. Wind is dispersing and moving the clouds above so the sky becomes clear and there is great clarity. It is best to endure lowly conditions with modesty so the efforts can be gradual. If you allow time to take care of things, you can gain a great power of penetrating the spirits of others. No person can be dominant without the permission of submission. Who or what then is really dominant? Wind doubled has great power.

The Lines (爻, Yao)

First Six (初 六, Chu Liu)
Advancing and withdrawing.
Advantage for the resolute warrior.

進退. 利 武 人 之 貞.

Every battle has a time when advancing is appropriate, and a time for retreating. It is between these two actions that the warrior should plan his next moves. Advantage goes to those who avoid indecision and can remain resolute.

Second Nine (九 二, Jiu Er)
Submission is beneath the couch. Diviners and wizards are employed, but they are confused. Auspicious. Without fault.

巽 在 牀 下. 用 史 巫 紛 若.
吉. 无 咎.

#57 Submission (Xun)

Crouching down to get beneath the couch so you cannot be clearly seen, the wizards and diviners come one after another to foretell your future, but they are all confused. Still, you made no errors and this is all very auspicious, showing that you need to search for the obstacles on your own.

Third Nine (九 三, Jiu San)
Repetition of Submission. Regret.   頻巽. 吉.

Too much divination and asking for divine assistance brings trouble. Just make a decision and stay with it. Too many opinions only cause trouble, so just remain submissive and follow the movement, otherwise there will be regret.

Fourth Six (六 四, Liu Si)
Regret vanishes. Game is to be snared   悔亡. 田獲三品.
in three ways.

There are no concerns at hand, as you have three different ways of snaring game in the fields. This shows that all variants and factors have been thought out, and this brings good fortune.

Fifth Nine (九 五, Jiu Wu)
Resoluteness is auspicious. Regret vanishes.   貞吉. 悔亡. 无不利.
Everything is advantageous. Not having   无初有終. 先庚三日.
in the beginning, but having in the end.   後庚三日. 吉.
Before restoration three days. After
restoration three days. Auspicious.

There are no worries as the foretelling was auspicious. Even if the beginning does not seem auspicious, the end will be. Three days before and three days after the Keng Shen Day [5] is extremely auspicious. Cautiously and carefully reform yourself. Be resolute in your submission.

Topmost Nine (上 九, Shang Jiu)
The Submission is beneath the couch.   巽在牀下. 喪其資斧. 貞凶.
Losing wealth and axe. Resoluteness
brings misfortune.

Crouching down to get beneath the couch so you cannot be clearly seen. Your wealth and axe are then stolen. This unfortunate situation shows you have allowed the submission to go too far and now you are losing yourself. Do not continue the submission.

---

5   *Keng Shen* is a spirit reporting day that occurs on the 57th day of the new year.

Alternate English Translations for the Hexagram of Xun, 巽

The Symbol of Bending to Enter [S]
The Gentle (The Penetrating, Wind) [WB]
The Penetrating Wind [CS]
The Root [RS]
Willing Submission, Gentleness, Ground [K]
The Symbol of Penetration [CC]
Wind [C]
Proceeding Humbly [H]
Gentle Wind—Submissiveness [N]
Penetration (Wind) [L]
Penetration [B]

The Great Symbolism (大象, Da Xiang) says,

The Wind following itself. This is Xun.   隨風巽.
The superior person, according with this,   君子以命行事.
repeats commands and acts on affairs.

Sexagenary Placement

Heavenly Stem: Yi 乙 (2nd Stem, Yin)—**Wood** (木, Mu)
Earthly Branch: Wei 未 (8th Branch, Yin)—**Goat** (羊, Yang)
Represents the *Year of the Wood Goat* (32nd Year of the Sixty-Year Cycle)
Years: 1895 – 1955 – 2015 – 2075

Trigram Correlations

Upper Gua (Wind)

Xun 巽   **Represents:** Wind, Wood, Eldest Daughter
Actions: Gentleness, Grounding, Penetrating, Spreading
Influences: Prosperity, Abundance, Wealth
Shape: Rectangle   **Color:** Purple
Body: Waist and hips   **Season:** Beginning Summer
Moon Phase: Waxing Gibbous
Animals: Earthly Fowl, Celestial Golden Rooster
Directions: Southwest (BH), Southeast (AH)
Nine Palaces Numbers: Fu Xi: **9**
    Yu the Great: Ho River Map, **2**—Lo River Script, **4**
Internal Alchemy: Breath and Mobilizing Qi
    Qi Center: Yu Zhen (Jade Pillow)
    Qi Meridian: Yin Wei Mai (Yin Preserving Vessel)

#57 Submission (Xun)

Lower Gua (Wind)

Xun 巽
Represents: Wind, Wood, Eldest Daughter
Actions: Gentleness, Grounding, Penetrating, Spreading
Influences: Prosperity, Abundance, Wealth
Shape: Rectangle **Color:** Purple
Body: Waist and hips **Season:** Beginning Summer
Moon Phase: Waxing Gibbous
Animals: Earthly Fowl, Celestial Golden Rooster
Directions: Southwest (BH), Southeast (AH)
Nine Palaces Numbers: Fu Xi: **9**
  Yu the Great: Ho River Map, **2**—Lo River Script, **4**
Internal Alchemy: Breath and Mobilizing Qi
  Qi Center: Yu Zhen (Jade Pillow)
  Qi Meridian: Yin Wei Mai (Yin Preserving Vessel)

Associated Developed Hexagrams of Xun

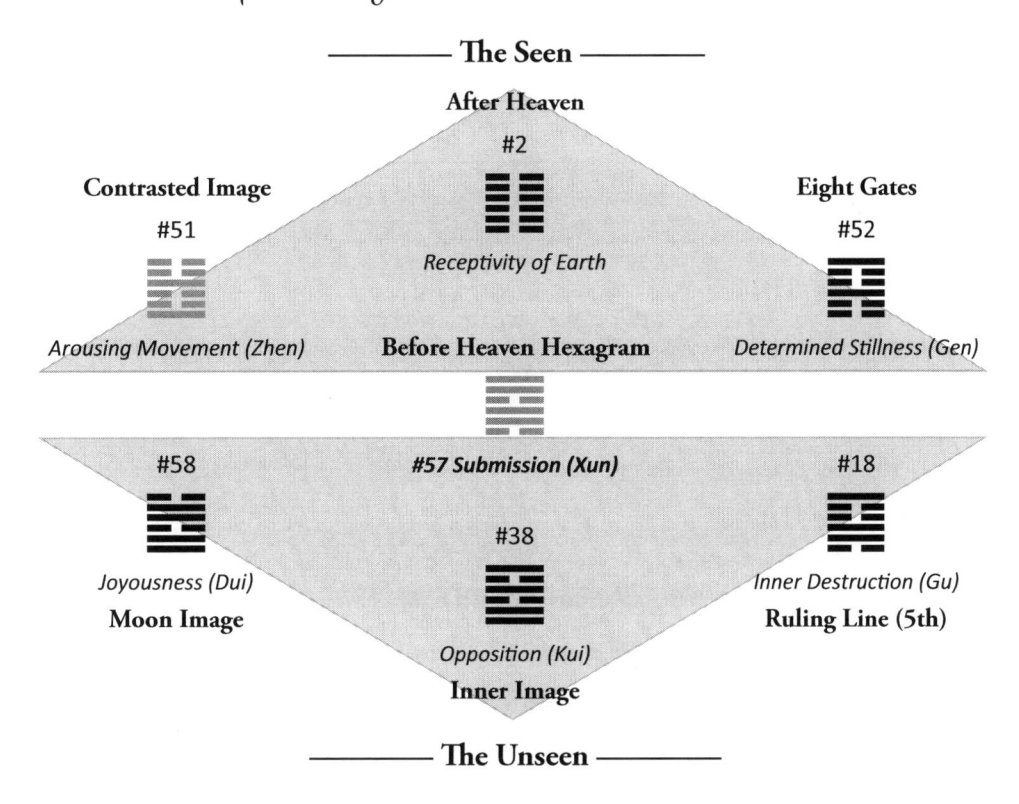

——— **The Seen** ———

After Heaven
#2
Receptivity of Earth

Contrasted Image
#51
Arousing Movement (Zhen)

Eight Gates
#52
Determined Stillness (Gen)

Before Heaven Hexagram

#57 Submission (Xun)

#58
Joyousness (Dui)
Moon Image

#38
Opposition (Kui)
Inner Image

#18
Inner Destruction (Gu)
Ruling Line (5th)

——— **The Unseen** ———

Dui 兑

Joyousness

58

Dui (Valley) above
兑 上
Dui Shang
Dui (Valley) below
兑 下
Dui Xia

Moon/Yin Image

The Prediction (彖, Tuan)

Joyousness:
Perseverance. Advantage in being resolute.

兑. 亨. 利 貞.

This image indicates that success will soon come. Everything goes well and it is a very good time for divination. The joy is very infectious and spontaneous, even the most hardened of hearts are softened. Joy generated from inner conviction and resolve will win over everyone. Others will come with lasting support. Valley doubled shows great openness, great pleasure, and great joy. All things flow into valleys, and valleys accept everything, thus there is great stimulation and absorption of energy and knowledge. The valley is the lowest place and is closest to the Dao.

The Lines (爻, Yao)

First Nine (初 九, Chu Jiu)
Harmonious Joyousness.
Auspicious.

和 兑. 吉.

There is harmony, peace, contentment, and auspiciousness.

Second Nine (九 二, Jiu Er)
Sincere Joyousness. Auspicious.
Regret vanishes.

孚 兑. 吉. 悔 亡.

Create an environment of joy and cheerfulness, then all can be auspicious and all worries gone.

Third Six (六三, Liu San)
Promise of rewards for Joyousness.   來兌. 凶.
Misfortune.

There is misfortune when too much ill-gossip and too many unfulfilled promises occur over an anticipated joy.

Fourth Nine (九四, Jiu Si)
Deliberating Joyousness, not yet   商兌未寧. 介疾有喜.
peaceful. Bordering on illness,
but will have joy.

The conversation is very cheerful, but nothing is settled. A decision about what path to follow needs to be determined. An illness is starting to fester, but it will go away.

Fifth Nine (九五, Jiu Wu)
Trusting in those who divest.   孚于剝. 有厲.
There is danger.

Those you trust in are revealing their true intentions. They only seek to take things away from you. Your faith has been given to the unworthy. This is dangerous.

Topmost Six (上六, Shang Liu)
Guiding Joyousness.   引兌.

Be a guide for others to experience joy and pleasure. Joy can be taught and given to others, so be a teacher of Joyousness.

Alternate English Translations for the Hexagram of Dui, 兌

The Symbol of Joy [S]   *Joyful* [H]
The Joyous, Lake [WB]   *Joyousness* [L] [N]
Joy [B] [C] [CS]   *The Open* [RS]
Open [K]   *The Symbol of Pleasure* [CC]

The Great Symbolism (大象, Da Xiang) says,

Connected Marshes. This is Dui.	麗澤. 兌.
The superior person, according with this, makes discussion a common practice with friends and companions.	君子以朋友講習.

Sexagenary Placement

Heavenly Stem: Xin 辛 (8th Stem, Yin)—**Metal** (金, Jin)
Earthly Branch: Chou 丑 (2nd Branch, Yin)—**Ox** (牛, Niu)
Represents the *Year of the Metal Ox* (38th Year of the Sixty-Year Cycle)
Years: 1901 – 1961 – 2021 – 2081

Trigram Correlations

Upper Gua (Valley)

Dui 兌
- **Represents:** Valley, River, Lake/Marsh, Youngest Daughter
- **Actions:** Joyous, Opening, Stimulating
- **Influences:** Family, Future, Collecting, Pleasure, Absorbing, Complacency.
- **Shape:** Introverted Triangle   **Color:** Brown
- **Body:** Mouth   **Season:** Beginning Spring
- **Moon Phase:** Waning Gibbous
- **Animals:** Earthly Goat, Celestial Great Roc
- **Directions:** Southeast (BH), West (AH)
- **Nine Palaces Numbers:** Fu Xi: 5
  - Yu the Great: Ho River Map, 4—Lo River Script, 7
- **Internal Alchemy:** Po (Earthly) Spirit
  - Qi Center: Xuan Guan (Mysterious Pass)
  - Qi Meridian: Yang Wei Mai (Yang Preserving Vessel)

#58 Joyousness (Dui)

Lower Gua (Valley)

☱ **Dui** 兑

Represents: Valley, River, Lake/Marsh, Youngest Daughter
Actions: Joyous, Opening, Stimulating
Influences: Family, Future, Collecting, Pleasure, Absorbing, Complacency.
Shape: Introverted Triangle   **Color:** Brown
Body: Mouth   **Season:** Beginning Spring
Moon Phase: Waning Gibbous
Animals: Earthly Goat, Celestial Great Roc
Directions: Southeast (BH), West (AH)
Nine Palaces Numbers: Fu Xi: 5
   Yu the Great: Ho River Map, 4—Lo River Script, 7
Internal Alchemy: Po (Earthly) Spirit
   Qi Center: Xuan Guan (Mysterious Pass)
   Qi Meridian: Yang Wei Mai (Yang Preserving Vessel)

Associated Developed Hexagrams of Dui

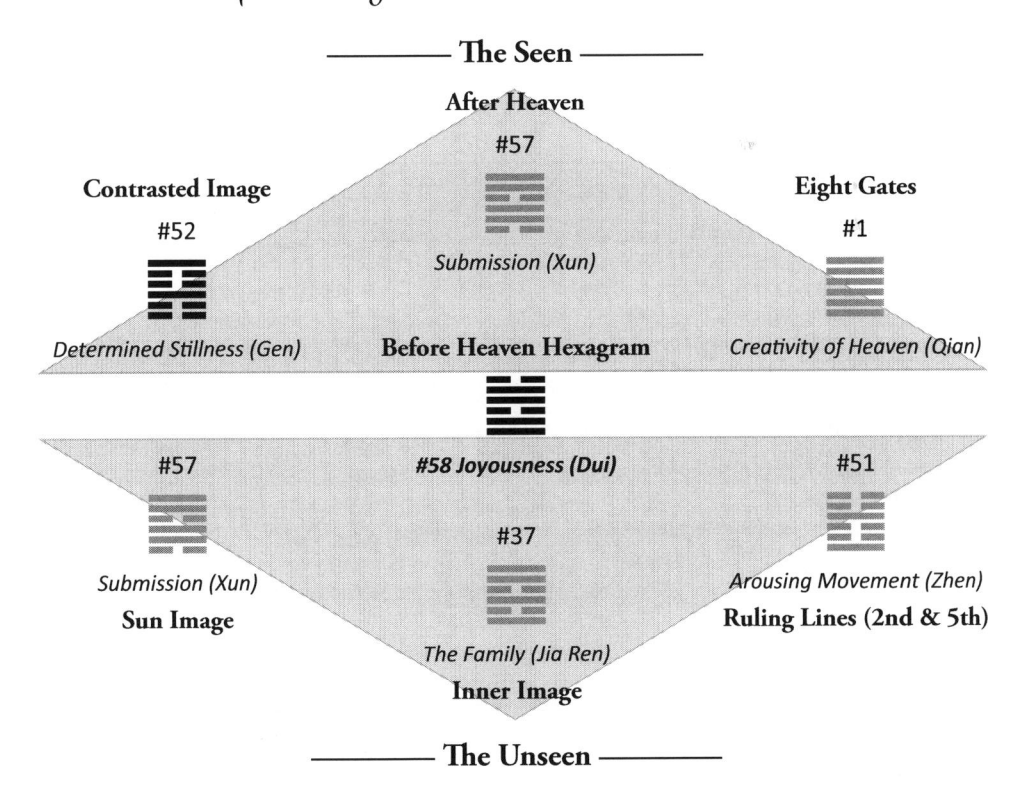

——— **The Seen** ———

After Heaven
#57
Submission (Xun)

Contrasted Image
#52
Determined Stillness (Gen)

Before Heaven Hexagram

Eight Gates
#1
Creativity of Heaven (Qian)

#58 Joyousness (Dui)

#57
Submission (Xun)
Sun Image

#37
The Family (Jia Ren)
Inner Image

#51
Arousing Movement (Zhen)
Ruling Lines (2nd & 5th)

——— **The Unseen** ———

Huan

Dispersion

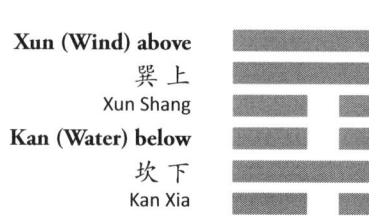

59

渙

Xun (Wind) above
巽上
Xun Shang
Kan (Water) below
坎下
Kan Xia

Sun/Yang Image

The Prediction (彖, Tuan)

Dispersion:
Perseverance. The king has approached the temple. Advantage in fording the great stream. Advantage in being resolute.

渙. 亨. 王假有廟.
利涉大川. 利貞.

Take the time and effort to examine yourself so you can stop the misfortune of your conduct. Dispersion shows a flood without any dams to control it. Even the king comes to the temple to seek assistance. There is benefit in leaving to cross the great water, being determined to do it. This shows there is a gentle dispersion of past obstacles resulting in a fresh, positive energy being released into your life. Your sense of being isolated or alone is passing, as are your more selfish motives. All is brought to success.

The Lines (爻, Yao)

First Six (初 六, Chu Liu)
Using a strong horse to go to the rescue. Auspicious.

用拯馬壯. 吉.

The horse you ride upon to go to the rescue is strong and correct. This shows resoluteness about being more selfless, and this brings about good fortune.

Second Nine (九 二, Jiu Er)
Dispersion is hurried and the opportunity is seized. Regret vanishes.

渙奔其机. 悔亡.

The flow of dispersion quickly passes the stairs leading through your front door, so you are able to move freely about your house. This shows positive qi is entering your home. All worries vanish. Now is not the time to engage in divisiveness and the harboring of ill feelings

Third Six (六 三, Liu San)
Dispersion of the self. Without regret. 　　涣 其 躬. 无 悔.

You are caught in the flood, but it causes you no worries. This is the time for the ego to disperse and to let go of attachments to your own self-interests.

Fourth Six (六 四, Liu Si)
Dispersion of his communities. 　　涣 其 羣. 元 吉. 涣 有 丘.
Great auspiciousness. Dispersion 　　匪 夷 所 思.
of the hills he possesses. The ordinary
do not contemplate this.

The flooding went through the entire village, yet repairs and improvements are already being made. Unexpected hills were found to sit upon during the flooding. This shows to use wisdom during dispersion because great accumulation may result from it.

Fifth Nine (九 五, Jiu Wu)
Great groans and sweating from 　　涣 汗 其 大 號. 涣 王 居. 无 咎.
Dispersion. Dispersion of the king's
dwelling. Without fault.

The flooding was overwhelming and people screamed and perspired in fear. The flood even reached the king's palace, but no serious damage occurred. Through generosity, obstacles and crises are overcome.

Topmost Nine (上 九, Shang Jiu)
Dispersion of his own blood. Going away 　　涣 其 血. 去 逖 出. 无 咎.
and being separate from a far distance.
Without fault.

Injury occurred during the flood, but you were able to escape from the flooded area, and no further danger will follow. It is wise to keep a safe distance from the situation.

Alternate English Translations for the Hexagram of Huan, 渙

The Symbol of Dispersion [CC] [S]
Dispersion (Dissolution) [WB]
Dispersion (Disintegration) [CS]
Scattering, Disintegration, Dispersal [B]
Dispersal [C]
Dispersing [H] [K] [RS]
Dispersion [L] [N]

The Great Symbolism (大象, Da Xiang) says,

Wind moving above Water. This is Huan. 風行水上. 渙.
The ancient kings, according with this, 先王以亨于
persevered with the sovereigns 帝立廟.
and established temples.

Sexagenary Placement

Heavenly Stem: Bing 丙 (3rd Stem, Yang)—**Fire** (火, Huo)
Earthly Branch: Chen 辰 (5th Branch, Yang)—**Dragon** (龍, Long)
Represents the *Year of the Fire Dragon* (53rd Year of the Sixty-Year Cycle)
Years: 1856 – 1916 – 1976 – 2036

Trigram Correlations

Upper Gua (Wind)

Xun 巽
- **Represents:** Wind, Wood, Eldest Daughter
- **Actions:** Gentleness, Grounding, Penetrating, Spreading
- **Influences:** Prosperity, Abundance, Wealth
- **Shape:** Rectangle   **Color:** Purple
- **Body:** Waist and hips   **Season:** Beginning Summer
- **Moon Phase:** Waxing Gibbous
- **Animals:** Earthly Fowl, Celestial Golden Rooster
- **Directions:** Southwest (BH), Southeast (AH)
- **Nine Palaces Numbers:** Fu Xi: **9**
    Yu the Great: Ho River Map, **2**—Lo River Script, **4**
- **Internal Alchemy:** Breath and Mobilizing Qi
    Qi Center: Yu Zhen (Jade Pillow)
    Qi Meridian: Yin Wei Mai (Yin Preserving Vessel)

#59 Dispersion (Huan)

Lower Gua (Water)

Kan 坎

Represents: Water, Moon, Springs/Streams, Middle Son
Actions: Peril, Danger, and Difficulty.
Influences: Abysmal Life Path and Vocation
Shape: Wave **Color:** Black
Body: Ears **Season:** Autumn (Autumn Equinox)
Moon Phase: First Quarter
Animals: Earthly Pig, Celestial White Tiger
Directions: West (BH), North (AH)
Nine Palaces Numbers: Fu Xi: 4
   Yu the Great: Ho River Map, 7—Lo River Script, 1
Internal Alchemy: Essence, Jing, Lead
   Qi Center: Shuang Guan (Double Pass)
   Qi Meridian: Chong Mai (Penetrating Vessel)

Associated Developed Hexagrams of Huan

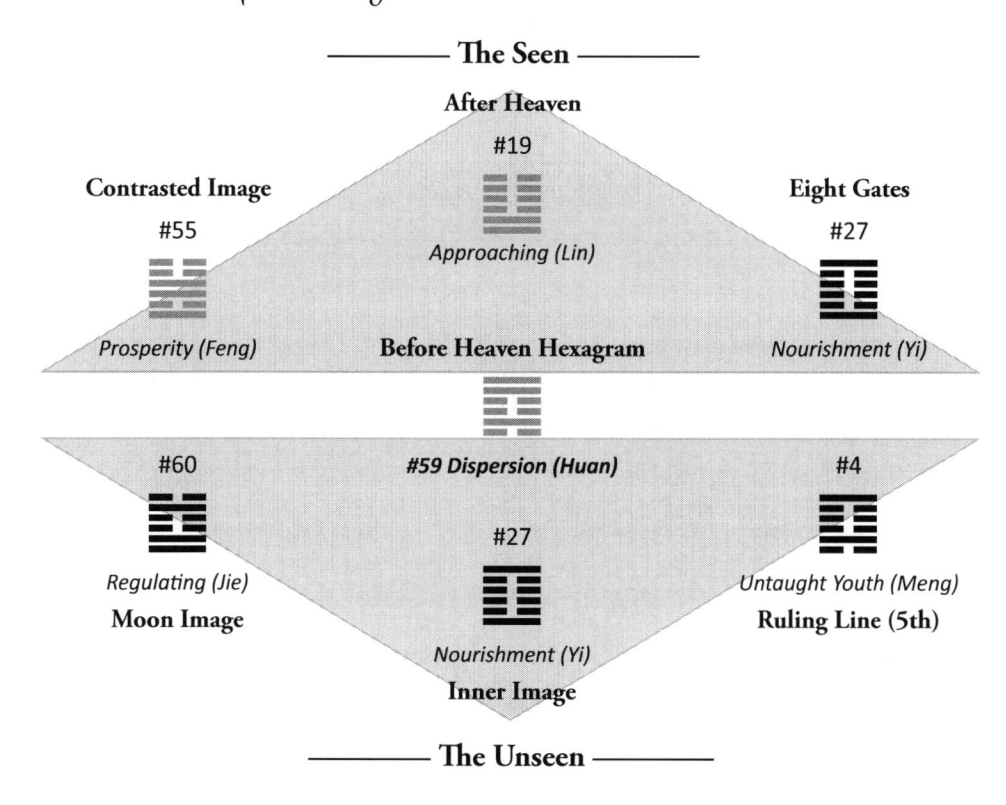

—— **The Seen** ——

After Heaven
#19
Approaching (Lin)

Contrasted Image
#55
Prosperity (Feng)

Eight Gates
#27
Nourishment (Yi)

Before Heaven Hexagram

#59 Dispersion (Huan)

#60
Regulating (Jie)
Moon Image

#27
Nourishment (Yi)
Inner Image

#4
Untaught Youth (Meng)
Ruling Line (5th)

—— **The Unseen** ——

Jie

節

Regulating

60

Kan (Water) above
坎 上
Kan Shang
Dui (Valley) below
兌 下
Dui Xia

Moon/Yin Image

The Prediction (彖, Tuan)

Regulating:
Perseverance. If the Regulating
is difficult and bitter, there will be
no ability to be resolute.

節. 亨. 苦 節 不 可 貞.

This image reflects the idea that no one person can do all things perfectly. Each person has his or her own endowments and failings. Hence, in regulating your affairs, if you find it too difficult to move forward you will not acquire the necessary skills. But one should always persevere and work through the difficulties and bitterness. Regulating also implies frugality in your actions and expenditures. Understand that regulating is a matter of applying the right measure, not too much and not to little. Know your strengths and weaknesses so you can determine your own correct path.

The Lines (爻, Yao)

First Nine (初 九, Chu Jiu)
Not going out the courtyard door.
Without fault.

不 出 戶 庭. 无 咎.

It is best to stay home and regulate yourself. In this way you will make no errors. Be patient and discreet about those you invite into your courtyard.

Second Nine (九 二, Jiu Er)
Not going out the courtyard gateway.
Misfortune.

不 出 門 庭. 凶.

In this situation, it's best to go out of your house because there's something in your house that needs to be removed. This is a time for action and you must move with resoluteness, otherwise misfortune will come.

Third Six (六 三, Liu San)
No Regulating of the rules,   不 節 若. 則 嗟 若. 无 咎.
causes lament. Without fault.

If you are not frugal you will lament. Still, no great disasters will occur. To be extravagant will only bear bitter fruit.

Fourth Six (六 四, Liu Si)
Quietly Regulating. Perseverance.   安 節. 亨.

If you can find peace and contentment in being frugal and regulating your life, everything will be good.

Fifth Nine (九 五, Jiu Wu)
Willing Regulating. Auspicious.   甘 節. 吉. 往 有 尚.
To go onward has honor.

Finding contentment in frugality and regulating your life will be auspicious. You will receive a much deserved reward. Yet, be fair and tempered in attempting to regulate others. Be an example of frugality and regulation, not a preacher, then people will honor you.

Topmost Six (上 六, Shang Liu)
Difficult and bitter Regulating. Resoluteness   苦 節. 貞 凶. 悔 亡.
brings misfortune. Regret vanishes.

If thinking that frugality and regulating are too difficult this will result in an even more difficult future. Going on without being frugal and regulating, you can never be free of miseries.

Alternate English Translations for the Hexagram of Jie, 節

The Symbol of Restrictive Regulations [S]   *Restricting* [H]
Limitations [WB]   *Self-Restraint* [N]
Restraint (Limitations) [CS]   *Articulating* [K] [RS]
Restraint [B]   *Limitation* [L]
Discipline [C]   *The Symbol of Regulated Restrictions* [CC]

The Great Symbolism (大象, Da Xiang) says,

Above the Marsh there is Water. This is Jie.	澤上有水. 節.
The superior person, according with this, regulates numbers and measures while discussing acts of virtue.	君子以制數. 議德行.

Sexagenary Placement

Heavenly Stem: Jia 甲 (1st Stem, Yang)—**Wood** (木, Mu)
Earthly Branch: Chen 辰 (5th Branch, Yang)—**Dragon** (龍, Long)
Represents the *Year of the Wood Dragon* (41st Year of the Sixty-Year Cycle)
Years: 1844 – 1904 – 1964 – 2024

Trigram Correlations

Upper Gua (Water)

Kan 坎   **Represents:** Water, Moon, Springs/Streams, Middle Son
Actions: Peril, Danger, and Difficulty.
Influences: Abysmal Life Path and Vocation
Shape: Wave   **Color:** Black
Body: Ears   **Season:** Autumn (Autumn Equinox)
Moon Phase: First Quarter
Animals: Earthly Pig, Celestial White Tiger
Directions: West (BH), North (AH)
Nine Palaces Numbers: Fu Xi: 4
    Yu the Great: Ho River Map, 7—Lo River Script, **1**
Internal Alchemy: Essence, Jing, Lead
    Qi Center: Shuang Guan (Double Pass)
    Qi Meridian: Chong Mai (Penetrating Vessel)

#60 Regulating (Jie)

Lower Gua (Valley)

☱ Dui 兌

Represents: Valley, River, Lake/Marsh, Youngest Daughter
Actions: Joyous, Opening, Stimulating
Influences: Family, Future, Collecting, Pleasure, Absorbing, Complacency.
Shape: Introverted Triangle   **Color:** Brown
Body: Mouth   **Season:** Beginning Spring
Moon Phase: Waning Gibbous
Animals: Earthly Goat, Celestial Great Roc
Directions: Southeast (BH), West (AH)
Nine Palaces Numbers: Fu Xi: 5
   Yu the Great: Ho River Map, 4—Lo River Script, 7
Internal Alchemy: Po (Earthly) Spirit
   Qi Center: Xuan Guan (Mysterious Pass)
   Qi Meridian: Yang Wei Mai (Yang Preserving Vessel)

Associated Developed Hexagrams of Jie

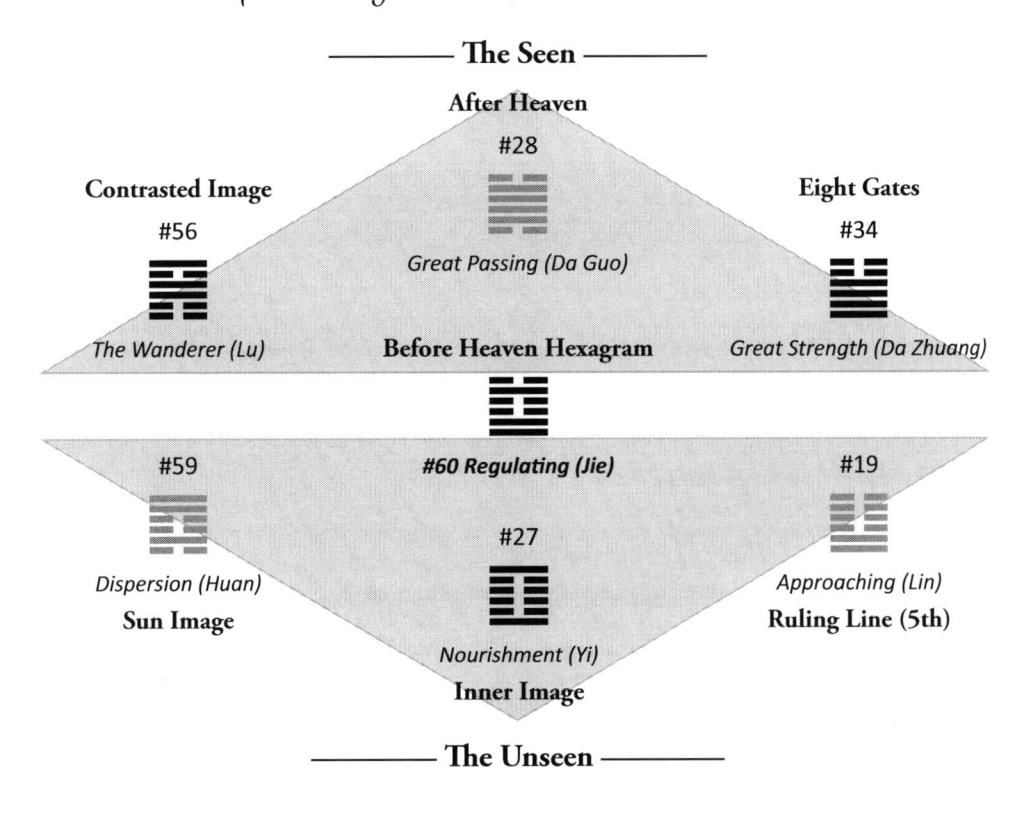

——— **The Seen** ———

After Heaven
#28
Great Passing (Da Guo)

Contrasted Image
#56
The Wanderer (Lu)

Eight Gates
#34
Great Strength (Da Zhuang)

Before Heaven Hexagram
#60 Regulating (Jie)

#59
Dispersion (Huan)
Sun Image

#27
Nourishment (Yi)
Inner Image

#19
Approaching (Lin)
Ruling Line (5th)

——— **The Unseen** ———

243

Zhong Fu 中孚

Inner Truth

61

Xun (Wind) above
巽 上
Xun Shang

Dui (Valley) below
兌 下
Dui Xia

Moon Eclipse/Yin Image

The Prediction (彖, Tuan)

Inner Truth:
Pigs and fishes are auspicious.
Advantage in fording the great stream.
Advantage in resoluteness.

中孚. 豚魚吉. 利涉大川. 利貞.

This image indicates to be suspicious and wary of those who are in authority. Yet, fat pigs and fishes bring good fortune because they are auspicious omens. Getting rid of your prejudices will enable you to truly appreciate others, and give you a new sense of truth about things. Therefore, crossing a great river and being resolute about doing so is beneficial, because injustices will be seen with a new revived clarity.

The Lines (爻, Yao)

First Nine (初 九, Chu Jiu)
To ponder is auspicious. Being with
others brings unrest.

虞吉. 有他不燕.

You are happily lost in thought and enjoying the good fortune you feel has been bequeathed to you, yet someone or something appears and startles you.

Second Nine (九 二, Jiu Er)
The crane cries out from the dark [Yin] side
of the hill. Her fledgling responds in song.
I have a goblet of good wine. I shall
share my rewards with you.

鳴鶴在陰. 其子和之.
我有好爵. 吾與爾靡之.

You hear a crane cry out from the other side of the hill, and her young offspring also joins in. This is an omen of good fortune so you invite friends to come and drink good wine with you.

Third Six (六三, Liu San)
Having defeated the opposition.　　　　得敵. 或鼓或罷. 或泣或歌.
Now beating the drum, now quiet,
now weeping silently, and now singing.

Your enemies have been defeated, but those around you respond in different ways: some happily beat the drums, others grow silent, some weep, while others sing out.

Fourth Six (六四, Liu Si)
The moon is nearly full. A team　　　　月幾望. 馬匹亡. 无咎.
of horses vanishes. Without fault.

Under the light of the full moon your horses have run off, but this causes no disaster as they return.

Fifth Nine (九五, Jiu Wu)
Has sincerity in taking hold of others.　　有孚攣如. 无咎.
Without fault.

Someone who seeks to harm you is bound and restrained. Everything is good.

Topmost Nine (上九, Shang Jiu)
Making the sound of a cockcrow　　　翰音登于天. 貞凶.
so it may rise into Heaven.
Resoluteness brings misfortune.

A rooster that is being readied for a sacrificial ceremony escapes and flies off into the sky. This is an auspicious omen. Do not seek to recapture it or misfortune will ensue.

Alternate English Translations for the Hexagram of Zhong Fu, 中孚

The Symbol of Central Sincerity [S]　　　*Innermost Sincerity* [H]
Inner Truth [WB]　　　　　　　　　　*Faithfulness* [N]
Inner Sincerity (Truth) [CS]　　　　　　*The Center Conforming* [RS]
Inward Confidence and Sincerity [B]　　*Inner Truthfulness* [L]
Faithfulness in the Center [C]　　　　　*Centering Connecting* [K]
The Symbol of Truth [CC]

The Great Symbolism (大象, Da Xiang) says,

Above the Marsh there is Wind. This is Zhong Fu. The superior person, according with this, discusses matters of litigation and delays executions.

澤上有風.中孚.
議獄緩死.

☱ Sexagenary Placement

Heavenly Stem: Wu 戊 (5th Stem, Yang)—**Earth** (土, Tu)
Earthly Branch: Chen 辰 (5th Branch, Yang)—**Dragon** (龍, Long)
Represents the *Year of the Earth Dragon* (5th Year of the Sixty-Year Cycle)
Years: 1868 – 1928 – 1988 – 2048

Trigram Correlations

Upper Gua (Wind)

☴ **Xun** 巽
- **Represents:** Wind, Wood, Eldest Daughter
- **Actions:** Gentleness, Grounding, Penetrating, Spreading
- **Influences:** Prosperity, Abundance, Wealth
- **Shape:** Rectangle   **Color:** Purple
- **Body:** Waist and hips   **Season:** Beginning Summer
- **Moon Phase:** Waxing Gibbous
- **Animals:** Earthly Fowl, Celestial Golden Rooster
- **Directions:** Southwest (BH), Southeast (AH)
- **Nine Palaces Numbers:** Fu Xi: **9**
  - Yu the Great: Ho River Map, **2**—Lo River Script, **4**
- **Internal Alchemy:** Breath and Mobilizing Qi
  - Qi Center: Yu Zhen (Jade Pillow)
  - Qi Meridian: Yin Wei Mai (Yin Preserving Vessel)

#61 Inner Truth (Zhong Fu)

Lower Gua (Valley)

☱ **Dui** 兑
Represents: Valley, River, Lake/Marsh, Youngest Daughter
Actions: Joyous, Opening, Stimulating
Influences: Family, Future, Collecting, Pleasure, Absorbing, Complacency.
Shape: Introverted Triangle   **Color:** Brown
Body: Mouth   **Season:** Beginning Spring
Moon Phase: Waning Gibbous
Animals: Earthly Goat, Celestial Great Roc
Directions: Southeast (BH), West (AH)
Nine Palaces Numbers: Fu Xi: 5
   Yu the Great: Ho River Map, 4—Lo River Script, 7
Internal Alchemy: Po (Earthly) Spirit
   Qi Center: Xuan Guan (Mysterious Pass)
   Qi Meridian: Yang Wei Mai (Yang Preserving Vessel)

Associated Developed Hexagrams of Zhong Fu

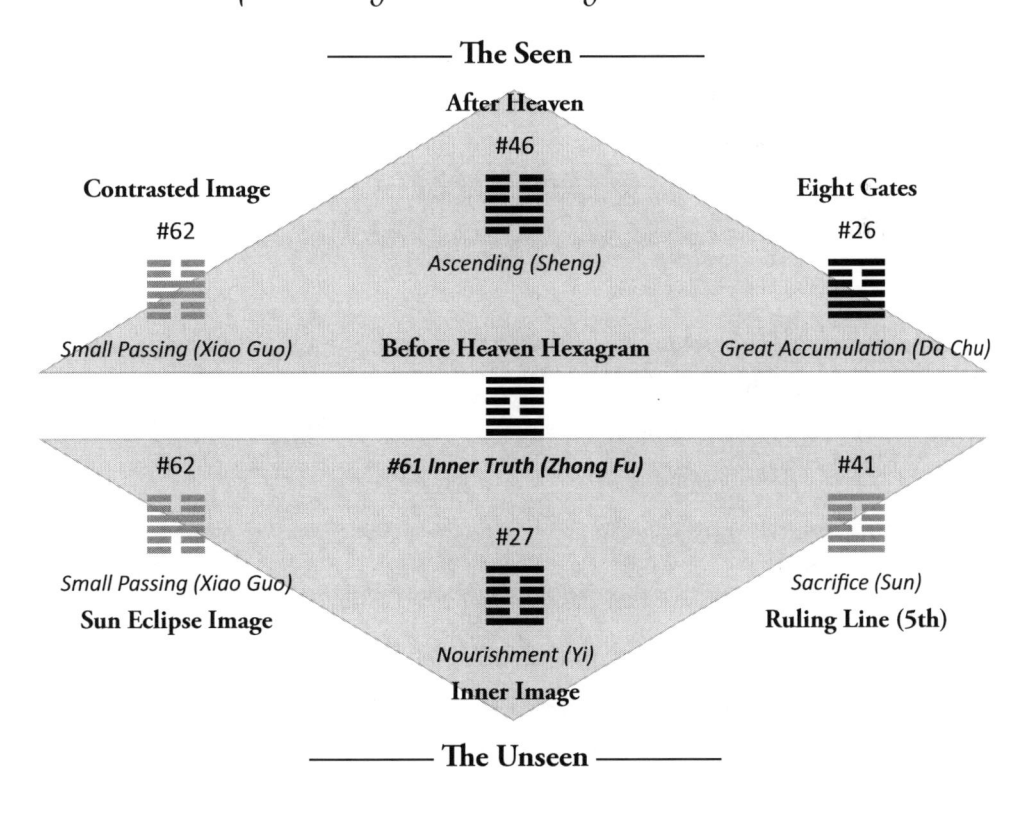

───── **The Seen** ─────

After Heaven
#46
Ascending (Sheng)

Contrasted Image
#62
Small Passing (Xiao Guo)

Eight Gates
#26
Great Accumulation (Da Chu)

Before Heaven Hexagram

#61 Inner Truth (Zhong Fu)

#62
Small Passing (Xiao Guo)
Sun Eclipse Image

#27
Nourishment (Yi)
Inner Image

#41
Sacrifice (Sun)
Ruling Line (5th)

───── **The Unseen** ─────

Xiao Guo

Small Passing

小過

62

Zhen (Thunder) above
震上
Zhen Shang
Gen (Mountain) below
艮下
Gen Xia

Sun Eclipse/Yang Image

The Prediction (彖, Tuan)

Excess of the Small:
Perseverance. Advantage in resoluteness.   小過.亨.利貞.
Ability in small affairs, no ability   可小事不可大事.
in great affairs. Sounds handed down   飛鳥遺之音.
by flying birds. It is not fitting to ascend,   不宜上宜下.大吉.
but fitting to descend. Great and auspicious.

People find contentment in taking care of the small things, so pay attention to the details. Hence, this image is showing that there is too much talking and too little action. Seek to complete small business transactions and not the big ones. Birds flying overhead are chirping, so it is not correct to think of ascending. If you climb, you will fall. Rather, it is great and auspicious to descend and be humble, and to be unpretentious in your actions.

The Lines (爻, Yao)

First Six (初 六, Chu Liu)
The flying bird causes misfortune.   飛鳥以凶.

A bird flies away because it is sensing danger close at hand. If attempting to fly away, to avoid a problem, it will bring misfortune.

Second Six (六 二, Liu Er)
Passing by his grandfather, and then meeting   過其祖.遇其妣.
the grandmother. Not reaching for his ruler,   不及其君.
but meeting his minister. Without fault.   遇其臣.无咎.

Bypassing the grandfather you meet with the grandmother, and bypassing the leader you meet with a subordinate. This brings no errors or mistakes, but is showing that you are unprepared. All you can do is try your best.

Third Nine (九 三, Jiu San)
No excessive protection. Following someone leads to violence. Misfortune.　　弗過防之. 從或戕之. 凶.

You have done nothing wrong but did not protect yourself as you should have. Do not follow other people's causes or revolts as it will lead to violence and bring misfortune.

Fourth Nine (九 四, Jiu Si)
Without fault. No passing by, but meeting. To go forward is dangerous and one must be cautious. No use for perpetual resoluteness.　　无咎. 弗過遇之. 往厲必戒. 勿用永貞.

So far you have made no errors, but do not think you have passed them by, for dangers will come to meet you. Do not think you can force your way through this situation.

Fifth Six (六 五, Liu Wu)
Dense clouds and no rain. From my western border. The duke shoots his arrows and takes hold of a bird in a cavern.　　密雲不雨. 自我西郊. 公弋取彼在穴.

Dark clouds have moved in from the West, but these have not brought any rain. A person of high rank shoots his arrows at a bird, hits it, but now has to retrieve it from the cavern into which it fell.

Topmost Six (上 六, Shang Liu)
No meeting, but passing by. The birds fly far off. Misfortune. It is right to say that there will be calamities from Heaven and injury.　　弗遇過之. 飛鳥離之. 凶. 是謂災眚.

He cannot find the cavern the bird fell into. But the bird was only slightly injured and has now flown away. This is a bad omen and brings misfortune. The actions of the high-ranking person has insulted Heaven and so injury will befall him.

Alternate English Translations for the Hexagram of Xiao Guo, 小過

The Symbol of Excess in Small Things [S]
Preponderance of the Small [WB]
Outer Preponderance [CS]
The Small Get By [B]
Predominance of the Small [C]
The Symbol of Minor Preponderance [CC]

Little Exceeding [H]
Minor Excess [N]
The Small Exceeding [RS]
Slight Excess [L]
Small Traverses [K]

The Great Symbolism (大象, Da Xiang) says,

Above the Mountain is Thunder. This is Xiao Guo. The superior person, according with this, passes beyond reverence in conduct, passes beyond emotions in sorrow, passes beyond frugality in expenditure

山上有雷.小過.
君子以行過乎恭.
喪過乎哀.用過乎儉.

Sexagenary Placement

Heavenly Stem: Wu 戊 (5th Stem, Yang)—**Earth** (土, Tu)
Earthly Branch: Xu 戌 (11th Branch, Yang)—**Dog** (狗, Gou)
Represents the *Year of the Earth Dog* (35th Year of the Sixty-Year Cycle)
Years: 1898 – 1958 – 2018 – 2078

Trigram Correlations

Upper Gua (Thunder)

Zhen 震
- **Represents:** Thunder, Earthquake, Eldest Son
- **Actions:** Arousing, Shaking, Initiating
- **Influences:** Foundations, Past Actions, Excitement.
- **Shape:** Vertical Column **Color:** Green
- **Body:** Feet and legs **Season:** Beginning Winter
- **Moon Phase:** Waning Crescent
- **Animals:** Earthly Dragons, Celestial Dragon-Horse
- **Directions:** Northeast (BH), East (AH)
- **Nine Palaces Numbers:** Fu Xi: **3**
  Yu the Great: Ho River Map, **8**—Lo River Script, **3**
- **Internal Alchemy:** Mind-Intention

Qi Center: Dan Tian (Elixir Field)
Qi Muridian: Yin Qiao Mai (Yin Heel Vessel)

Lower Gua (Mountain)

Gen 艮   **Represents:** Mountain, Towers, Youngest Son
Actions: Stillness, Binding, Stopping
Influences: Knowledge, Wisdom, Skill, Determination
Shape: Vertical Column   **Color:** Blue
Body: Hands and arms   **Season:** Beginning Autumn
Moon Phase: Waxing Crescent
Animals: Earthly Dog, Celestial Vermilion Snake
Directions: Northwest (BH), Northeast (AH)
Nine Palaces Numbers: Fu Xi: 7
    Yu the Great: Ho River Map, **6**— Lo River Script, **8**
Internal Alchemy: Hun (Heavenly) Spirit
    Qi Center: Jing Men (Essence Gate)
    Qi Meridian: Yang Qiao Mai (Yang Heel Vessel)

Associated Developed Hexagrams of Xiao Guo

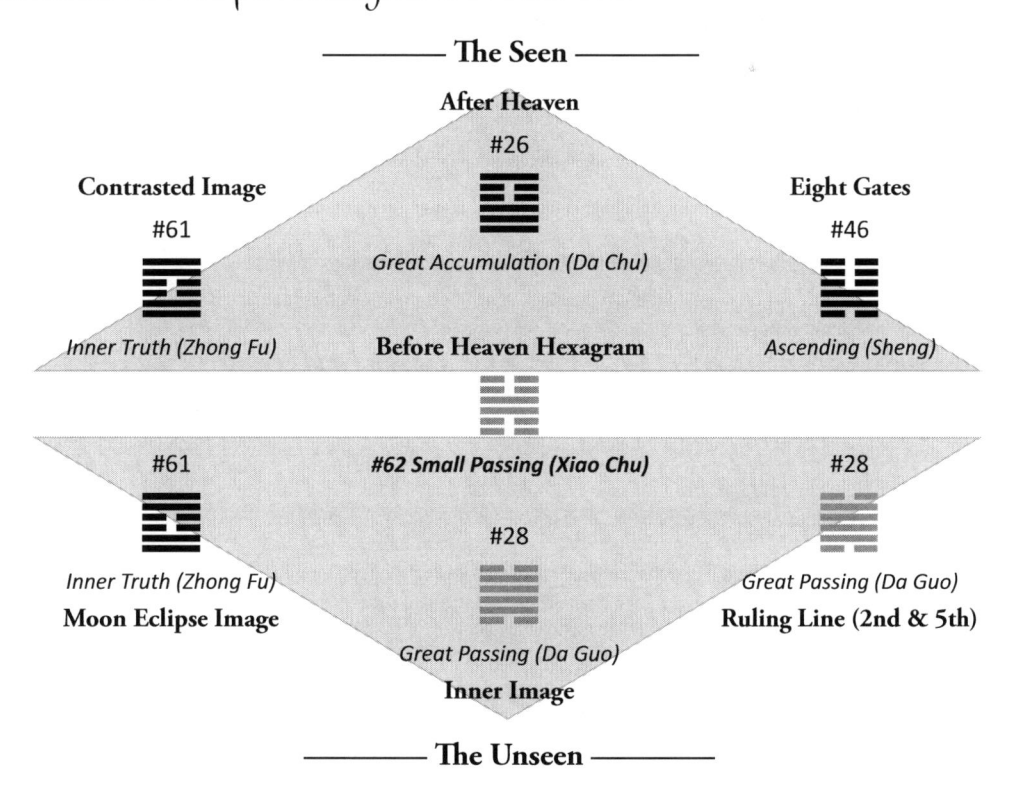

——— **The Seen** ———

After Heaven
#26
Great Accumulation (Da Chu)

Contrasted Image
#61
Inner Truth (Zhong Fu)

Eight Gates
#46
Ascending (Sheng)

Before Heaven Hexagram

#62 Small Passing (Xiao Chu)

#61
Inner Truth (Zhong Fu)
Moon Eclipse Image

#28
Great Passing (Da Guo)

#28
Great Passing (Da Guo)
Ruling Line (2nd & 5th)

Inner Image

——— **The Unseen** ———

Ji Ji

After Completion

63

既濟

Kan (Water) above
坎 上
Kan Shang
Li (Fire) below
離 下
Li Xia

Moon/Yin Image

The Prediction (彖, Tuan)

After Completion:
Perseverance. Small advantage in being resolute. The beginning is auspicious. The end is disorderly.

既濟. 亨. 小利貞. 初吉. 終亂.

This image shows to persevere in the things you know. Do not attempt to take on untried things, as they will bring too much disorder and frustration into your life. All appears to be perfect and everything is going your way, yet this is no time to be lax. Remain resolute and cautious, and pay close attention to the details of the situation. In the beginning, everything feels auspicious, but in the end there will be troubles.

The Lines (爻, Yao)

First Nine (初 九, Chu Jiu)
Dragging his wheels, his tail gets wet. Without fault.

曳其輪. 濡其尾. 无咎.

When dragging your cart across the water, the back of the cart gets submerged, but this is no cause for concern. This shows to remain calm and collected in the midst of excitement.

Second Six (六 二, Liu Er)
The wife loses the screens of her carriage. She does not pursue them. In seven days they will be regained.

婦喪其茀. 勿逐. 七日得.

When riding in her carriage, the silk screens fall off, but she can spare no time to look for them. They are recovered in seven days, so the situation is of no concern.

#63 After Completion (Ji JI)

Third Nine (九 三, Jiu San)
Gaozong chastised the Demon Region.
But it took three years to subdue it.
Inferior people should not be employed.

告宗伐鬼方.三年克之.
小人勿用.

The Emperor Gaozong (of the Yin Dynasty) went to defeat the Demon Region, but he could not win for three long years. His soldiers became so exhausted they could not fight in any other battles or campaigns.

Fourth Six (六 四, Liu Si)
He owns silk garments, but wears old ragged clothes. All day long he is on guard.

繻有衣袽.終日戒.

He does not wish to damage his fineries nor to put on airs. To the end of each day he guards himself against revealing his wealth.

Fifth Nine (九 五, Jiu Wu)
The eastern neighbor sacrificed an ox,
but not like the simple spring sacrifice
of the western neighbor. Through this
sincerity he received blessings.

東鄰殺牛.不如西鄰
之禴祭.實受其福.

The neighbor to the east makes a sacrificial offering to the gods by killing an ox. The neighbor to the west bathed and planted flowers. The western neighbor received the most benefits and blessings from Heaven. This shows that making grand displays can result in little reward.

Topmost Six (上 六, Shang Liu)
Wetting his head. Danger.

濡其首.厲.

The river being crossed is too deep and the head gets submerged. This is dangerous because it shows smugness and a self-congratulatory attitude.

Alternate English Translations for the Hexagram of Ji Ji, 既濟

The Symbol of What Is Already Past [S]
After Completion [B] [CS] [WB]
Settled [C]
Already Fulfilled [H]

After Crossing the Water [N]
Already Fording [RS] [K]
Completion [L]
The Symbol of Accomplishment [CC]

The Great Symbolism (大象, Da Xiang) says,

Above Fire dwells Water. This is Ji Ji.	水在火上. 既濟.
The superior person, according with this,	君子以思患而
is mindful of wrongdoing and is	豫防之.
thereby prepared to guard against it.	

Trigram Correlations

Upper Gua (Water)

☵ **Kan** 坎   **Represents:** Water, Moon, Springs/Streams, Middle Son
Actions: Peril, Danger, and Difficulty.
Influences: Abysmal Life Path and Vocation
Shape: Wave   **Color:** Black
Body: Ears   **Season:** Autumn (Autumn Equinox)
Moon Phase: First Quarter
Animals: Earthly Pig, Celestial White Tiger
Directions: West (BH), North (AH)
Nine Palaces Numbers: Fu Xi: 4
    Yu the Great: Ho River Map, 7—Lo River Script, 1
Internal Alchemy: Essence, Jing, Lead
    Qi Center: Shuang Guan (Double Pass)
    Qi Meridian: Chong Mai (Penetrating Vessel)

Lower Gua (Fire)

☲ Li 離

Represents: Fire, Lightning, Sun, Middle Daughter
Actions: Clinging, Illuminating, Congregating
Influences: Fame, Reputation, Brightness, Elegance
Shape: Triangle   **Color:** Red
Body: Eyes   **Season:** Spring (Spring Equinox)
Moon Phase: Last Quarter
Animals: Earthly Rooster, Celestial Green Dragon
Directions: East (BH), South (AH)
Nine Palaces Numbers: Fu Xi: **8**
   Yu the Great: Ho River Map, **3**—Lo River Script, **9**
Internal Alchemy: Mercury, Qi
   Qi Center: Jiang Gong (Crimson Palace)
   Qi Meridian: Dai Mai (Belt Vessel)

Associated Developed Hexagrams of Ji Ji

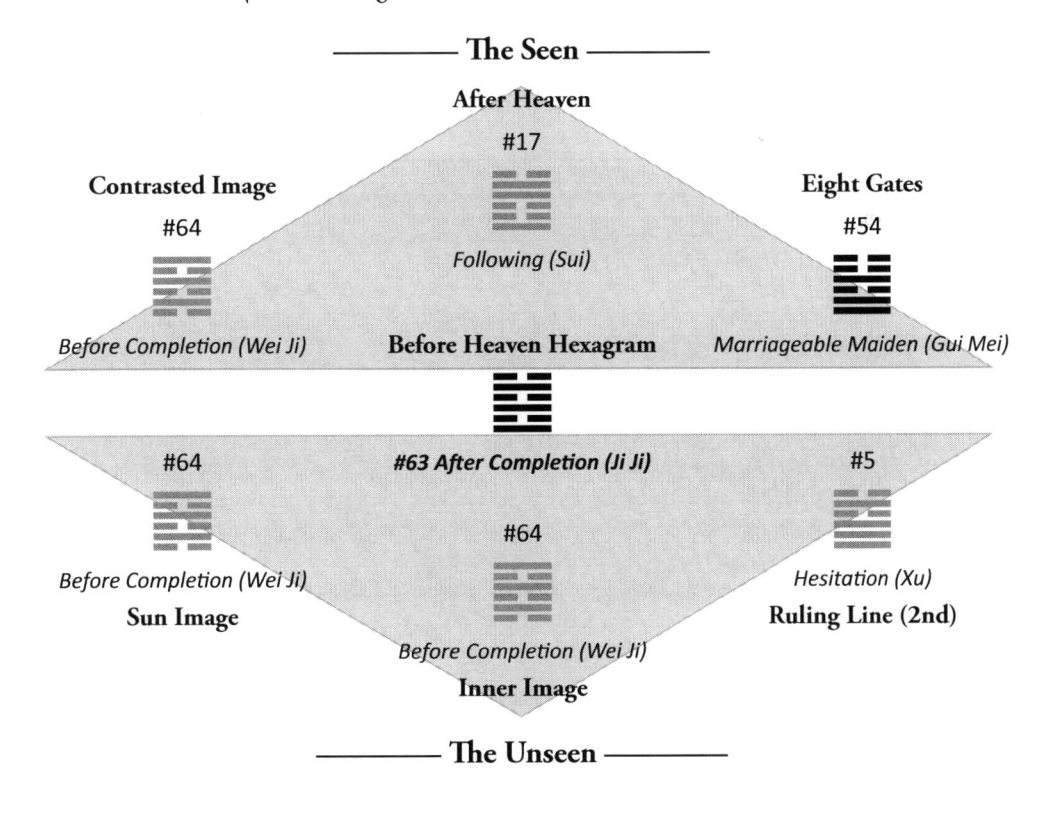

——— **The Seen** ———

After Heaven
#17
Following (Sui)

Contrasted Image
#64
Before Completion (Wei Ji)

Eight Gates
#54
Marriageable Maiden (Gui Mei)

Before Heaven Hexagram

#63 After Completion (Ji Ji)

#64
Before Completion (Wei Ji)
Sun Image

#64
Before Completion (Wei Ji)
Inner Image

#5
Hesitation (Xu)
Ruling Line (2nd)

——— **The Unseen** ———

Wei Ji — *Before Completion* — 64

未濟

Li (Fire) above
離 上
Li Shang
Kan (Water) below
坎 下
Kan Xia

Sun/Yang Image

The Prediction (彖, Tuan)

Before Completion:
Perseverance. The young fox nearly crosses the stream. Wets its tail. Nowhere is there advantage.

未濟. 亨. 小狐汔濟.
濡其尾. 无攸利.

This image reveals that everything is going well and as planned, yet there is a formidable task ahead. Like the fox treading upon ice, proceed with caution and prudence. The goal should be to focus and unite all your energies into one action. However, the river is not crossable at this time. The fox which does manage to cross the river will get its tail wet. This is not a good omen.

The Lines (爻, Yao)

First Six (初 六, Chu Liu)
Wets his tail. Regret.

濡其尾. 吝.

The fox's tail is wet and it proves to be very annoying and irritating. He demonstrates untimely enthusiasm and so fails in crossing the stream.

Second Nine (九 二, Jiu Er)
Drags back the carriage wheel.
With resoluteness it is auspicious.

曳其輪. 貞吉.

Determined to pull the cart across the river proves to be auspicious. This shows gathering energy while waiting for an opportune moment.

Third Six (六三, Liu San)

Before Completion, advancing brings 未濟征凶. 利涉大川.
misfortune. Advantage in fording
the great stream.

It is useless to attempt to conquer something at a distance. Better to cross the river and face it head on. This shows one is unprepared for the task at hand and so must wait.

Fourth Nine (九四, Jiu Si)

Resoluteness is auspicious. Regret vanishes. 貞吉. 悔亡. 震用伐鬼方.
Agitation is useful in chastising the Demon 三年有賞于大國.
Region. In three years rewards from
the kingdom will be reaped.

Stay with your plan and all worries will disappear. It is better to agitate the opposition than to attack directly. In three years you will achieve success. This shows a situation where it is better to engage in immediate actions, otherwise the long-term opportunity could be lost.

Fifth Six (六五, Liu Wu)

Resoluteness is auspicious. No regrets. 貞吉. 无悔. 君子之光.
The brilliance of a wise person. 有孚吉.
Having sincerity is auspicious.

Stay with your plan and all worries will vanish. The wise person is glorious in subduing the opposition. Good fortune comes from being true to yourself and sharing with others.

Topmost Nine (上九, Shang Jiu)

Has sincerity in his drinking of spirits. 有孚于飲酒. 无咎.
Without fault. One's own head gets wet. 濡其首. 有孚失是.
Having sincerity, still losing the right.

There is no error in drinking with your opposition, but if getting too drunk, the opposition will leave and nothing will be accomplished. This shows carelessness destroying good fortune.

Alternate English Translations for the Hexagram of Wei Ji, 未濟

The Symbol of What Is Not Yet Past [S]
Before Completion [B] [CS] [L] [WB]
Unsettled [C]
The Symbol of What Is Not Yet Accomplished [CC]

Not Yet Fulfilled [H]
Before Crossing the Water [N]
Not Yet Fording [K] [RS]

The Great Symbolism (大象, Da Xiang) says,

Above Water dwells Fire. This is Wei Ji. Superior persons, according with this, are cautious in discriminating their affairs and dwelling places.

火在水上. 未濟.
君子以慎辨物
居方.

Trigram Correlations

Upper Gua (Fire)

Li 離

Represents: Fire, Lightning, Sun, Middle Daughter
Actions: Clinging, Illuminating, Congregating
Influences: Fame, Reputation, Brightness, Elegance
Shape: Triangle   **Color:** Red
Body: Eyes   **Season:** Spring (Spring Equinox)
Moon Phase: Last Quarter
Animals: Earthly Rooster, Celestial Green Dragon
Directions: East (BH), South (AH)
Nine Palaces Numbers: Fu Xi: **8**
    Yu the Great: Ho River Map, **3**—Lo River Script, **9**
Internal Alchemy: Mercury, Qi
    Qi Center: Jiang Gong (Crimson Palace)
    Qi Meridian: Dai Mai (Belt Vessel)

#64 Before Completion (Wei Ji)

Lower Gua (Water)

Kan 坎 **Represents:** Water, Moon, Springs/Streams, Middle Son
Actions: Peril, Danger, and Difficulty.
Influences: Abysmal Life Path and Vocation
Shape: Wave **Color:** Black
Body: Ears **Season:** Autumn (Autumn Equinox)
Moon Phase: First Quarter
Animals: Earthly Pig, Celestial White Tiger
Directions: West (BH), North (AH)
Nine Palaces Numbers: Fu Xi: 4
   Yu the Great: Ho River Map, 7—Lo River Script, 1
Internal Alchemy: Essence, Jing, Lead
   Qi Center: Shuang Guan (Double Pass)
   Qi Meridian: Chong Mai (Penetrating Vessel)

Associated Developed Hexagrams of Wei Ji

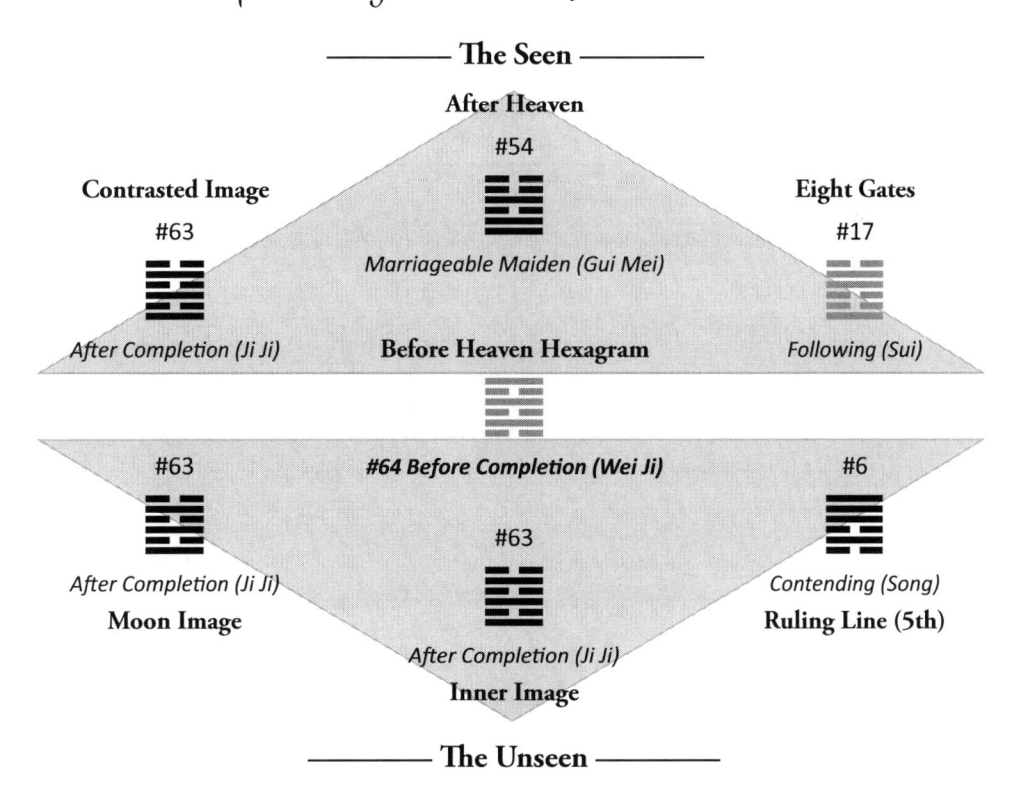

——— **The Seen** ———

After Heaven
#54
Marriageable Maiden (Gui Mei)

Contrasted Image
#63
After Completion (Ji Ji)

Before Heaven Hexagram

Eight Gates
#17
Following (Sui)

#64 Before Completion (Wei Ji)

#63
After Completion (Ji Ji)
Moon Image

#63
After Completion (Ji Ji)
Inner Image

#6
Contending (Song)
Ruling Line (5th)

——— **The Unseen** ———

About the Author

Stuart Alve Olson, long-time protégé of Master T.T. Liang (1900–2002), is a teacher, translator, and writer on Daoist philosophy, health, and internal arts. Since the early 1970s, he has studied and practiced Daoism and Chinese Buddhism. As of 2014, Stuart has published twenty books, many of which now appear in several foreign-language editions.

Daoism Books

- *The Immortal: True Accounts of the 250-Year-Old Man, Li Qingyun* by Yang Sen (Valley Spirit Arts, 2014).
- *Being Daoist: The Way of Drifting With the Current* (Valley Spirit Arts, 2014)
- *The Jade Emperor's Mind Seal Classic: The Taoist Guide to Health, Longevity, and Immortality* (Inner Traditions, 2003).
- *Tao of No Stress: Three Simple Paths* (Healing Arts Press, 2002).
- *Qigong Teachings of a Taoist Immortal: The Eight Essential Exercises of Master Li Ching-Yun* (Healing Arts Press, 2002).

Forthcoming

- *Clarity and Tranquility: A Daoist Guide on the Meditation Practice of Tranquil Sitting.*
- *Refining the Elixir: The Internal Alchemy Teachings of Daoist Immortal Zhang Sanfeng* (Daoist Immortal Three Peaks Zhang Series).
- *Seen and Unseen: A Daoist Guide for the Meditation Practice of Inner Contemplation.*
- *The Yellow Emperor's Yin Convergence Scripture.*
- *The Actions and Retribution Treatise.*

Taijiquan Books
Chen Kung Series

- *Tai Ji Qi: Fundamentals of Qigong, Meditation, and Internal Alchemy,* vol. 1 (Valley Spirit Arts, 2013).
- *Tai Ji Jin: Discourses on Intrinsic Energies for Mastery of Self-Defense Skills,* vol. 2 (Valley Spirit Arts, 2013).
- *Tai Ji Bing Shu: Discourses on the Taijiquan Weapon Arts of Sword, Saber, and Staff,* vol. 6 (Valley Spirit Arts, 2014).

Forthcoming Books in Chen Kung Series

- *Tai Ji Quan: Practice and Philosophy of the 108-Posture Solo Form,* vol. 3 (Valley Spirit Arts, 2015).

- *Tai Ji Tui Shou & Da Lu: Mastering the Eight Operations of Sensing Hands and Greater Rolling-Back,* vol. 4 (Valley Spirit Arts, 2015).
- *Tai Ji San Shou: Dispersing Hands Exercises for Mastering Intrinsic Energies Skills,* vol. 5 (Valley Spirit Arts, 2015).

- *Tai Ji Quan Treatise: Attributed to the Song Dynasty Daoist Priest Zhang Sanfeng,* Daoist Immortal Three Peaks Zhang Series (Valley Spirit Arts, 2011).
- *Imagination Becomes Reality: 150-Posture Taijiquan of Master T.T. Liang* (Valley Spirit Arts, 2011).
- *The Wind Sweeps Away the Plum Blossoms: Yang Style Taijiquan Staff and Spear Techniques* (Valley Spirit Arts, 2011).
- *Steal My Art: The Life and Times of Tai Chi Master T.T. Liang* (North Atlantic Books, 2002).
- *T'ai Chi According to the I Ching—Embodying the Principles of the Book of Changes* (Healing Arts Press, 2002).
- *T'ai Chi for Kids: Move with the Animals,* illustrated by Gregory Crawford (Bear Cub Books, 2001).

Kung-Fu
- *The Complete Guide to Northern Praying Mantis Kung Fu* (Blue Snake Books, 2010).

  Forthcoming
  - *18 Lohan Exercises* (Valley Spirit Arts, 2015).

Check out Stuart's author page at Amazon:
www.amazon.com/author/stuartalveolson

About the Publisher

Valley Spirit Arts offers books and DVDs on Daoism, taijiquan, and meditation practices primarily from author Stuart Alve Olson, longtime student of Master T.T. Liang and translator of many Daoist-related works.

Its website provides teachings on meditation and internal alchemy, taijiquan, qigong, and kung fu through workshops, private and group classes, and online courses and consulting.

For more information as well as updates on Stuart Alve Olson's upcoming projects and events, please visit: www.valleyspiritarts.com

About the Sanctuary of Dao

Established in 2010, the Sanctuary of Dao is a nonprofit organization dedicated to the sharing of Daoist philosophy and practices through online resources, yearly meditation retreats, and community educational programs. The underlying mission of the Sanctuary of Dao is to bring greater health, longevity, and contentment to its members and everyone it serves.

Please visit www.sanctuaryofdao.org for more information about the organization and its programs.

Chart for Determining Hexagrams

Trigrams Lower \ Upper	Qian	Dui	Li	Zhen	Xun	Kan	Gen	Kun
Qian	#1 Creativity of Heaven	#43 Decision	#14 Great Possession	#34 Great Strength	#9 Small Accumulation	#5 Hesitation	#26 Great Accumulation	#11 Peacefulness
Dui	#10 Treading	#58 Joyousness	#38 Opposition	#54 Marriageable Maiden	#61 Inner Truth	#60 Regulating	#41 Sacrifice	#19 Approaching
Li	#13 People United	#49 Revolution	#30 Distant Brightness	#55 Prosperity	#37 The Family	#63 After Completion	#22 Adornment	#36 Diminishing Light
Zhen	#25 Innocence	#17 Following	#21 Mastication	#51 Arousing Movement	#42 Increase	#3 Beginning Difficulties	#27 Nourishment	#24 Returning
Xun	#44 Pairing	#28 Great Passing	#50 The Cauldron	#32 Constancy	#57 Submission	#48 The Well	#18 Inner Destruction	#46 Ascending
Kan	#6 Contending	#47 Oppression	#64 Before Completion	#40 Liberation	#59 Dispersion	#29 The Abyss	#4 Untaught Youth	#7 The Army
Gen	#33 Retreating	#31 Attraction	#56 The Wanderer	#62 Small Passing	#53 Gradual Movement	#39 Difficult Obstruction	#52 Determined Stillness	#15 Modesty
Kun	#12 Adversity	#45 Collecting	#35 Advancement	#16 Joyful Ease	#20 Contemplation	#8 Union	#23 Removing	#2 Receptivity of Earth

264

Made in the USA
Middletown, DE
07 June 2015